Unlikely Heroes

Contemporary Holocaust Studies

SERIES EDITORS

Ari Kohen
Gerald J. Steinacher

Unlikely Heroes

The Place of Holocaust Rescuers in Research and Teaching

Edited by **ARI KOHEN** and **GERALD J. STEINACHER**

University of Nebraska Press
LINCOLN & LONDON

An earlier version of Gerald Steinacher and Brian Barmettler's chapter, "The University in Exile and the Garden of Eden: Alvin Johnson and His Rescue Efforts for European Jews and Intellectuals," was published in *Reassessing History from Two Continents: Festschrift Günter Bischof*, ed. Martin Eichtinger, Stefan Karner, Mark Kramer, and Peter Ruggenthaler (Innsbruck: Innsbruck University Press, 2013): 49–68, reprinted with permission.

Library of Congress Cataloging-in-Publication Data
Names: Kohen, Ari, 1977–, editor. | Steinacher, Gerald, editor.
Title: Unlikely heroes: the place of Holocaust rescuers in research and teaching / edited by Ari Kohen and Gerald J. Steinacher.
Description: Lincoln; London: University of Nebraska Press, [2019] |
Series: Contemporary holocaust studies | Includes bibliographical references and index.
Identifiers: LCCN 2018047771
ISBN 9781496208927 (cloth: alk. paper)
ISBN 9781496216304 (epub)
ISBN 9781496216311 (mobi)
ISBN 781496216328 (pdf)
Subjects: LCSH: Righteous Gentiles in the Holocaust—Study and teaching. | Holocaust, Jewish (1939–1945)—Study and teaching. | Holocaust, Jewish (1939–1945), in textbooks.
Classification: LCC D804.65 .U56 2019 | DDC 940.53/183507—dc23
LC record available at https://lccn.loc.gov/2018047771

Set in Minion Pro by E. Cuddy.

There is an evil which most of us condone and are even guilty of: indifference to evil. We remain neutral, impartial, and not easily moved by the wrongs done unto other people. Indifference to evil is more insidious than evil itself; it is more universal, more contagious, more dangerous. A silent justification, it makes possible an evil erupting as an exception becoming the rule and being in turn accepted.

—Rabbi Abraham Joshua Heschel, *Essential Writings*

Contents

Unlikely Heroes

Introduction

ARI KOHEN AND GERALD J. STEINACHER

The vast, vast majority of classes and books on the Holocaust are rightly centered around the experiences of victims, with additional and important attention given to perpetrators, resisters, and to bystanders. But rescuers—those who took serious risks or made difficult sacrifices to attempt to save people who faced persecution—occupy a prominent space as well. This is quite surprising, given that incidents of rescue were relatively few, with rescuers likely making up less than 1 percent of the population in Nazi-occupied Europe.[1] But, in the popular imagination, as inspiring figures, role models of how people should behave, they are far more present than these numbers would suggest. Rescue was a clear act of resistance, and a very dangerous one, which is one of the main reasons these stories speak to us, challenge us, inspire us, and encourage us to consider how we would act if we found ourselves in a similar situation.

The title of this volume, *Unlikely Heroes*, hints at two meanings of the word "unlikely." First, it rightly notes that rescuers were very few in number and therefore the experience of rescue was "unlikely." In addition, the use of "unlikely" in the title should also remind us that people are not born rescuers, just as they are not born perpetrators. Those rare gentile rescuers made the difficult and extremely dangerous decision to act on behalf of others—often deciding to act again and again, on a daily basis—not because such actions were encoded in their DNA but because they chose to see the common humanity they shared with a person in need.

That said, the entire notion of the humanitarian hero has changed radically, seemingly arising out of nowhere. Individual rescuers were rarely honored or remembered, or treated as role models, in the immediate postwar period. After some initial reckoning and addressing questions of guilt and responsibility, the world tried to "move on." In the 1950s few were willing to talk about their experiences in the recent past. This was particularly true for societies with many perpetrators like Germany or Austria. Stories of individual rescuers, those who stood out and resisted, would also challenge widespread narratives and self-exculpating views of the postwar years. Many Germans claimed that they were victims too, a society held hostage by a small gang of criminal leaders. According to this version of events, the regime was totally in control, and resistance was impossible. Resisters and rescuers, although small in number, certainly challenged this absolute claim.[2]

A certain hesitation regarding the status of individuals who resisted the Nazis might also have to do with culture. In Europe, particularly in largely Catholic countries, the community might be prioritized over the individual.[3] Individual aspirations and standing out are often met with distrust and judgment. Of course, in countries that were occupied by Nazi Germany, resistance was emphasized, and individual stories were chosen to showcase this aspect of the history of the war. In countries that fell under the sway of the Soviet Union after 1945, for example, the focus of these stories was almost exclusively on Communist resistance groups and partisan fighters, while the particular fate of Jews was downplayed and the role of those who risked their lives to rescue Jews was often ignored.

Many of the brave men and women who are today regarded as Righteous went largely unrecognized seventy years ago and might even have been singled out for abuse by their co-nationals. Red Cross delegate Friedrich Born and Swiss vice-consul Carl Lutz saved thousands of Jews in Budapest, but on their return from Hungary neither Lutz nor Born received thanks from their Swiss homeland. Instead, Lutz was accused of overstepping his authority, and Born's death in 1963 went unnoticed. Both would ultimately achieve recognition in Switzerland for their extraordinary acts of rescue, but only after they were officially recognized as Righteous by Yad Vashem, Israel's Holocaust Memorial and Museum in Jerusalem. The Righteous Among the Nations are the 26,513 non-

Jewish men and women from 51 countries who have been designated for honor through a process of identification and verification that began in 1963. Each one took great risks to save Jews during the Holocaust: "Rescue took many forms and the Righteous came from different nations, religions and walks of life. What they had in common was that they protected their Jewish neighbors at a time when hostility and indifference prevailed."[4]

Looking back from our excellent vantage point today, at a time when the moral heroism of the Righteous is well known and celebrated as the very best of humanity, it is surprising how even the best-known rescuers of the Shoah were unheralded or even literally unknown in the postwar years. Red Cross official Louis Haefliger, who helped to liberate the notorious Mauthausen concentration camp in Austria, was fired from his job. Swiss police officer Paul Grüninger, who helped Jewish refugees cross into Switzerland, lost his position and was humiliated because of the actions he took.[5] Even the now world-renowned Oskar Schindler lived in poverty and obscurity after the war, surviving on donations from the Jews whose lives he had saved after his numerous business enterprises failed. And the famous Swedish humanitarian Raoul Wallenberg was little known at the time of his disappearance in 1945. Except for a few diplomats, his extended family, and the people he worked to save, few had heard about him and his rescue work.

What changed so that these outcasts and outsiders came to be recognized as heroes? And why have the actions of a relatively small number of humanitarian heroes come to occupy such a large space in the consciousness of those who study World War II and, especially, the Holocaust?

In part, we can attribute the change to a shift in thinking, especially in North America, about heroism in general. Historically, discussions of heroism centered around extraordinary individuals whose actions were inimitable and changed the course of human history. Over time, however, there was a discernable shift that occurred, putting the *ordinary* individual whose *actions* were extraordinary front and center. While the actions of ordinary men and women might not reshape their society or change history, they could impact the lives of those around them in positive ways.

Thus, this change moved heroism from the realm of the gods to the realm of mortals, effectively democratizing the entire concept and allowing people to celebrate the pro-social actions of their parents, friends, and neighbors.[6] While we might still celebrate characters like Achilles, a demigod whose brutal battlefield heroics bring about the eventual downfall of Troy, we can also now put alongside him a character like Atticus Finch, the small-town lawyer who stands up against the prejudice that surrounds him. While this change can be traced as far back as Plato and his casting of Socrates as an Everyman hero, it is also clear that rethinking what qualifies as heroism continued into the Enlightenment era—consider Jean-Jacques Rousseau's thoughts on the uses and also the dangers of heroes for republicanism—and that it continues to be updated, and struggled with, in the present day.[7]

That said, our thinking about heroism clearly has continued to change dramatically in the aftermath of two world wars and the Holocaust. While we in North America continue to celebrate the battlefield heroics of citizen-soldiers—consider the popularity of *Band of Brothers* or *Saving Private Ryan*, for example—we are also on the lookout for the common man or woman who stands up for others or saves a life. In fact, we have moved so far in the direction of seeking out those examples of pro-social heroics by ordinary people that we even go looking for them on the battlefield now and we have difficulty figuring out what to say about battlefield heroes who are *not* helping others. As Ari Kohen notes, over the past decade, "The [Congressional] Medal of Honor has only been awarded to two living servicemen for 'conspicuous gallantry' in Iraq and Afghanistan; in both cases, the men risked their lives to save the lives of others in a manner that was regarded as distinctly notable."[8] One reason, perhaps, for this ongoing shift is the way that academic research has changed.

From a methodological point of view, rescue was seen as a form of resistance in the immediate postwar years. When countries documented their resistance to Nazi occupation, they also included cases of rescue. As mentioned above, to a fairly significant extent this was the result of a political motivation to minimize one's own society's guilt or responsibility for the extent of collaboration with the Nazi and Fascist forces. But then, beginning in the early 1960s, Yad Vashem collected testimonial material about gentile rescuers of Jews and presented positive, heroic narratives of those who acted on behalf of others without remuneration of any kind. Those who helped in exchange for money, possessions, food, sex, and so on fail to make the cut and thus are not presented. In addition to the way that Yad Vashem has popularized these moral heroes—for example in a series of books stretching across three decades now by Mordecai Paldiel, the long-serving director of the Department of the Righteous Among the Nations at Yad Vashem—so too have sociologists and psychologists started to change their focus. In the aftermath of the Holocaust, researchers dug deeply into the problem of evil in an attempt to work out how ordinary people could perpetrate unspeakable crimes against their fellow men.[9] But the flip side of that research is the problem of good, and researchers are now methodically digging into the motivations of those individuals who take heroic action on behalf of others.[10] That change, and the expanding study of heroism, were spurred in no small part by the research specifically into the actions and motivations of Holocaust rescuers in the 1980s by Samuel Oliner and Pearl Oliner, as well as Nechama Tec and Mordecai Paldiel.[11] In the past two decades, Christian churches have cultivated their own rescuers, a factor that plays a major part in the popular imagination of these communities, and scholars have increasingly begun to look at rescue as a form of civil disobedience, connected as well to the study of Jewish self-help and Jewish resistance.[12]

With a view to meaningfully contributing to this growing body of research, the present volume collects papers from the 2017 Sommerhauser Symposium on Holocaust Education, a biennial workshop that began in 2015 under the auspices of the Harris Center for Judaic Studies at the University of Nebraska-Lincoln. This first volume in a new series from the University of Nebraska Press, called *Contemporary Holocaust Studies*, addresses rescue in the Holocaust by looking at the ways in which scholars, politicians, and filmmakers consider not only individual rescuers like Raoul Wallenberg and Oskar Schindler but also humanitarian organizations and their efforts. Because we feel strongly that stories about heroism in the Holocaust can play a positive role in our own society, as it demonstrates the power of individuals even in the face of terrible brutality, we focus not only on scholarship but also on teaching about the role of rescuers in high schools and universities. Thus, there is a great deal of new and exciting research here to interest scholars of the Holocaust and a general audience interested in the Holocaust and human rights, presented alongside discussion questions to motivate high school and university educators to teach this material in their classes. This approach will be a hallmark of the series, as our aim is to bring new research from well-known and up-and-coming researchers directly into the classroom by including teachers in the symposia and in the preparation of each volume. This is not simply one more in a long line of academic publications for fellow academics; rather, it is also intended to appeal to educators in high schools, to be used for university undergraduate courses, and for other educational settings.

The need for Holocaust education for a wider public is very timely and obvious. Recent studies in the United States show that knowledge about the Holocaust is fading. For example, according to one widely quoted study, 41 percent of Americans and 66 percent of millennials can't say what Auschwitz was. And 52 percent of Americans falsely assume Hitler took power in Germany by force.[13] State governments are aware of these problems and react with legislation. In 2018, both the Kentucky and the Connecticut legislatures passed laws requiring basic Holocaust education in state high schools. With this volume we help to bridge the gap between academic researchers and nonacademic educators. In particular, high school teachers can serve as excellent multipliers to get academic research "out there" among the general public. This is the innovative and main aim of our series. There are not many book series like this, in either North America or in Europe. Despite the repeated efforts and public statements made to address this problem, more work is necessary because the gap between academia and classroom teaching seems to be widening rather than closing.

Bringing together university professors and high school educators, as well as individuals with local and national expertise, is a central aspect of our concept of the Sommerhauser Symposium, this volume, and the whole book series. High school teachers focus more on pedagogy and their own experience in the classroom, academic historians more on new research findings. This explains why the contributions of part 1 are written in a different style and structure from those found in part 2. This difference in style exists by design, in the same way that the questions for each chapter are included for a specific purpose; they are tied directly to the nature of this project and, in our minds, represent a real strength of the project.

The aim of this collection is not to provide an all-encompassing work about "rescuers" or the phenomenon of rescue. The topic is too large to cover exhaustively, of course, but doing so is also not our aim. We use a few examples in this volume to illustrate research findings and teaching techniques related to Holocaust rescuers in order to show the issues at stake. We open with some new research on the phenomenon of rescue and resistance during the Holocaust. Roy Koepp looks at the reasons for the rather young history of academic scholarship on rescuers and provides an overview of most recent scholarship. According to Koepp, it was mainly the efforts of Yad Vashem as well as individual rescuers and writers that first shed light on these histories long before academic historians followed suit. Benjamin Frommer presents some results from his ongoing research on rescuers in Prague and the Czech lands. A general overview about the situation in Nazi-annexed Bohemia and Moravia is followed by some biographical cases of the Righteous from the Protectorate. Frommer shows that help for Jews was limited and more common and successful in the case of gentile resister groups, who could provide the necessary contacts and preplanning. In the following chapter Mark Celinscak uses the liberation of the concentration camp Bergen-Belsen as a case study to underline that liberation should not be understood as a moment, but rather a process that took weeks, if not months or years. In his contribution Celinscak also provides insights into the "liberators'" experiences, when these "ordinary soldiers" were quite suddenly confronted with mass murder, torture, and immense suffering. Celinscak's chapter highlights the connection between rescue and liberation and pushes the conversation about rescue in an interesting direction that is not often discussed. In particular, discussions of rescue tend to focus exclusively on people like Miep Gies, who was central to the efforts to hide Anne Frank and her family in Holland. While those sorts of rescuers are moral exemplars without a doubt, their stories often highlight the ways in which rescue was incomplete or could only be accomplished on a very small scale. What Celinscak's chapter articulates is an alternative way of thinking about rescue, one that places "ultimate rescue" front and center and encourages readers to grapple with the idea that liberation (whether intentional or not) resulted in freedom for those who were liberated, whereas rescue efforts (as in the case of Anne Frank) quite often were incomplete. Rebecca Erbelding, in her chapter about the War Refugee Board (WRB), looks closely at the first U.S. government agency created to help and rescue civilian victims of Nazi persecution. Although the WRB was founded quite late, in January 1944, its achievements were nonetheless significant. The authority of the U.S. government paired with very committed individuals made a difference. As Erbelding reminds us, many Americans were involved in the Holocaust in various roles—often as liberators, but also as bystanders. Ultimately, the Holocaust was a European phenomenon; however, it is particularly present in American life. Michael Dick illustrates this idea by focusing on the famous example of Raoul Wallenberg, a Swedish-born businessman turned diplomat and rescuer. After briefly detailing Wallenberg's biography and activities in Hungary, Dick treats the story and memory of Wallenberg as a case study of the "Americanization of the Holocaust." Gerald Steinacher and Brian Barmettler examine the biography of Alvin Johnson, a founder and director of the New School for Social Research in New York. Johnson saved dozens of academics from Nazi-occupied Europe, bringing them to the United States and finding them jobs. Given the very restrictive immigration policy at the time, this was not an easy task, and Johnson proved both very inventive and persistent. The drive and stubbornness exemplified by Johnson raise all sorts of questions for demystifying the ways in which ordinary people respond to finding themselves in situations that call for extraordinary action.

The second section of the book transitions to the ways in which rescue can be used in teaching the Holocaust to a multiplicity of audiences, specifically high school students and university undergraduates. Lawrence Baron's contribution is based on his extensive research of recurring patterns in rescuer behavior and experience. In this chapter, Baron provides practical advice for classroom teaching about the complexities of rescuer motivations through selected film scenes. Taking up the idea of using film to highlight the phenomenon of rescue, Mark Gudgel surveyed 420 teachers across the United States on the question of which are the most commonly used films for teaching the Holocaust in U.S. classrooms. Twenty-five percent of them still use 1993's *Schindler's List* in their classes. Gudgel summarizes his research results and the challenges and possibilities involved in effectively using film for Holocaust education.[14] Finally, Liz Feldstern and Amanda Ryan take one of the largest rescue operations during the Holocaust and explain how it came to inspire an essay contest for high school students in Nebraska and Iowa. This contest, called Tribute to the Rescuers, was founded to raise awareness of the Danish response to the Holocaust, in which ordinary citizens organized a fleet of fishing vessels to ferry thousands of their Jewish neighbors to safety in neutral Sweden in 1943.

Taken together, these contributions represent a serious and thought-provoking look at contemporary research on Holocaust rescuers, combined with a focus on bringing that research to students. While we have organized the chapters into sections focused on research and on teaching, we believe Holocaust researchers will find much of interest in the teaching chapters and vice versa; for that reason, we have called on veteran Holocaust educators Liz Feldstern and Donna Walter to provide discussion questions throughout in order to make every chapter as useful as possible to teachers and researchers alike. These questions for students are aimed to facilitate the exchange of thoughts and to deepen the understanding of the materials presented; they are specifically intended for students in middle school, high school, and undergraduate college classes.

We are grateful to Liz and Donna for their willingness to craft those discussion questions, to Lawrence Baron for contributing widely to the selected bibliography and filmography in this volume, and to all of the scholars and educators who joined us in Lincoln, Nebraska, for the thought-provoking discussions throughout the Sommerhauser Symposium in April 2017. For the ability to conduct these biennial symposia, we are very thankful for the generous support from siblings Peter Sommerhauser and Eileen Sommerhauser Putter, who established a supporting fund in loving memory of their father, Lou Sommerhauser, and in honor of their grandparents, Albert and Babette, who were murdered in Nazi concentration camps. Additional support for the 2017 symposium was provided by the University of Nebraska's Forsythe Family Program on Human Rights and Humanitarian Affairs, the Harris Center for Judaic Studies, and the History Department. The editors thank the Harris Center for financial support in preparing the manuscript, and also want to thank the University of Nebraska Press, and specifically our editor, Alisa Plant, as well as Harris Center Director Jean Cahan, for their enthusiasm and support of this entire project.

Notes

1. In their seminal book, *The Altruistic Personality: Rescuers of Jews in Nazi Europe* (New York: Free Press, 1988), Samuel P. Oliner and Pearl M. Oliner estimate that "somewhere between 50,000 and 500,000 non-Jews risked their lives and frequently those of their families to help Jews survive," but note that the lower figure is probably more accurate "if the definition of rescue is limited to those who risked their lives without monetary compensation." They also point out that "even the highest estimate, a million, represents less than one-half of 1 percent of the total population under Nazi occupation" (1–2).

2. One prominent example of a resister, who has recently gained additional recognition through the film *13 Minutes*, is Georg Elser, a German carpenter and watchmaker who almost killed Hitler singlehandedly. Elser's case shows the amount of knowledge and insight that an ordinary citizen living under a totalitarian regime could have at the time. An earlier film, 1989's *Seven Minutes*, brought some recognition to Elser's story, though positive portrayals of Elser were finally brought into the mainstream only with the 1999 publication of the Hellmut G. Haasis biography *Den Hitler jag' ich in die Luft: Der Attentäter Georg Elser* [I will blow up Hitler: The would-be assassin Georg Elser] (Berlin: Rowohlt, 1999). See also the case of Claus Schenk von Stauffenberg, now the most famous of a group of officers and Nazi officials who attempted to assassinate Hitler in 1944. Stauffenberg now serves as a role model for young officers of the German army, who are encouraged to critically challenge authority and resist blind obedience.

3. One exception would be religious martyrs thought of as witnesses of faith and therefore role models for society.

4. For more on the Righteous, see Yad Vashem's website: http://www.yadvashem.org/righteous/statistics. One of the early academic publications on the topic, the proceedings of a conference held in 1974 by Yad Vashem, is *Rescue Attempts during the Holocaust* (Jerusalem: Yad Vashem, 1977).

5. For more on Born, Haefliger, and Lutz, see Gerald Steinacher, *Humanitarians at War: The Red Cross in the Shadow of the Holocaust* (Oxford: Oxford University Press, 2017).

6. See Ari Kohen, *Untangling Heroism: Classical Philosophy and the Concept of the Hero* (New York: Routledge, 2014).

7. See Rousseau's "Discourse on the Virtue Most Necessary for a Hero" and also Christopher Kelly, "Rousseau's Case for and against Heroes," *Polity* 30, no. 2 (Winter 1997): 347–66.

8. Kohen, *Untangling Heroism*, 172n3.

9. Stanley Milgram, "Behavioral Study of Obedience," *Journal of Abnormal and Social Psychology* 67, no. 4 (1963): 371–78; and Philip Zimbardo, *The Lucifer Effect: Understanding How Good People Turn Evil* (New York: Random House, 2007) are two of the best-known examples from the field of psychology, though both have also recently come in for criticism regarding the validity of their findings. Holocaust historians like Christopher Browning and Jan Gross have also contributed significantly to the popular understanding of humanity's dark side. See Christopher Browning, *Ordinary Men: Reserve Police Battalion 101 and the Final Solution in Poland* (New York: Aaron Asher Books/HarperCollins, 1992); and Jan Tomasz Gross, *Neighbors: The Destruction of the Jewish Community in Jedwabne* (Princeton NJ: Princeton University Press, 2001).

10. For example, see Zeno Franco, Kathy Blau, and Philip Zimbardo, "A Conceptual Analysis and Differentiation between Heroic Action and Altruism," *Review of General Psychology* 15, no. 2 (2011): 99–113; Brian Riches, "What Makes a Hero? Exploring Characteristic Profiles of Heroes Using Q-Method," *Journal of Humanistic Psychology* 58, no. 5 (September 2018): 585–602; and Ari Kohen, Matt Langdon, and Brian Riches, "The Making of a Hero: Cultivating Empathy, Altruism, and Heroic Imagination," *Journal of Humanistic Psychology* (May 2017), https://doi.org/10.1177%2F0022167817708064.

11. Samuel P. Oliner and Pearl M. Oliner, *The Altruistic Personality: Rescuers of Jews in Nazi Europe*, (New York: Free Press, 1988), 1–3. See Nechama Tec, *When Light Pierced the Darkness: Christian Rescue of Jews in Nazi-Occupied Poland* (Oxford: Oxford University Press, 1986) and *Resistance: Jews and Christians Who Defied the Nazi Terror* (Oxford: Oxford University Press, 2013) as well as Mordecai Paldiel, *The Path of the Righteous: Gentile Rescuers of Jews during the Holocaust* (Hoboken NJ: KTAV Publishing, 1993) and *Saving the Jews: Amazing Stories of Men and Women Who Defied the "Final Solution"* (Rockville MD: Schreiber, 2000).

12. See, for example, James M. Glass, *Jewish Resistance during the Holocaust: Moral Uses of Violence and Will* (Basingstoke: Palgrave, 2004); Israel Gutman, *Resis-*

tance: The Warsaw Ghetto Uprising (Boston: Houghton Mifflin, 1994); Nechama Tec, *Resilience and Courage: Women, Men, and the Holocaust* (New Haven CT: Yale University Press, 2003) and *Defiance: The Bielski Partisans* (Oxford: Oxford University Press, 1993); Jacques Semelin, Claire Andrieu, and Sarah Gensburger, eds., *Resisting Genocide: The Multiple Forms of Rescue* (New York: Columbia University Press, 2011); and Martin Gilbert, *The Righteous: Unsung Heroes of the Holocaust* (New York: Henry Holt, 2003). For an excellent overview on the subject, see Bob Moore, ed., *Survivors: Jewish Self-Help and Rescue in Nazi-Occupied Western Europe* (Oxford: Oxford University Press, 2010).

13. See "Holocaust Is Fading from Memory, Survey Finds," *New York Times*, April 12, 2018.

14. Mark Gudgel, "A Mixed-Methods Study of the Use of Film by American Secondary School Educators in Teaching about the Holocaust," PhD diss., Regent University, 2015. See also Alex Grobman, *Those Who Dared: Rescuers and Rescued: A Teaching Guide for Secondary Schools* (Los Angeles: Martyrs Memorial and Museum of the Holocaust of the Jewish Federation, 1995).

Part 1

Research about Rescue

1

Holocaust Rescuers in Historical and Academic Scholarship

ROY G. KOEPP

The last several decades have seen a marked interest by historians and other academics in the actions of people who rescued Jews during the Holocaust. This small subset of Holocaust studies has long been overlooked by most scholars, whose attention focused more on the crimes of the Nazis, the processes by which they sought to murder the Jews of Europe, and instances of Jewish resistance to genocide. However, utilizing the records of Yad Vashem, along with their own research, historians and other social scientists have begun to tell the story of Holocaust rescuers.

A key component of this research concerns trying to explain the causes for the heroic activity of rescuers. Though this topic has engaged academics, it is no mere academic exercise. For some, like Leonard Grob, it provides a blueprint to empower future generations. He writes, "The witness of rescuers during the Holocaust thus does more than shake up our assumptions about a fundamentally self-serving human nature. Their witness inspires us to follow in the ways they lead. Rescuers help us know that we have it within ourselves to repair the world."[1] The scholarship produced on Holocaust rescuers points to three main reasons why people saved Jews: altruism, religion, and resistance to the imperatives of German policy.

The number of people who engaged in Holocaust rescue is sadly rather small. According to Samuel and Pearl Oliner, the number of people who engaged in rescue fluctuates between fifty thousand and five hundred thousand individuals. The exact number may never be known with precision because a not insignificant number of rescuers lost their lives both during World War II and after. Moreover, the higher number includes many people who helped Jews not only for the reasons listed above but for baser reasons as well. If one takes the criteria that the Holocaust remembrance authority Yad Vashem use to determine the "Righteous Among the Nations," the lower number of fifty thousand seems more likely.[2] However, Martin Gilbert points out that "in almost every instance where a Jew was saved, more than one non-Jew was involved in the act of rescue, which in many cases took place over several years. 'In order to save one Jew,' writes Elisabeth Maxwell, referring to the French experience,' it required ten or more people in every case.'"[3]

In the first few decades after 1945 few historians paid any attention to the story of Holocaust rescuers. Most scholarship investigated the genocide committed against the Jews of Europe, focusing on the steps that led to the Holocaust, the processes the Nazis used to carry it out, and the suffering of the victims. Raul Hilberg's monumental study, *The Destruction of the European Jews*, remains the quintessential example of this early scholarship.[4] In addition, other historians, like Yitzhak Arad, preferred to write about aspects of Jewish resistance, both in the ghettoes and in the camps.[5] Moreover, a great deal of resistance emerged to the idea of investigating rescuers because of the deeply held belief that by highlighting the story of rescuers, authors would lessen people's willingness to confront the truth of the Holocaust. One survivor epitomized this sentiment succinctly when she wrote to Martin Gilbert, arguing that "the focus is shifting away from the crimes."[6]

As it happened, many rescuers preferred it that way. Despite their undoubted heroism in saving Jews in Nazi-occupied Europe, very few came forward with their stories. As Patrick Henry notes, many rescuers—like those they saved—wanted to move on with their lives following the war and reflected the historical amnesia that affected all European societies in the first decade and a half following 1945. Additionally, some feared that the latent antisemitism in their societies might lead to retribution if people knew what they had done for Jews during the Holocaust. Finally, nearly all felt as if they had done nothing truly remarkable, that their actions were those that normal people would have carried out.[7] This last sentiment defined rescuers even as people began to recognize their efforts. When Yad Vashem honored Tine zur Kleinsmiede in Israel she noted, "Anyone would have done the same thing, in my place. Any decent person, that is."[8]

As a result, the earliest research done on Holocaust rescuers did not come from academia but from three major sources: Yad Vashem, the Holocaust Martyrs' and Heroes' Remembrance Authority; the efforts of individual authors to highlight the stories of individual rescuers—often motivated by religious reasons; and from the publication of a handful of memoirs of individual rescuers who decided to tell their stories, like the French pastor André Trocmé. Of the three, the efforts of Yad Vashem were of particular importance for the development of research on rescuers.[9]

Founded in 1953 by the Israeli Knesset (Parliament), the organization had as one of its principal goals to investigate and honor non-Jewish rescuers during the Holocaust. As Mordecai Paldiel notes, this aspect of Yad Vashem's work did not begin until 1962, with the creation of the Commission of the Righteous, a board that looks at rescue cases and judges whether the person(s) in question deserves the title "Righteous Among the Nations." Those given this prestigious award receive a medal and certificate and have their names inscribed in the Garden of the Righteous at Yad Vashem, though the tradition of planting a tree for the honoree has been discontinued due to lack of space. As of 2012 Yad Vashem has awarded the title of "Righteous Among the Nations" to 23,200 individuals from all over Europe.[10]

The work of Yad Vashem impacted academic research on rescuers in several ways. First, due to its own research into determining the Righteous as well as documenting the horrors of the Holocaust, the organization has compiled a significant archive to aid those interested in the stories of rescuers and provide a springboard for further research. Second, the criteria that Yad Vashem uses to determine the Righteous have guided scholars in delineating who could be a rescuer. These standards include the willingness to risk one's own life to save Jews from deportation and extermination, personal involvement in the rescue of Jews (regardless of outcome), performing actions that sprang from humanitarian concerns and not out of a desire for compensation, the absence of physical harm to Jews or others, and the documentation of these activities from survivors either through oral testimony or incontrovertible documentary evidence of their actions. Finally, the research of Yad Vashem identified the types of aid that qualified as rescue. These included sheltering or hiding Jews, helping them to assume new identities, helping to transport them to safer locales, and hiding children who found themselves separated from their parents.[11]

Academic research on Holocaust rescue began in earnest in the 1980s. Much of this scholarship, then and now, was interdisciplinary in nature, with contributions made from a variety of academic fields, including, in addition to history, sociology, psychology, theology, and medicine. Utilizing the primary source material at Yad Vashem, these scholars added contemporary interviews with rescuers and those they rescued. Of primary importance in these studies of Holocaust rescue, beyond describing the heroism of the rescuers, was discerning the reasons why rescuers saved Jews in German-occupied Europe. Those who engaged in rescue did so for a variety of reasons, with a great deal of overlap regarding their motivations. In the process of investigating these causes, scholars have created an impressive body of scholarship on the subject of Holocaust rescue. Keeping that in mind, there are three main motivations that scholars have identified for the actions of Holocaust rescuers that form the remainder of this article. These are altruism, religion, and resistance.

The first major causal factor highlighted by academic researchers is the idea of altruism. This interpretive school springs from the research of psychologist and sociologists who first began exploring the rescuer phenomenon in the 1980s. In initial studies, authors took the criteria set forth by Yad Vashem that to be considered one of the Righteous, rescuers had to save Jews without regard to their own personal safety or to personal profit. These standards formed the basis for one of the seminal works on Holocaust rescuers, *The Altruistic Personality*, published in 1988 by Samuel and Pearl Oliner. Samuel Oliner, a sociology professor and a survivor of the Holocaust saved by non-Jews, directed the research for this book through the Altruistic Personality and Prosocial Behavior Institute at Humboldt State University that he founded in 1982. Along with his wife, Pearl Oliner, and a team of researchers, Oliner and his staff interviewed seven hundred people in Poland, Germany, France, the Netherlands, Italy, Denmark, Belgium, and Norway. Those subjects selected included rescuers, nonrescuers, and survivors. Cross-checking their findings with Yad Vashem and other archives, the Oliners created a profile of the typical rescuer, one with certain characteristics that served as a guide to their behavior during the Holocaust.[12]

They identified this composite type as an altruistic personality. The people identified as such in the study shared several traits in common. The first concerned upbringing. Those engaged in rescue tended to come from close-knit families where parents placed a premium on the values of communication and caring. The homes in which rescuers grew up were laxer in terms of discipline but still maintained high standards of behavior associated with empathy for others. This fostered a high degree of self-worth and a strong moral core that reacted positively when it saw its values threated. These people tended to help others instinctively, or when asked. By contrast, people from more authoritarian environments tended to have weak familial relationships and viewed interactions with other people in a more transactional way.[13]

Influenced by the ideas set forth in *The Altruistic Personality*, other scholars have sought to deepen the analysis by advancing ideas that complemented or challenged the findings that the Oliners made. Lawrence Baron has highlighted a couple of these. One was the theory of marginalization advanced by Perry London. He argued that people who saw themselves as outcasts in society would identify more with Jews because of their outsider status. This would lead to higher incidences of rescue or sheltering of Jews. A variation on this theory, advanced by the sociologist Nechama Tec, argued that marginalized populations tended to see themselves as more independent and autonomous in terms of their decision making. A second argument, advanced by Douglas Huneke and Eva Fogelman, posits that some rescuers were compelled to save Jews due to a well-developed sense for human suffering that came from trauma, whether it was illness, handicap, or the loss of a loved one. Finally, most researchers looking at psychological or social characteristics of rescuers note that a not-too-insignificant number of rescuers had personal relationships and attachments to the Jews they helped save.[14]

The idea of altruism put forward in *The Altruistic Personality* has had, and continues to have, a decided influence on rescuer research. Not only has it inspired several studies from people associated with the Oliners' research project, but altruism as a motivating force is one that is elastic and can encompass many different types of rescuers and situations, including those for whom religion or resistance are the main reasons given for rescue.[15] For instance, reflecting on the Danish rescue of Denmark's Jewish population in October 1943, Arthur Cohen notes that Danish society had a civic culture that acknowledged diversity in unity and emphasized "civic virtue, moral responsibility, and clarity of self-understanding."[16] He claimed that these values led the people of Denmark to resist German orders to give up their Jews for transportation east. This "act of resistance," he argued, would have been carried out for any Danish minority community.[17]

Similarly, for the people of the French town of Le Chambon-sur-Lignon and its surrounding plateau the rescue of Jews was seen not only as an act of resistance, one based in the religious sentiments of its primarily Protestant population, but in the fact that the region had sheltered religious dissidents for centuries regardless of religious persuasion, in manner reminiscent of the characteristics of altruism.[18] This elasticity makes the psycho-social ideas surrounding altruism one of the more fruitful ways to interpret the phenomenon of Holocaust rescuers.

The second major causal factor for Holocaust rescue looked at by academic researchers concerns the religious motivations of the rescuers. The desire to help save Jews due to deeply held religious beliefs is a topic that has captured the public imagination. For the vast majority of people, their knowledge of Holocaust rescue comes primarily from stories involving devout Christians engaged in rescue. The most well known of these involves the story of Corrie ten Boom, a Dutch woman recognized by Yad Vashem as a Righteous person, whose very religious Dutch family rescued and hid

Jews during war. After her arrest, imprisonment, and release, her story became famous due in large part to ten Boom's activism in favor of reconciliation, her activities as an evangelist, and the publication of her memoir, *The Hiding Place*.[19] The prevalence of stories like those of Corrie ten Boom, while inspiring and comforting to many Christians, was not universally welcomed by survivors, many of whom regarded it as a distraction from the crimes of the Holocaust.[20]

The first academic investigations of rescuers inspired by religion emerged in 1986 with the publication of Nechama Tec's *When Light Pierced the Darkness*. Tec, like many researchers at the time, approached the topic from a sociological perspective. Her study took place in her native Poland, where she had survived the Holocaust in Lublin. She found that many Poles that helped Jews did so out of compassion, with a smaller minority doing so for base reasons only. Most rescuers represented a cross-section of Polish society, with the largest numbers consisting of farmers, workers, and intellectuals, while the middle classes did the least to save Polish Jews. Of particular interest in Tec's study was her assessment of the role of the Catholic Church, an institution that played a significant role in the lives of many Poles. Tec notes that, during the Holocaust, the church, both the clergy and laity, adopted a relatively neutral stance regarding Nazi genocide. Despite the efforts of some members of the church, particularly Polish nuns, to hide (and baptize) Jewish children, very little was accomplished by Polish clergy. Tec argues that had the church done more as an institution, this might have inspired even more Poles to save Jews from destruction.[21]

Another author who has looked at the religious motivations for Holocaust rescue is Pearl M. Oliner. Her study *Saving the Forsaken: Religious Culture and the Rescue of Jews in Nazi Europe* builds on the work of *The Altruistic Personality*. In this study, Oliner looked at rescuers who were deeply religious, moderately religious, and irreligious to see how these differing identification levels impacted who sought to save Jews, and why. A second goal of the study was to investigate how the Protestant-Catholic divide impacted the question of rescue. The ideal type of religious rescuer would have had a highly developed sense of what Oliner calls "outgroup altruism." Her findings were that none of the groups or subgroups had a majority of members that would qualify as "outgroup altruistic" in terms of group culture, but that within each division there existed a small group of people who identified significantly with the outgroup. When compared to bystanders and nonrescuers, they scored significantly higher in all the criteria that Oliner utilized in the study to determine "outgroup altruism." The different cultures of Protestants and Catholics, one more dialectical, the other more analogical and imaginative, led to instances of what she called "consequential altruism" in relation to rescuers. "Consequential altruism" is an act that led to a good outcome, whether or not it did for the person engaged in rescue.[22]

The third factor that historians and other academics have identified to explain the motivations of Holocaust rescuers is the idea of "rescue as resistance." This has become a more prominent aspect of research on rescuers, and one grounded less in sociological theories than in historical research. As with the other two motivations highlighted by scholars, the concept of "resistance" is a fluid one that sees many people who engaged in rescue having other motivations. In fact, one could argue, as was done recently at the 2017 Sommerhauser Symposium, that every act of rescue is, on some level, an act of resistance. While true, scholars who have argued for resistance serving as a primary cause for the rescue of Jews have stipulated that, for these types of rescuers, the imperative to take a strong stance against the ideological and racial program of the Nazi regime became the primary focal point for collective action by groups of individuals or organizations. Reasons rooted in altruism and religion still played a significant role in the actions of these groups, but they served as contributing causes rather than the primary factor.

More recently, scholars emphasizing the idea of rescue as resistance have attempted to redesign the basic paradigm through which people have looked at Holocaust rescuers. In the edited volume *Resisting Genocide*, editors Claire Andrieu, Sarah Gensburger, and Jacques Semelin outline how this new conceptualization looks. First, they have for the most part discarded the psycho-sociological framework that has guided so much of the literature on rescuers. Instead they draw more heavily on concepts that guide other academic disciplines like history and political science. Second, they have rejected individualist explanations in favor of collective efforts, emphasizing the group effort over the individual story.[23] Third, they have made geography an important element in efforts at rescue, emphasizing the proximity of rescuers to those Jews they could rescue. Finally, the context in which rescue takes place occupies a prominent place in these studies. According to Jacques Semelin, the emphasis on the social environment in which instances of rescue take place allows scholars to remove what he calls the "artificial barriers" between those who resisted and those who did not, allowing scholars to look at mundane, even anonymous, actions as elements of what he calls "civil resistance."[24]

Even before the conceptual rethink, much of the scholarship related to rescue as resistance utilized many of the ideas put forward in that volume. Moreover, historians and scholars who have written in this vein have identified three types of collective action. The first category consists of ad hoc acts of rescue. These encounters often organized on a moment's notice and were organic in nature. The activities they undertook almost never sustained themselves beyond the initial period of rescue, and often the impetus for saving Jews tended to be unique to the group of people involved. A second category consists of nonviolent rescue through informal networks. This involved more people, and their activities persisted for several years. They often set up links with other resistance groups, both non-Jewish and Jewish, for material support and, in the case of the latter, for help with sheltering and transporting Jews out of Nazi-occupied Europe. The last category consisted of organized efforts to rescue Jews, primarily through resistance organizations. Resistance movements that helped Jews did so primarily for ideological reasons. Jewish resistance bands primarily led the way here, though other European groups helped Jews similarly.

Nathan Stoltzfus wrote one of the first books that made the case for rescue as a form of resistance. *Resistance of the Heart*, published in 1996, not only became one of the first books to explicitly argue for rescue as an element of resistance, it remains one of the best examples of the first, improvised, form of collective action. Stoltzfus's study looked at the famous Rosenstrasse Protest of February 27 to March 6, 1943. This demonstration took place following the "Factory Action" of February 27, when the Gestapo rounded up Jewish men as part of an effort to remove the remaining Jews from Berlin. What made these men different from other Jews the Nazis deported was the fact that they had German wives who, to that point, had not divorced them in spite of intense state pressure for them to do so. These women reacted to the arrest of their husbands by holding a protest outside the factory on the Rosenstrasse, where the Gestapo held them. They persisted in maintaining their vigil outside the factory for a full week before Berlin gauleiter Joseph Goebbels ordered their release. All the men detained at Rosenstrasse survived the war.[25]

The events of the Rosenstrasse certainly bear all the hallmarks of an improvised collective action. The spouses of the men only found out they had been arrested over the course of the several days of the "Factory Action," as the Gestapo had acted suddenly. Informal networks spread the news about what had happened, what one of the women referred to as "mouth radio." The demonstrations in front of the factory also formed on an ad hoc basis. Women showed up on the first day in small groups that built until a sizeable group of nearly two hundred could be seen. The protesters worked together over the course of the week, coordinating visits to the Rosenstrasse and providing each other with the necessities needed to maintain a constant vigil. Finally, as many of the women noted to Stoltzfus in his interviews with them, the only demand they made in their protest was the return of their husbands—nothing more. Once the Gestapo released their husbands, the protests ceased and the Nazis continued to carry out deportations of Jews from Berlin.[26]

Did the women of the Rosenstrasse, however, constitute an element of resistance to the Nazi regime? Stoltzfus makes a case for this. The wives' motivations, though rooted in very personal matters, forced them to come together and support one another. Moreover, these women, though coming from different walks of life, found themselves by circumstance in the same social milieu, an important element for resistance movements. Geographically, they all had proximity to the Jewish husbands they intended to save. Finally, the collective action they undertook also had the effect of forcing a change in course in this one instance, though one must note that it did not stop the genocide fully underway in the East.[27]

In spite of the inspiring story that Stoltzfus relays in *Resistance from the Heart*, the notion of the Rosenstrasse women as rescuers and resisters has come under scrutiny from German historian Wolf Gruner. In articles in the journal *Central European History*, Gruner argues that there is no documentary evidence that the Gestapo or the Reich Central Security Office (RSHA) had made any plans to deport Jews in protected mixed marriages to the East. The infamous "Factory Action" that had captured these men had been aimed at "full Jews," with the intent to ship them to death camps in the East. Gruner asserts that the release of these men by the regime, which Stoltzfus claims came about due to the actions of their wives, had been planned all along. In no way, however, does Gruner believe that the intentions of the German authorities in Berlin vis-à-vis these men detracts in any way from the courage of the women of the Rosenstrasse, many of whom had no knowledge of the inner discussions of government officials in the SS or the Nazi Party.[28] Stoltzfus disputes Gruner's depiction of these events, noting that much of Gruner's sourcing comes from a security document from the provinces that stipulates the regime planned no such deportation. Such disputes show the difficulty that scholars run into when dealing with historical documentation that is incomplete.[29]

Another example of an improvised collective action to rescue Jews informed Bryan Mark Rigg's 2004 study, *Rescued from the Reich*. Rigg's account details an international effort involving the American State Department and high-ranking members of the German army and government to smuggle a prominent Lubavitcher rabbi, Joseph Isaac Schneersohn, out of Nazi-occupied Poland in February and March 1940. The men involved in the operation from the German side had complicated reasons for participating in the rescue. This was particularly true of both Helmuth Wohltat, the man who administered the Four-Year Plan for Hermann

Goering and who felt that it would serve Germany's interests to permit prominent Jews to leave Europe, and Admiral Wilhelm Canaris, the head of German military intelligence, who, though an early supporter of Hitler and the Nazi regime, eventually became a significant and silent critic and eventually joined the group that tried to assassinate Hitler in July 1944. Meanwhile, Ernst Bloch, the army officer who searched for, found, and spirited Schneersohn out of Poland, was protected by Canaris even though he himself was a *Mischling*, a person of mixed German and Jewish heritage as defined by the Nazis in their infamous 1935 Nuremberg Laws. Though these men succeeded in carrying out a successful rescue, this type of operation never happened again because it lacked the international support that the rabbi's rescue had. Each of the men on the German side, apart from Canaris, would continue to serve the Third Reich loyally to the end of the regime.[30]

Rigg's study provides readers with a superb example of the type of "anonymous rescue" highlighted by Jacques Semelin. The context for rescue occurred in the flush of Germany's victory against Poland in 1939, and in a period when Nazi authorities were still in the process of organizing the territories they had conquered, along with the Jews who now came under their control. The men involved in the operation from the German side, while loyal servants to the Third Reich, all had reasons for wanting to see this operation succeed. Circumstances led them to deal with Americans who also desired to see the rabbi safely escorted to the New World.[31]

Another example of anonymous rescue has been provided by German historian Karl-Heinz Schoeps, who looked at the case of two German soldiers who served in the city of Vilnius during the German occupation there. Major Karl Plagge and Sergeant Anton Schmid both sought to rescue Jews from mass murder in a region where the infamous Einsatzgruppe A operated. Plagge ran a motor pool garage for the German army. The workers he hired came from the Jewish ghetto in Vilnius, workers he treated well and sought to protect from the SS on several occasions. As one Jewish survivor stated, "Major Plagge was better than Schindler. . . . He made no money. He did it only to help Jews." Asked after the war why he had rescued Jews, Plagge stated that he wanted to emulate the character of Dr. Rieux from Albert Camus's 1947 novel, *The Plague*, a man who never gave up trying to help people during an outbreak of the bubonic plague even as his efforts seemed destined to fail.[32]

Like Major Plagge, Sergeant Anton Schmid sought to help Jews escape the machinery of death operating around Vilnius, and like the major he attempted to do this through employment of Jews in a workshop. In Schmid's case, he operated a workshop at a collecting point for German soldiers. Overall, he hired 103 Jewish men and women to work in his shop, even procuring for them identity papers that allowed them to leave the ghetto. Unlike Major Plagge, Schmid met an unfortunate end. Arrested in February 1942, the army court-martialed and executed him in April 1942. His crime was providing Jewish partisan groups with weapons and transportation. While Schoeps believes that these two men most likely did not know each other, he asserts that it would be unlikely that either could have carried out their rescue work without the knowledge of, and possibly tacit cooperation, of other German soldiers—all of whom remain anonymous.[33]

The second type of collective action formed the basis of Patrick Henry's 2007 study, *We Know Only Men*. This work looked at the rescue operations that took place in the plateau region of Vivarais-Lignon in south-central France, and in particular in the village of Chambon-sur-Lignon. During World War II several thousand Jews sheltered in the region, and for many it became the way station for spiriting them out of France. The massive effort was organized by Protestant and Catholic clergymen. The figure most important in this regard was Pastor André Trocmé, who organized many of the safe houses in the region. Henry's depiction of the rescue work in this region came about primarily through a seven-hundred-page document produced in 1979 after a symposium had brought many of the participants together to tell their stories for the first time.[34]

Henry's account shows how the motivations that earlier scholars had highlighted in tales of individual rescuers were still very important in collective rescue operations. For many of the people in the region, the imperatives of Christianity provided the impetus to help save Jews. However, the religious impulse was tempered due to the historical development of the region. Vivarais-Lignon had long been a center for Huguenots in France. Henry notes that the long history of being a hated minority in their own country created a great deal of empathy toward the plight of French and foreign Jews who sought refuge in the region. It also made them disdainful of Nazi ideology and barbarism as well as the collaboration of the Vichy regime. André Trocmé spoke for this disgust in a sermon delivered on June 23, 1940 (the day after France's surrender). During this address he implored his parishioners to resist any orders that violated the teachings of Christ, stating, "No government can force us to kill; we have to find the means of resisting Nazism without killing people."[35]

Attempts to rescue the Jews on the plateau were far more organized, and persisted for a lot longer than in other areas of France. When France fell to the Nazis, many Jews began to hide out in the region. However, after the Vichy regime began to round up Jews on behalf of the Germans in July 1942, more organized rescue operations were put in place. Trocmé and his associates set up a series of safe houses where Jews and others sought shelter and where volunteers identified those who could help them. The people in the region often moved Jews from place to place based on when Vichy, and later German, authorities conducted raids. The large presence of Jews hiding in the region was well known to the Germans and their French collaborators, and many of the people involved in the rescue operation found themselves harassed and arrested. The Germans took André Trocmé into custody in February 1943 for his activities, but they released him just before the camp the Germans held him in sent its prisoners "to the East." His cousin Daniel Trocmé, however, was not so lucky. The Gestapo arrested him on June 29, 1943, and sent him to several concentration camps before eventually killing him at Majdanek in March 1944.[36]

Perhaps most important, the rescuers in the Vivarais-Lignon plateau also reached out to other networks in their efforts. According to Henry, this gave them access to provide material comforts to the Jews they hid, and allowed them to facilitate the escape of Jews from France. Some of these organizations were of a humanitarian nature, such as the American Friends Service Committee in Marseilles that provided Trocmé and his group with food, clothing, and other practical items. Equally important were the ties between Trocmé and elements of the resistance, particularly the Jewish resistance, which operated in the area. These units provided intelligence to Trocmé and his followers and facilitated their departure from the region through the Swiss border. This coordination made it much easier for Trocmé and his associates to save Jews from the Germans in such large numbers.[37]

The help that Jewish resistance groups gave to André Trocmé provides a good example of the third category of collective rescue, that defined through networks and resistance organizations. These associations formed the basis of the French historian Lucien Lazare's 1996 book, *Rescue as Resistance*. This study looked at Jewish resistance groups that operated in France during World War II, their efforts to save as many Jews as possible from the German net, and the effect that these had on Jewish life in France after the war.

The efforts of the Jewish resistance in France during the Holocaust stood in marked contrast to the state of Jewish life in France before the outbreak of World War II. French Jews had long had to deal with the virulence of antisemitism in their country, dating back to the Dreyfus Affair and even earlier. However, anti-Jewish feeling had become a significant problem in the 1930s. The Great Depression, which started in France somewhat later than in other countries, resulted in economic dislocation that led to renewed attacks on Jews by many people in France. The governments of the late Third Republic, never the most stable of states, proved unequal to the task of reviving the French economy. Xenophobia led to repressive legislation against foreign workers and immigrants in 1938. This hit many French Jews hard, as many of them had immigrated to France only within the last generation or two. However, the law itself had a galvanizing effect on French Jews and led to the birth of many of the organizations that would defend the community during the Holocaust.[38]

The German occupation of northern France in June 1940 furthered this process along by leading to centralization among the various groups founded in the late 1930s. This led to France having one of the largest, and most diverse, Jewish resistance organizations in Europe. While some of these resistance cadres participated in military action against the German invaders, the main area where Jewish associations organized resistance to the Germans was in the areas rescuing and hiding Jews.[39]

The activities of the Jewish resistance naturally had a profound effect on the course of the Holocaust in France. Lazare notes that because of these units' efforts, three out of four Jews present in France at the time of the surrender in 1940 survived the Holocaust. This included nearly ten thousand Jewish children that these groups saved from the transportation to the death camps in the East. As a result, the number of Jewish children in France murdered during the Holocaust was half the number of adults (27 percent of Jewish adults compared to 13.8 percent of Jewish children).[40]

Jewish resistance groups achieved this remarkable feat by providing those Jews who went underground with the material needs for survival. This included money, fake identity papers, ration cards, and safe houses. They worked with informal networks like André Trocmé's to shelter Jews and sometimes place Jewish children with gentile families. They also sought to liberate those Jews held in internment camps waiting transport to the East. Finally, they smuggled Jews out of occupied France through Switzerland or Spain. Lazare argues that, as a result of their activities during the Holocaust, Jewish life in France, which was moribund prior to World War II, experienced a renaissance after 1945.[41]

The efforts of the wider European resistance to save Jews from the Nazis and their collaborators have recently become the interest of the historian Emil Kerenji. Traditionally, historians have acknowledged that European resistance groups provided assistance to networks that helped to shelter Jews (particularly in eastern Europe) or allowed escaped Jews to join their organizations as fighters but have not really explored actions by resistance movements to rescue large numbers of Jews. Nor have scholars looked at the rescue of Jews as an aspect of ideological or programmatic imperatives. Kerenji's 2016 article, "Your Salvation Is the Struggle against Fascism," which looks at the efforts of the Yugoslavian resistance to rescue Jews, is an attempt to correct this picture.

The focal point of Kerenji's study concerns the Rab operation of

September 1943, when Yugoslavian partisans liberated 2,500 Jews from an Italian internment camp on the island just off the coast of Croatia prior to their transportation to the death camps. The impetus for the partisan's raid on the camp came from the Yugoslavian Communist Party's desire to create a Yugoslavian national identity that took anti-Fascism as its motivating force. The rescue of the Jews from Rab thus became, in Kerenji's words, "an ideological imperative" that inspired the partisans, who were located at great remove from most of the centers of Jewish life in Yugoslavia, to seek to save them. Once they had spirited the Jews off Rab, the partisans, rather than arrange for transportation out of Europe, brought them back to their home region and placed them in several villages controlled by the partisans. They were thus protected this way for the duration of the war.[42]

The rescue of Jews as an ideological imperative also drove the members of a German life reform group known as the Bund (League). This organization, founded in 1924 in Essen, was one of the more progressive associations in Weimar Germany. Mark Roseman, who has studied the Bund, notes that after the Nazis rise to power in 1933, the Bund set itself a new task, resistance to the Nazi regime. This took several forms. The first was to keep themselves broadly informed about what was happening in the country. The second was to help political dissidents and the persecuted flee Germany. Over time this included German Jews in increasing numbers, despite the negative views they held regarding organized religion. Their reasons for involving themselves in rescue efforts stem from the group's belief in the "continuum between political principles and habitual behavior."[43] This allowed them time and again to quietly save Jews from deportations, provide them safe hiding spaces, and create identities that would allow them to start a new life.

Academic research into the efforts of individuals and groups to save Jews during the Holocaust did not become an area of focus until well after World War II. This belated interest was due to several factors: the desire of the first generation of Holocaust scholars to investigate the genocide perpetrated against the Jews in all its facets; the unwillingness of rescuers themselves to come forward with their stories due to fears of retribution and a desire to move on with their lives; and the belief, strongly held by some survivors, that discussion of rescuers took the focus away from the magnitude of the crimes committed and the suffering endured. This left the field to Yad Vashem, an organization tasked with investigating and honoring those worthy of the title "Righteous Among the Nations." The criteria utilized to conduct those investigations would significantly shape Holocaust research.

However, once interest in the story of Holocaust rescuers came to the fore by the beginning of the 1980s a vibrant and diverse research agenda developed, one that sought to explain the motivations that guided people engaged in rescue. Initially this agenda was interdisciplinary in nature and driven by psychologists and sociologists. Their theories about what motivated rescuers derived in large part from the research criteria of Yad Vashem as well as a desire to find a particular personality type that would serve as the quintessential rescuer. This paradigm also impacted those scholars that sought to highlight the role of religion. It has only been within the last two decades that we have witnessed a shift in research away from theoretical ideas in favor of those that highlight context, social groups, ideological fixations, and structures that in general inform the ideas of historians and other scholars in the social sciences. This has allowed a new generation of scholars to emphasize resistance, along with altruism and religion, as a major reason why the few who saved Jews did so.

Questions for Further Discussion

- How common do you think rescue efforts were during the Holocaust?
- Historians believe less than 1 percent of people who could have helped during the Holocaust actually made an effort to do so. Are you surprised by this small percentage—why/why not?
- Considering that such a small percentage of people were rescuers, how much emphasis (classroom time) do you think should be spent on this topic?
- Apart from the three main reasons given at the beginning of this chapter—altruism, religion, and resistance to imperatives

of German policy—can you think of other factors that might have influenced rescuers?

- Do you think that people are more likely to help a stranger, or someone they know personally?
- Conduct an Internet search to learn about the Jewish population of various European countries prior to World War II. You will find that the Jewish population ranged from a small fraction of a percent in some countries, to nearly 1 percent of the German population, to around 10 percent in Poland. Would you guess that there is any correlation between these percentages and the percentages of rescuers per country?
- Tine zur Kleinsmiede said, "Anyone would have done the same thing, in my place. Any decent person, that is." What this suggests, however, is that 99 percent of people in Europe during the Holocaust were not 'decent' human beings. If that seems unreasonable, what other factors might explain why so few people became rescuers?
- With the kind of information collected by Yad Vashem regarding more than twenty-three thousand rescuers, what kind of academic questions do you think could be asked? What questions do you have about rescuers and acts of rescue during the Holocaust?
- If upbringing and family environment are influential in an individual's likelihood to be a rescuer, what should a society do in order to encourage this type of behavior/personality?
- In thinking about the collective act of rescue that took place in Denmark and the emphasis on Danish "civic culture," what kind of "civic culture" do you think our society has? How can a "civic culture" be measured?
- What *values* would determine the actions of your neighbors/friends/family/self in a dangerous situation?
- Though much research has focused on the religious motivations for rescue efforts, the findings have not been conclusive. Some rescuers were "deeply religious," some were "moderately reli-

gious," and some were "irreligious." To add to an understanding of this topic, research other types of religious rescuers, beyond Protestant and Catholic Christians. Try searching for Muslim rescuers in Albania, or the efforts of the American Friends Service Committee or of the Unitarian Church.

- Would you consider the Rosenstrasse Protest actions of non-Jewish German women who were married to Jewish men to be resistance? Why/why not? Do you consider them to be rescuers? With nearly two hundred women protesting in a public place for a week, many people saw the protest and were aware of what was going on. The event was also covered in the international press at the time. But the wives were not joined by others in their weeklong vigil. Why do you think that was?
- Having a personal experience of feeling like an "outsider" can help each of us to show empathy toward the suffering of others. And this "outsider" experience does not have to be as pronounced as being persecuted or belonging to a "hated minority." Think about the ways in which you have been a stranger, a newcomer, or were not part of a particular group. What helped you in this circumstance? How can you help others in a similar situation?

Notes

1. Leonard Grob, "Rescue during the Holocaust—and Today," *Judaism* 46, no. 1 (Winter 1997): 98–107.

2. Samuel P. Oliner and Pearl M. Oliner, *The Altruistic Personality: Rescuers of Jews in Nazi Europe* (New York: Free Press, 1988), 1–3.

3. Martin Gilbert, *The Righteous: The Unsung Heroes of the Holocaust* (New York: Henry Holt, 2003), xx.

4. Raul Hilberg, *The Destruction of the European Jews* (New Haven CT: Yale University Press, 1961).

5. Gilbert, *The Righteous*, xvii. For an example of Jewish resistance against their destruction, see Yitzhak Arad, *Ghetto in Flames: The Struggle and Destruction of the Jews of Vilna in the Holocaust* (Jerusalem: Yad Vashem, 1980).

6. Quoted in Gilbert, *The Righteous*, xviii.

7. Patrick Henry, *We Know Only Men: The Rescue of Jews in France during the Holocaust* (Washington DC: Catholic University of America Press, 2007), 137–41. On historical amnesia in Europe, see Tony Judt, *Postwar: A History of Europe Since 1945* (New York: Penguin, 2005), 197–225.

8. As quoted in Gilbert, *The Righteous*, 437–38.

9. Henry, *We Know Only Men*, 137–41.

10. Mordecai Paldiel, "Righteous Gentiles and Courageous Jews: Acknowledging and Honoring Rescuers of Jews," *French Politics, Culture, and Society* 30, no. 2 (Summer 2012): 135–40.

11. Paldiel, "Righteous Gentiles," 135–40.

12. Oliner and Oliner, *The Altruistic Personality*, 2–15.

13. Oliner and Oliner, *The Altruistic Personality*, 249–60.

14. Lawrence Baron, "Integrating the New Psycho-Social Research about Rescuers into the Teaching of Holocaust Courses," *Shofar: An Interdisciplinary Journal of Jewish Studies* 10, no. 2 (Winter 1992): 97–107.

15. For three examples, see Ellen Land-Weber, *To Save a Life: Stories of Holocaust Rescue* (Urbana: University of Illinois Press, 2000); Lawrence Baron, "The Dutchness of Dutch Rescuers: The National Dimension of Altruism," in Pearl M. Oliner et al., eds., *Embracing the Other: Philosophical, Psychological, and Historical Perspectives on Altruism* (New York: New York University Press, 1992), 306–27; and Bob Moore, *Victims and Survivors: The Nazi Persecution of Jews in the Netherlands 1940–1945* (London: Arnold, 1997).

16. Arthur A. Cohen, "Observations on the Danish Rescue," in *The Rescue of the Danish Jews: Moral Courage Under Stress*, ed. Leo Goldberger (New York: New York University Press, 1987), 191–94, quote on 192.

17. Cohen, "Observations," 192.

18. Henry, *We Know Only Men*, preface, 25–29.

19. Corrie ten Boom, *The Hiding Place* (New York: Bantam, 1974).

20. Gilbert, *The Righteous*, xviii.

21. Nechama Tec, *When Light Pierced the Darkness: Christian Rescue of Jews in Nazi Occupied Poland* (Oxford: Oxford University Press, 1986).

22. Pearl M. Oliner, *Saving the Forsaken: Religious Culture and the Rescue of Jews in Nazi Europe* (New Haven CT: Yale University Press, 2004), 1–17, 135–48, and 149–62.

23. Claire Andrieu, "Rescue: A Notion Revisited," in *Resisting Genocide: The Multiple Forms of Rescue*, ed. Claire Andrieu, Sarah Gensburger, and Jacques Semelin (New York: Columbia University Press, 2011), 495–506.

24. Jacques Semelin, "From Help to Rescue," in *Resisting Genocide: The Multiple Forms of Rescue*, ed. Claire Andrieu, Sarah Gensburger, and Jacques Semelin (New York: Columbia University Press, 2011), 1–14.

25. Nathan Stoltzfus, *Resistance of the Heart: Intermarriage and the Rosenstrasse Protest in Nazi Germany* (New Brunswick NJ: Rutgers University Press, 1996), 209–57.

26. Stoltzfus, *Resistance of the Heart*, 209–57.

27. Stoltzfus, *Resistance of the Heart*, 258–77.

28. Wolf Gruner and Ursula Marcum, "The Factory Action and the Events at the Rosenstrasse in Berlin: Facts and Fictions about 27 February 1943, Sixty Years Later," *Central European History* 36, no. 2 (2003): 179–208.

29. Nathan Stoltzfus, "Historical Evidence and Plausible History: Interpreting the Berlin Gestapo's Attempted 'Final Roundup' of Jews (also known as the 'Factory Action')," *Central European History* 38, no. 3 (2005): 450–59.

30. Bryan Mark Rigg, *Rescued from the Reich: How One of Hitler's Soldiers Saved the Lubavitcher Rebbe* (New Haven CT: Yale University Press, 2004), 197–208.

31. Rigg, *Rescued from the Reich*, 197–208.

32. Karl-Heinz Schoeps, "Holocaust and Resistance in Vilnius: Rescuers in 'Wehrmacht' Uniforms," *German Studies Review* 31, no 3 (October 2008): 497–501.

33. Schoeps, "Holocaust and Resistance," 501–6.

34. Henry, *We Know Only Men*, 7.

35. Henry, *We Know Only Men*, 123.

36. Henry, *We Know Only Men*, 25–63.

37. Henry, *We Know Only Men*, 65–105.

38. Lucien Lazare, *Rescue as Resistance: How Jewish Organizations Fought the Holocaust in France*, trans. Jeffrey M. Green (New York: Columbia University Press, 1996), 23–31.

39. Lazare, *Rescue as Resistance*, 23–31.

40. Lazare, *Rescue as Resistance*, 23–31.

41. Lazare, *Rescue as Resistance*, 310–12.

42. Emil Kerenji, "'Your Salvation Is the Struggle against Fascism': Yugoslav Communists and the Rescue of Jews, 1941–1945," *Contemporary European History* 25, no. 1 (2016): 57–74.

43. Mark Roseman, "Surviving Undetected: The 'Bund,' Rescue and Memory in Germany," in *Resisting Genocide: The Multiple Forms of Rescue*, ed. Claire Andrieu, Sarah Gensburger, and Jacques Semelin (New York: Columbia University Press, 2011), 465–79.

2

The Saved and the Betrayed

Hidden Jews in the Nazi Protectorate of Bohemia and Moravia

BENJAMIN FROMMER

In his magisterial study of the Theresienstadt ghetto, H. G. Adler commented, "In no other country occupied by Hitler, not even in Germany itself, was 'illegal' rescue so rare as in the territory of the 'Protectorate.'"[1] Over two volumes, Adler actually devoted only a few pages to life outside the ghetto in the Protectorate of Bohemia and Moravia, the dominion the Nazis created over what remained of these two, mainly Czech-speaking, provinces after the Munich Pact of autumn 1938 and the German occupation in March 1939. Nonetheless, Livia Rothkirchen, one of the foremost émigré historians of the Shoah in Bohemia and Moravia, initially shared Adler's assessment: "Yet we do not have many cases of self-sacrifice on record; the Righteous among [the Czechs] were but few."[2] For decades this negative assessment remained the dominant view, until the preeminent Czech scholar of the Holocaust, Miroslav Kárný, challenged Adler to produce evidence for his claim that "only 424 [Jews] survived till liberation underground in Bohemia and Moravia."[3] Adler could not support his assertion, but Kárný himself offered only conjecture for his counterclaim that many more Jews may have in fact hidden successfully in the Protectorate.[4] Following Kárný, in her later work Rothkirchen adopted a more positive view of Czech conduct, but the cases of rescue she offered, while notable and laudatory, did not substantially refute her earlier skepticism.[5]

This chapter attempts to pick up where Adler, Kárný, and Rothkirchen left off. The secretive nature of hiding, and the many decades that have elapsed since 1945, make it highly unlikely that we will ever be able to determine exactly how many Jews hid successfully in the Protectorate, not to mention how many tried to go underground but tragically failed. We should, however, be able to get a better sense of both the scope and the patterns of hiding. To that end, I first analyze several extant sources that we can use to document attempts to hide. Then I sketch out several different cases, including those of Jews who sought to go underground but were discovered.

When German troops marched into Prague in March 1939 and established the Protectorate, they added nearly 120,000 Jews and approximately 7 million Czech gentiles to the Nazi empire. Despite the persistence of antisemitism, the Jews of Bohemia and Moravia counted among the most integrated in the world at that time, and the local Czech fascist movement remained remarkably weak throughout the 1930s in comparison to neighboring lands.[6] Following the German occupation, the region's Jews found themselves subject to an ever more repressive regime of sanctions that isolated them from the majority gentile population and deprived them of their livelihoods. Nazi policy initially concentrated on robbing the Jews of their possessions and forcing them to emigrate. Bohemian and Moravian Jews joined the queues for foreign visas after their German and Austrian co-religionists and, therefore, only 30,000 of them managed to escape before the end of legal emigration in September 1941. The following month, the newly appointed acting Protector, SS-Obergruppenführer Reinhard Heydrich, ordered the first mass transport train of Jews from the Protectorate to the Lodz ghetto. From 1941 to 1943, the Germans sent trains of more than 80,000 Jews to walled ghettos, the vast majority first to the former military town of Theresienstadt (Terezín), which for most was only a way station on the way to death in Treblinka, Auschwitz, and elsewhere. In the last months of the war, transport trains brought several thousand intermarried Jews and so-called *Mischlinge* (mixed-race offspring) to Theresienstadt. Of the 68,000 Bohemian and Moravian Jews deported beyond the borders of the Protectorate to ghettos, concentration camps, and extermination centers, only 3,371 were recorded as having survived the war. Several thousand more, mainly the intermarried and their offspring, remained at Theresienstadt until liberation. By the end of the occupation in 1945, the Jewish community of

Bohemia and Moravia had been reduced to less than 10 percent of its prewar size.

We can classify rescue and hiding in the Protectorate over the course of the occupation into five general categories. First, from the Munich Pact of autumn 1938 until the beginning of mass transports in autumn 1941, rescue primarily took the form of efforts to help Jews emigrate from the region legally or clandestinely. In all, approximately 14,000 left Bohemia and Moravia prior to the occupation, and another 30,000 Jews emigrated from the Protectorate with Nazi authorization in the subsequent two years, although a significant portion of those may have perished in countries that were later occupied by Germany. An unknown, though much smaller number of Jews fled illegally over the border to still-independent Poland in the spring of 1939 or to Nazi-allied Slovakia and Hungary later in the war, when those two countries seemed to offer safer haven. Emigration, whether open or clandestine, often relied on help from individuals and organizations, which ultimately saved tens of thousands of Jewish lives.[7] During the same period, a second, far smaller group of potential victims avoided identification and registration in the first place and thus never became subject to deportation orders. Others acquired false papers and new names. The high degree of assimilation and secularization in the region meant that people whom the Nazis considered to be Jews had never been recorded by the Jewish community. Some managed to hide "in plain sight" for the entire war or only until someone denounced them to the authorities.

Two further groups of Jews went underground in the final two years of the occupation. The third consists of those Jews who were either intermarried with gentiles or were the children of such unions. At first, collectively exempted from deportation until 1944, most "Aryan-related" (*arisch-versippt*) Jews received summonses to appear for forced labor and transport only during the last year of the war. In contrast to the victims of earlier transports, the intermarried and their children had far greater opportunities to hide because they had non-Jewish relatives who could aid and shelter them. Furthermore, by the winter of 1944–45, the Jews and their rescuers had a clearer sense of the ultimate goal of deportation and could be confident that they needed to avoid detection for a matter of months till the defeat of Nazi Germany and the end of the occupation. The fourth group comprises Jews, both from Bohemia and Moravia and originally from elsewhere, who escaped the death marches from concentration camps in Nazi-occupied Poland in spring 1945 and hid in the Protectorate for a few months or elsewhere until liberation.

The fifth group, the main subject of this article, comprises those Jews who received and ignored summonses for mass transport from October 1941 through January 1943. Unlike in the earlier period, Jews in those years faced the prospect of imminent deportation and the high likelihood (albeit often unknown to the victims) of death. Unlike the intermarried Jews and the death-march escapees, who went underground with knowledge of the outcome and pending end of the war, Jews who ignored transport orders in the years 1941–43 and the gentiles who hid them both faced the prospect of indefinite life-threatening illegality. The rest of this chapter concentrates on those cases, which fit Jacques Semelin's definition of rescue: "acts of sheltering and aiding a person who is . . . marked for destruction."[8]

Finding the Hidden

Regardless of the accuracy of Adler's exact figure, the limited sources we have support his general claim (and Rothkirchen's initial assessment) that hiding from deportation was rare in the Protectorate during the period of mass transports. Nazi records and reports from Ostrava and Olomouc, two of the largest Jewish communities outside of Prague, show how few of those cities' Jews did not report for deportation and how few of the missing had likely gone underground. In Ostrava, only 4 of 864 summoned Jews failed to report for the September 21, 1942, transport to Theresienstadt. Of those 4, the Germans quickly determined that 2 had committed suicide. Another one was seventy-seven years old at the time and was unlikely to set out on her own. Two days later, another transport train left Ostrava without a single missing person. At the end of the month, the Germans counted 20 Jews who had failed to appear for deportation. On further investigation, the Gestapo had 8 of them in detention in Brno and another had been deported to Theresienstadt the day before. Ultimately, from a total of 3,682 Jews deported from Ostrava that month, the Gestapo considered only 11 of them to be potentially in flight.[9] Similarly, the numerous community of Olomouc counted 11 Jews "missing" at the end of 1942. Official records from June 1943 show 13 missing Jews, who represented 0.4 percent of the Jews deported from the city the previous year.[10] Even among the young and politically engaged, who might seem most likely to avoid transport, hiding was rare. Of the approximately 2,000 members of the Zionist group Hechaluz in the Protectorate, only about 20 did not appear for transport.[11]

Kárný suggested "police announcements of missing persons" as a possible source for future historians. He noted that Nazi reports on the number of "missing" Jews bounced around between 341 and 379 and claimed that, whenever the total got higher, the Germans reduced it because high numbers looked bad. Kárný further noted that overnight at the end of 1942, the Germans removed 1,111 missing Jews from the record and claimed "that 'adjustment' was supposed to remove from the statistics individuals who had disappeared by going underground, fleeing [the country] or in some other way."[12] Kárný's assumptions, however, rested, first, on an incongruent simultaneous belief both in the reliability of the original lists and the unreliability of the reductions and, second, on the supposition that the Nazis would have rather let more than 1,000 Jews survive than admit that they had gone underground. To the contrary, we know from all over occupied Europe the horrific ends to which the Germans went to find missing Jews. The absence of any significant "Jew hunts" in the Protectorate, akin to what happened in occupied Poland, would seem to provide negative proof for any belief among Germans officials that many were in fact in hiding. As the Gestapo's own investigations into the Ostrava transports indicate, the names likely included individuals who had died of natural causes or suicide, who were in hospitals or jails, or, most critically, who had already been arrested individually and sent directly to concentration camps (where most perished).[13] The Germans likely removed other names because Jews had been transported together with relatives from a different location than where they had been originally registered.

Another possible source for information about hiding and rescue are the more than one thousand interviews conducted since the 1990s by researchers from the Jewish Museum of Prague.[14] We are limited in our ability to generalize from these interviews by the nature of the sample: it includes only those survivors who were young enough in the 1940s to have lived long enough to be able to testify in recent decades. That group, however, arguably was the most likely to hide (in the case of young adults) or be hidden (in the case of children). Of the more than one thousand interviews, however, the summaries for little more than two dozen mention that the survivor had hidden in some fashion during the occupation. That sample can be fairly evenly divided in three groups. Eight testifiers escaped from death marches in 1945 and hid in the Protectorate for the last few months of the war. Nine, who were either married to gentiles or had one non-Jewish parent, hid for anywhere from two to ten months in 1944–45 after the Germans had begun mass deportations of intermarried Jews and their offspring. Of the original sample, only nine interviewees were Jews who tried to hide during the period of mass transports to Theresienstadt and beyond (roughly from 1941 to 1943). Five of those nine were eventually caught, one survived the war in Vienna, and another escaped with her family to Slovakia and Hungary. Of the remaining two, one went underground with her intermarried mother after 1943 when her "Aryan" father died. In other words, only one of the collection of testimonies came from a so-called "full Jew" who had spent the war in hiding in the Protectorate in the care of gentiles. Little wonder then that in her interview she recalled a sense of loneliness after the war when none of the other Jewish children in the orphanage could relate to her experience. Decades later she noted: "I thought that I was the only one who had survived that way; that all the [Bohemian and Moravian] Jews had been in concentration camps."[15]

Yad Vashem's list of the Righteous Among the Nations offers another possible source, with its own challenges and limitations. The very idea of recognizing gentiles who saved Jews without compensation originated as a means to promote positive diplomatic relations between European countries and the nascent state of Israel. For nearly a decade after Israel approved the concept, Yad Vashem did not even have a procedure or established body to review nominations. By the time the commission did begin to review applications, many Jews who had been saved thanks to the aid of others had already passed away.[16] The latter point mattered because for someone to receive the honorific, a Jewish survivor has to testify on his or her behalf, a stipulation that effectively limits recognition to those who successfully saved a Jew who then lived long enough to make the decision to speak out. Moreover, different countries' governments and civic institutions have demonstrated various levels of commitment at varying times to finding and promoting individual Righteous and their stories. To give but one example of the lists' inadequacies, consider, on the one hand, Bulgaria, where concerted civic and political action prevented the deportation of the country's entire native Jewish population of some fifty thousand persons, and, on the other, neutral Switzerland, which infamously prevented Jews from entering its territory. Bulgaria has only twenty gentiles recognized as Righteous Among the Nations, while Switzerland has seventy-nine.[17]

As of 2016, the Czech Republic section of the Righteous recognized 116 individual saviors in 62 distinct groups, a number that we cannot characterize as a lot or a little except perhaps in comparison with Slovakia, which had 576 recognized rescuers by that time.[18] Of the Czech saviors, moreover, fewer than half the cases concerned gentiles who helped native Bohemian and Moravian Jews avoid deportation from their homeland in the Protectorate to Nazi ghettos and camps during the period of mass transports from 1941 to 1943. Instead, the majority of recognized cases fell into three groups: four instances where gentiles helped Jews avoid death in concentration camps; twelve cases of Czechs who hid survivors of death marches at the very end of the war; and, most strangely, sixteen cases of rescue that occurred in German-occupied Poland and Ukraine. In those cases, native Ukrainians of Czech nationality saved local Jews, but neither the rescuers nor the rescued had ever been Czechoslovak citizens. Their benevolent actions took place hundreds of miles from the Protectorate of Bohemia and Moravia. Their praiseworthy acts of rescue do not tell us anything about life in the Protectorate and attempts there to evade deportation.[19] In all, from the original 116 cases, there are 27 clearly documented cases of Righteous who acted to save Jews in the Protectorate during the first six years of the occupation (March 1939 to March 1945). Among those 27 cases, we find clear and courageous cases of altruistic and life-endangering rescue, perhaps all the more noteworthy because of their apparent rarity.

The Saved

Among the best-documented cases in the Righteous list for the Czech Republic is that of Heda Kaufmannová, the author of the only detailed memoir of hiding in the Protectorate. Heda and her brother, Viktor Kaufmann, active members of a resistance group, decided that they would go underground if and when they received summonses to appear for deportation.[20] In the end, Viktor "submerged" himself when he feared that he would be arrested, but the Gestapo eventually caught him in 1941 and ultimately hanged him in Neubrandenburg in 1945. When Heda finally received her summons to transport in September 1942, she removed her star and hid for a night in the Jewish school in the center of Prague. Viktor's wife, Irma, also went underground at the same time. Together the two Jewish women found shelter with friends and contacts that they had developed through their and Victor's work in the resistance movement.

Kaufmannová hid for the first nine months in a friend's apartment but had to flee when the Gestapo discovered that she had been passing notes in clothing sent to Viktor in prison. At first she moved to another friend's studio, where she could sleep at night, but had to leave during each day. In her memoir, Kaufmannová described how she spent her daylight hours walking around the city or hiding among audience members in a movie theater. As the Gestapo closed in, that second location became untenable, and she began a two-week odyssey during which she repeatedly moved, first seeking shelter within Prague and then in the surrounding countryside. At each stop she faced the prospect of endangering her hosts. Kaufmannová commented, "an illegal can only be there where the hosts are not afraid, or don't show him that they are."[21] In the countryside, where she pretended to be a Czech gentile at risk of conscription for forced labor, she found a mixed reception, including villagers who refused to help her and others who sheltered her in exchange for compensation. Finally, old friends in Prague, Hana Málková and her daughter, Eva, brought Kaufmannová to join her sister-in-law, Irma, in their apartment.

Perhaps proving the Czech expression, "under the lamp is darkness," the Málkovás lived just around the corner from the Zentralstelle für jüdische Auswanderung (the Central Office for Jewish Emigration)—the SS office that organized the forced emigration and then deportation of Jews from the Protectorate. Although they had found shelter, the danger was far from over. In her memoirs, Kaufmannová described an existence that she likened to that of Anne Frank:

> For our security there were several rules: walk around the apartment silently . . . in slippers, and at the time when both Málková women were at work or shopping, it was better to just sit quietly. Even when they were home, the rule applied: speak softly, do everything quietly. When the Málkovás were gone it was of course not possible to turn on the water faucet or flush the toilet.[22]

Once, when a faucet was left open in the morning, Heda and Irma had to leave it running all day.[23] At night they could get some air standing at the far back of the balcony in the dark. The Málkovás' courageous acts included not only their rescue of Heda and Irma. In the last months of the war, Hana and Eva Málková took in a Jewish girl who escaped with six others from a death march. For a short while they also hid the girl's sister.[24]

Heda Kaufmannová survived in part because she had been active in the resistance. The contacts that she made through her underground political work, as well as the relationships that her brother had built over the years with his fellow doctors, offered her access to a network of gentiles who both opposed the occupation and were willing to risk their lives to act against it. Heda also demonstrated both those qualities. Nonetheless, even she proved unable to protect her own mother and only helped her to prepare for deportation. For Kaufmannová, moreover, one brave friend was far from enough. From the moment that she "submerged," she slept in at least eight different places, several of them for only one night. A number of gentile friends helped Kaufmannová, but several who provided material assistance (mainly food) simultaneously refused to let her sleep over in their homes. One constant in Kaufmannová's journey, which aligns with Heda Margolius Kovály's better-known experience of flight from a death march, is that men proved far less willing to shelter her than women.[25] On several occasions in Kaufmannová's odyssey, a husband either refused outright or demanded papers, even after the wife had promised to let her stay. In fact, Kaufmannová managed to stay more than a week only in places in which where no man lived.

The only diary we have of a Bohemian or Moravian Jew who successfully hid for an extended period of time in the Protectorate is that of Otto Wolf, a boy from the city of Olomouc. In 1940 Otto's family moved to the seemingly safer confines of the nearby small town of Tršice, but in June 1942 the Wolfs received a summons to return to Olomouc for transport to Theresienstadt. The family obeyed, or at least made it appear that way. A local man drove them in his cart to Olomouc, where they asked to be dropped off early so that they could visit a friend and doctor. The driver delivered the Wolfs' baggage to the collection point, but the Wolfs never arrived there. In his diary, Otto wrote, "we immediately steamed off our stars."[26] Instead, they walked all the way back to Tršice, where they arrived just before midnight and hid themselves in a refuge that had been arranged with a local gardener, Jaroslav Zdařil.

For the next two years they survived the summer in a shelter in the woods, and during the cold winter months they hid in Zdařil's small shed on his garden plot. Together with the help of other gentiles, including his parents, he provided the Wolfs with food, but as the war dragged into its fifth year, he suffered a near collapse from the stress. He became more hesitant about the risk and asked the Wolfs to move out. In April 1944, thanks to the help of a local dentist, Ludmila Tichá, who had already helped pay for their provisions, the Wolfs moved into the attic of another home, where they lived for nearly another year before they were again asked to relocate. In March 1945 they moved to their final hiding place in a neighboring village. On April 18, 1945, a Gestapo-ordered operation raided the village and captured the entire Wolf family along with a number of others. Intent on finding and punishing partisans, not Jews, the Gestapo released the women, girls, and older men, but then shot Otto Wolf along with eighteen others in a small hut. With only a few weeks till the end of the war, Otto's father, mother, and younger sister survived, but he did not.

The Wolf family's underground journey illustrates a number of aspects common to rescue in Europe. The Wolfs were certainly not alone in their attempt to avoid antisemitic regulations and sentiments by moving to the countryside. The Nazis specifically had condemned such evasion in their orders restricting the movement of Protectorate Jews.[27] Like "submariners" elsewhere, the Wolfs took the initiative to cover their tracks and find a hiding place.[28] They also had a number of helpers in the gentile community and even more who, at the least, did not tell any authorities what they knew. The Wolfs also had to move several times, but each move was arranged through their existing network. Cruelly, the family was not discovered in a raid designed to find Jews but in one focused on helpers of partisans.

The Betrayed

If the number of Jews who survived in hiding is unknown, then our knowledge of those who tried and failed is even less certain. The archives offer only sporadic hints from which we can attempt to reconstruct what led to discovery. For example, in August 1943 the Kladno Gestapo reported finding five Jews hiding in the village of Hinter Trebain (Zadní Třebaň) near Prague and arrested six others who helped them. One of the Jews had fled from "work in the Eastern Land."[29] The report contained no names, but this particular case of rescue can also be found among the list of the Righteous, which provides more details. In April 1943 four Jews, including two who had escaped from the Izbica ghetto in Lublin, found shelter with Růžena Šmídová and her son, Bodhan Bohun. Šmídová and Bohun hid them during the day in a bunker under the floor of the house's one room. In August 1943 the Gestapo arrested the fugitives and their rescuers and sent them to different camps, but all miraculously survived the war.[30]

Three cases of failed hiding from 1942 Moravia illustrate the challenges that Jews faced when they sought to avoid deportation from the Protectorate. When Erich Geiger, a forty-five-year-old lawyer who had converted to Catholicism, did not show up for deportation from Brno on May 15, 1942, the Germans immediately ordered a search for him.[31] According to Geiger's later interrogation by the Gestapo, he actually went underground on April 2. At that time he removed his yellow star and traveled to the city of Hradec Králové, where he hid for nearly a month. In the meantime, Czechoslovak parachutists shot and mortally wounded Reinhard Heydrich, the SS chieftain of the Protectorate, and the Germans initiated a massive search to discover the perpetrators and punish their alleged helpers. Amid daily announcements of executions, Geiger fled back to Brno because he was afraid that he would be reported as not having a registered address. He slept two nights in a city park but then decided to try to escape across the border to Slovakia. With that aim he headed southeast, where for nearly eleven days he slept at night in the forest. During the days he wandered the local villages and begged for and received food from local farmers. On June 10, 1942, he walked into the village of Střílky in the hope of finding a better hiding place.

On that very day the German reign of terror in reaction to Heydrich's assassination culminated in massacre of the entire male population of the Czech village of Lidice and the deportation of its women and children. At noon, nearly 170 miles to the east, the local teacher in Střílky showed up at the local Protectorate gendarme station and announced the presence of a stranger in the village. The teacher reported that the man had asked for a drink of water and then whether he could stay in the house. When the teacher refused, the stranger inquired whether there was a place to hide in the nearby forest. According to the protocol that the teacher signed later that day, he showed Geiger a spot to hide and then immediately went to report him. The Protectorate gendarmes arrested Geiger two hours later at the edge of the nearby woods, and the Gestapo picked him up later that day. Under interrogation Geiger did not betray either the people with whom he hid in Hradec Králové or the names of the farmers who fed him on the run in eastern Moravia. The Gestapo handed Geiger over to the Martial Law Court in Brno, which ordered his execution on June 17, 1942.[32]

Geiger's tragic fate illustrates the overwhelming challenges Jews faced if they did not report for deportation. The death of Heydrich and the ensuing repression could have led his helpers in Hradec Králové to rethink their aid and to request that Geiger leave. His subsequent wanderings around the countryside offer evidence of local farmers who kindly provisioned him with food and did not report him to the authorities as a vagrant or fugitive. But those farmers' help had its limits: None of them apparently offered Geiger a place to stay, a request that we can assume he made because we know he asked the same of the man who finally denounced him. Had just one of those kindly farmers found a spot for Geiger, he would not have approached the teacher in the village of Střílky. Finally, it seems clear that the teacher was Czech, not German, although the police reports never identify him as such, because a Jew on the run hardly would risk asking a German if he could stay for the night. In any case, Geiger's survival for a dozen days in the woods was only possible in the summer—and there were still three winters left before the end of the German occupation.

On the same day Geiger was hanged, the Brno martial law court also executed another Jewish man, Richard Bäck, and his daughter Hana, together with four Czech gentiles who had helped them hide: Antonín Novotný; Josef Střecha; Střecha's wife, Marie; and their almost seventeen-year-old son, Ladislav.[33] Bäck, a grain tradesman, and his wife, Bedřiška, who ran the village's general store, received summonses to report for transport from the Moravian Highlands city of Třebíč in May 1942. Bedřiška and the couple's younger daughter, Eva, reported for deportation, but Richard and the older daughter, Hana, did not.[34] For several weeks the two Bäcks hid, occasionally in homes, usually in the woods, together with another Jew, Leo Braun, who had already been reported as the only local Jew missing in July 1941.[35] The intensity of the German search for Heydrich's assassins, one of whom came originally from the Třebíč region, again had the side effect of undermining attempts to hide from deportation. On June 7 Bäck and his daughter came to the house of a Czech gendarme whose wife had already given them provisions on several occasions. According to the postwar testimony of the gendarme, he and his wife believed that neighbors had seen the Bäcks, and so he went to report on them before he himself was denounced. On their own initiative, the gendarmes from the neighboring station immediately organized a search and came upon three persons on the road. They managed to arrest the Bäcks, but Leo Braun escaped. When a massive search party led by the Gestapo found him in a neighboring field, Braun shot back, then turned his weapon on himself. Several days later he died of his wounds in a local hospital. In her assessment of the postwar trial of the Czech gendarme who first denounced the Bäcks, Jarka Vitámvásová concludes: "There is nothing in the testimony of the gendarmes that they had tried to disguise any clues which led to the discovery of the Jews. The Bäcks and Braun were discovered during an operation carried out by a Czech unit."[36]

Two weeks after the execution of the Bäcks and their helpers, the Brno court ordered the hanging of a medical doctor, Rudolf Goldmann, and his wife, Emilie, who had escaped from the collection camp in Třebíč. For a month the Goldmanns hid in the woods, in an old brickwork, and occasionally with several gentile families. When the Goldmanns sought shelter with a forest ranger, however, he refused, told them to leave the area, and then apparently denounced them. On June 24, 1942, the Gestapo surrounded the village and caught them. In the ensuing roundup, the Germans arrested members of two gentile families who had helped shelter the Goldmanns during the previous month. On June 30, 1942, the Brno court ordered the execution of the Goldmanns and eight Czech gentiles who had helped them. The entire Cejpek family—father, mother, son, and two daughters—was shot, along with the Plašil couple and another man, Jaroslav Obranský. The Goldmanns, as Jews, were hanged.[37]

Conclusion

The fates of the Bäcks, the Goldmanns, and Erich Geiger bore many similarities. All of them received help from non-Jews, but none of them found shelter for long, and ultimately their need to keep moving from place to place doomed them to betrayal. In each case the likely denouncer was a Czech in government employ (a teacher, a police officer, a forestry ranger). Perhaps if they had not had the misfortune to find themselves on the run immediately after Heydrich's assassination, they would not have been denounced by overzealous Czech officials. On the other hand, their tenuous existence in the forests and fields of the countryside depended on the relatively favorable temperatures in May and June. Without more permanent arrangements, like that the Wolfs found, they would not have lasted through the winter, not to mention the subsequent two. Similarly, Heda Kaufmannová proved unsuccessful in her attempt to hide in the countryside, where people feared the results of not registering visitors with the authorities. These examples illustrate that Jews certainly tried to hide from deportation, but their prospects for survival were extraordinarily slim if they could not rely on an already established network of contacts, especially during the terror that followed Heydrich's assassination.

The importance of networks and gentile contacts in these examples raises the contradictory relationship between resistance and rescue. On the one hand, Heda Kaufmannová's role in the Czech resistance proved critical to her survival. Similarly, Josef Krautman survived thanks to connections with persons active in the underground. In the small town of Zahrádky, on the hilly border between Bohemia and Moravia, Adolf Brchaň and his family hid Krautman from February 1943 till the end of the war. Krautman had met Adolf's brother, Joseph, through contacts in the Czech underground and fled across half the Protectorate in the tense days after Heydrich's assassination to seek shelter in Zahrádky. According to the Righteous Among the Nations report, Krautman "hid in the attic, in a niche whose entrance was concealed by hay" and "disguised as a woman and wearing a kerchief, . . . helped the family with its farm work."[38] In *Life with a Star*, Jiří Weil's iconic novel about the Holocaust in the Protectorate, the protagonist Roubíček's chance meeting with a worker in the underground proved critical to his decision to hide. Without the resister's persuasive arguments and open offer of help, Roubíček could not have imagined the possibility of not reporting for transport.[39]

For some members of the underground, helping someone to go underground (especially if the person was already a friend) may have seemed a logical extension of their resistance work. If contacts with the resistance were important to survival in the Protectorate, then the fact that the Czech underground was decimated in the wake of Heydrich's assassination, may have been a critically important impediment to successful hiding. In the Protectorate there were relatively few non-Jewish individuals who had already made the fundamental decision to risk their lives and live in illegality. In the case of the Netherlands, Marnix Croes observed that there was an inverse relationship between the intensity of resistance activity and the survival rate of Jews in hiding because attacks on Germans provoked reprisals that endangered those who sought to escape detection.[40] In the Protectorate, the massive German search for Heydrich's assassins resulted in the discovery of the Bäcks, the Goldmanns, and Erich Geiger in Moravia in 1942. Otto Wolf only perished because his family happened to be in the way of an antipartisan raid late in the war. It would seem that underground organizations, and especially contacts with them, could play a positive role in creating networks to save Jews. By contrast, armed resistance of the sort that resulted in the assassination of Heydrich in May 1942 and the partisan attacks of spring 1945 provoked mass search-and-reprisal operations that reduced the possibilities for Jews to hide and led to their discovery.

Whether Adler or Kárný was ultimately more correct in his assessment of the frequency of hiding and rescue depends in large part on what amount of life-risking one considers to be a lot or a little. In any case, the personal stories of escape and capture presented here represent only a fraction of the Jews who sought to hide from deportation, a group whose numbers we will never be able to conclusively determine. Consequently, there are limits to how far one can extrapolate about gentile rescuers from such extraordinary experiences. Further research can help us to better understand why particular individuals attempted to hide and why others risked their lives to support them. Nonetheless, the central narrative of the Holocaust in Bohemia and Moravia remains that of those who did not hide and did not survive.

Questions for Further Discussion

- Analyze a map of where Jews lived in pre–World War II Europe, such as https://www.ushmm.org/outreach/en/media_nm.php?MediaId=358. Then view Yad Vashem's list of *Righteous Among the Nations by Country*, https://www.yadvashem.org/righteous/statistics.html. How do these two resources compare? Where in occupied Europe was rescue more/less likely?
- What does it mean to hide "in plain sight"? What aspects of one's identity does this require one to deny?
- Are you surprised by how many different rescuers it took to hide just one Jewish person during the Holocaust?
- Why did the teacher that Erich Geiger approached do what he did? What choices did he have, and what choices did he make? How "guilty" or complicit was this teacher in Geiger's murder?

Notes

1. H. G. Adler, *Theresienstadt 1941–1945: Das Antlitz einer Zwangsgemeinschaft* [Theresienstadt, 1941–1945: The face of a coerced community], 2 vols. (Tubingen: J.C.B. Mohr, 1955), 15. All translations are the author's, unless otherwise noted.

2. Livia Rothkirchen, "Czech Attitudes towards the Jews during the Nazi Regime," *Yad Vashem Studies* 13 (1979): 319–20. Rothkirchen was referring to the Righteous Among the Nations list established by Yad Vashem in Israel (see below for more).

3. Miroslav Kárný, *"Konečné řesení": Genocida českých židů v německé protektorátní politice* ["Final Solution": The genocide of Czech Jews in German Protectorate policy] (Prague: Academia, 1991), 113.

4. Adler, *Theresienstadt*, 15; Jewish Museum of Prague (hereafter, JMP), Shoah collection, doc. DP/18/78/103/01; Kárný, *"Konečné řesení"*, 113.

5. Livia Rothkirchen, *The Jews of Bohemia and Moravia: Facing the Holocaust* (Lincoln NE and Jerusalem: University of Nebraska Press and Yad Vashem, 2005), 218–27.

6. By the five-year period from 1928 to 1933, interfaith unions made up 43.8 percent of all marriages involving a Jew in Bohemia. In traditionally more religious Moravia, the corresponding figure was still a substantial 30 percent. Kateřina Čapková, Michal

Frankl, and Peter Brod, "Czechoslovakia," in *The YIVO Encyclopedia of Jews in Eastern Europe*, vol. 1, ed. Gershon David Hundert (New Haven CT: Yale University Press, 2008), 376. The catchall party of the extreme Czech right, the National Fascist Community (Národní obec fašistická), earned only 2 percent of the popular vote in the 1935 general elections. Tomáš Pasák, *Český fašismus (1922–1945) a kolaborace (1939–1945)* [Czech fascism (1922–1945) and collaboration (1939–1945)] (Prague: Práh, 1999), 115.

7. For more, see Laura E. Brade and Rose Holmes, "Troublesome Sainthood: Nicholas Winton and the Contested History of Child Rescue in Prague, 1938–1940," *History and Memory* 29, no. 1 (Spring/Summer 2017): 3–40; Rothkirchen, *The Jews of Bohemia and Moravia*, 220–21.

8. Jacques Semelin, "Introduction: From Help to Rescue," in *Resisting Genocide: The Multiple Forms of Rescue*, ed. Jacques Semelin, Claire Andreu, and Sarah Gensburger; trans. Emma Bentley and Cynthia Schoch (New York: Oxford University Press, 2013), 6.

9. Národní archive (hereafter, NA), fond (f.) OVS/KT-OVS (AMV), (sign.) 101–653–1, strana (s.) 79–82.

10. Although Wolf Gruner argues that the thirteen missing Jews represent a high number (almost a fifth of the remaining Jews, along with those detained), nearly all of those remaining in the area were intermarried and, thus, not subject to the original transports. Instead, if the thirteen are counted from the total number deported in the summer of 1942, the percent who failed to appear for transport was 0.38 percent (13 of 3,458). Gruner further argues that there may have been more uncounted missing because of the limitations of the Gestapo's purview, but it seems as likely that some of the missing had previously died, been deported from another location, or were already in custody elsewhere in the Protectorate. Wolf Gruner, *Die Judenverfolgung im Protektorat Böhmen und Mähren: Lokale Initiativen, zentrale Entscheidungen, jüdische Antworten 1939–1945*. [The persecution of Jews in the Protectorate of Bohemia and Moravia: Local initiatives, central decisions, Jewish responses, 1939–1945] (Göttingen: Wallstein Verlag, 2016), 273.

11. Ruth Bondy, *"Elder of the Jews": Jakob Edelstein of Theresienstadt*, trans. Everlyn Abel (New York: Grove Press, 1989), 243.

12. Kárný, *Konečné řesení*, 20–21.

13. NA, fond (f.) OVS/KT-OVS (AMV), (sign.) 101–653–1, strana (s.) 79–82.

14. Interviews conducted primarily by Anna Hyndraková and Anna Lorencová, JMP, Oral History Collection, Oral History about the Shoah.

15. Her inability to relate to the other children soon drove her away from the home and back to the family that had hidden her. Interview with Jana D., February 22, 1999, JMP, no. 787, 13.

16. Sarah Gensburger, "From the Memory of Rescue to the Institution of the Title of 'Righteous,'" in *Resisting Genocide: The Multiple Forms of Rescue*, ed. Jacques Semelin, Claire Andreu, and Sarah Gensburger; trans. Emma Bentley and Cynthia Schoch (New York: Oxford University Press, 2013), 21–23.

17. For the list of Righteous Among the Nations arranged by country, see http://www.yadvashem.org/righteous/statistics.html, accessed October 18, 2016.

18. Although conditions in Nazi-allied wartime Slovakia differed substantially from those in the occupied Protectorate, the number of Jews in each territory was roughly similar (approximately 90,000 in both territories in 1941). Moreover, the different numbers of saviors cannot be explained by a divergent lack of interest on the part of the state, or a more hostile atmosphere toward rescuers on the part of officials, because Czechs and Slovaks lived under the same postwar regime until the end of 1992 (and the Slovak figures similarly proportionately outnumber the Czechs ones in the decades prior to the breakup of Czechoslovakia). Even if social pressure inhibited many saviors from coming forward in the postwar decades, the atmosphere among the Czech population was arguably less inhospitable than in Slovakia, which had a stronger tradition of antisemitism and greater identification with the wartime Nazi-allied state and its policies. See http://www.yadvashem.org/righteous/statistics.html, accessed October 18, 2016.

19. Without further evidence, Rothkirchen claimed, based on these numbers, that "Czechs residing outside the Protectorate . . . displayed more readiness to assist their Jewish acquaintances." Rothkirchen, *The Jews of Bohemia and Moravia*, 303–4.

20. Heda Kaufmannová, *Léta 1938–1945: Válečné vzpomínky* [The years 1938–1945: War memories] (Prague: Ústav pro soudobé dějiny AV ČR, 1999), 57.

21. Kaufmannová, *Léta 1938–1945*, 151.

22. Kaufmannová, *Léta 1938–1945*, 154.

23. Kaufmannová, *Léta 1938–1945*, 177.

24. Kaufmannová, *Léta 1938–1945*, 183–84.

25. Heda Margolius Kovály, *Under a Cruel Star: A Life in Prague, 1941–1968* (New York: Holmes & Meier, 1991), 30–33.

26. Otto Wolf, *Deník Otty Wolfa 1942–1945* [The diary of Otto Wolf, 1942–1945] (Prague: Institut Terezínské iniciativy-Sefer, 1997), 27.

27. NA, f. Ministerstvo vnitra-Nová registratura, k. 12041, sign. E-3341, 266.

28. Richard Lutjens, "Vom Untertauchen: 'U-Boote' und der Berliner Alltag" ["'Submarines' and everyday life in Berlin"] in *Leben und Sterben im Schatten der Deportation: Der Alltag der jüdischen Bevölkerung im Großdeutschen Reich 1941–1945* [Life and death in the shadow of deportation: The everyday life of the Jewish population in the Greater German Reich, 1941–1945], ed. Doris Bergen, Andrea Löw, and Anna Hájková (Munich: Oldenbourg, 2013), 49–64.

29. NA, f. Úřad Říšského protektora (ÚŘP), k. 278, S. 41–44.

30. See Šmídová family, accessed January 15, 2018, http://db.yadvashem.org/righteous/family.html?language=en&itemId=4017544.

31. Moravský Zemský Archiv (hereafter, MZA), f. B340 (Gestapo Brno), k. 35, inv.č. 21, 100–36–21.

32. MZA, f. B340 (Gestapo Brno), k. 35, inv.č. 21, 100–36–21; "JUDr. Erich Anton Geiger," *Internetová encyklopedie dějin Brna* [Internet encyclopedia of the history of Brno], accessed February 16, 2017, http://encyklopedie.brna.cz/home-mmb/?acc=profil_osobnosti&load=3776.

33. *Internetová encyklopedie dějin Brna*, "Popravy ve druhém stanném právu v Brně (Středa 17. června)" [Executions during the second period of martial law in

Brno (Wednesday, June 17)], accessed February 16, 2017, http://encyklopedie.brna.cz/home-mmb/?acc=profil_udalosti&load=4528.

34. Originally published in *Budišovský zpravodaj* no. 1/2001, JMP, Shoah Collection, doc. PERS/ZS/460/001.

35. Státní okresní archiv [State District Archive] Třebíč, f. Okresní úřad [District Office (OÚ)] Třebíč, pres. spisy, inv.č. 387, k. 45.

36. Jarka Vitámvásová, "Kolaborace jako způsob přežití. Židovský zpravodaj Gestapa z Třebíče a jeho zprávy z let 1942–1944," [Collaboration as a means of survival: A Jewish agent of the Třebíč Gestapo and his reports, 1942–1944], *Židé a Morava* [Jews and Moravia] 13 (2006):132–33.

37. In total, fourteen people connected to the case were executed. See "MUDr. Rudolf Goldmann," *Internetová encyklopedie dějin Brna*, accessed February 16, 2017, http://encyklopedie.brna.cz/home-mmb/?acc=profil_osobnosti&load=4752.

38. "Kolman Family," http://db.yadvashem.org/righteous/family.html?language=en&itemId=4442434, accessed November 10, 2016.

39. Jiří Weil, *Life with a Star*, trans. Rita Klímová, with Roslyn Schloss (Evanston IL: Northwestern University Press, 1998), 103.

40. Marnix Croes, "Researching the Survival and Rescue of Jews in Nazi Occupied Europe," in *Resisting Genocide: The Multiple Forms of Rescue*, ed. Jacques Semelin, Claire Andreu, and Sarah Gensburger; trans. Emma Bentley and Cynthia Schoch (New York: Oxford University Press, 2013), 78–79.

3

The Final Rescue?

Liberation and the Holocaust

MARK CELINSCAK

> Shall we, when the day of triumph comes, be easy in our hearts, our minds, and our consciences if we see the dead bodies . . . of human lives whom we could have saved, but whom we were not sufficiently strong, or courageous, or determined to rescue?
>
> —Samuel Sydney Silverman, Member of Parliament (UK), May 19, 1943

> The rate of extermination is such that no measures of rescue or relief, on however large a scale, could be commensurate with the problem. Every week and every month by which victory is brought nearer will contribute more to their salvation than any diversion of our war effort in measures of relief.
>
> —Osbert Peake, Under-Secretary of State for the Home Department (UK), May 19, 1943

Until recently, the study of the liberation of Nazi camps has been nearly absent from the ever-growing field of Holocaust studies. As the field has expanded, scholars have come to understand more about the origins of the Holocaust, the legal repression, resettlement and deportation, the camp system, methods of murder, resistance, and the death marches. However, much less has been known about the point of liberation, in particular, the days, weeks, and months that followed. By examining the period immediately after the Allies reached the camps we can reveal the true complexities of liberation as well as unearth the challenges faced by both survivors and liberators in the immediate postwar period.[1]

The study of liberation affords us a glimpse into how men and women both thought and acted when confronted by unimaginable suffering. The accounts of Allied military personnel often push against the notion that liberation was somehow a celebratory occasion, resulting in the end of the survivors' miseries in the camps.

These accounts help us understand that liberation was not a uniform moment in time; rather, it was a long, often trying process.

From the earliest research into the subject, scrutinizing the experiences of those involved in the Holocaust has been a particular concern for researchers. Raul Hilberg, first in his pioneering *The Destruction of the European Jews* (1961) and then in subsequent works, presents a triad of agents in the Holocaust known as the perpetrator, the victim, and the bystander.[2] For many scholars, these became the primary categories of participants involved in the Holocaust.

Perpetrators were those individuals involved in either constructing or carrying out anti-Jewish measures. At the other end of the spectrum were the victims: those targeted for destruction. Bystanders, undeniably the largest group in terms of sheer numbers, were individuals who were aware that Jews were being targeted by the Nazi regime but who did not actively assist nor persecute them. Neither a perpetrator nor victim, bystanders are a complex and contentious group.

To this triad, a fourth category of participant has emerged as a serious topic of study. Those who are called "rescuers" or "helpers" have become a focal point in contemporary Holocaust studies. In both scholarly research and popular media, rescuers have been elevated in the public consciousness. In Holocaust studies the term "rescue" relates to a wide range of activities that aided Jews during their persecution by the Nazi regime. Accordingly, and as this collection of essays clearly demonstrates, the topic of rescue has become a major subfield in the study and teaching of the Holocaust.

From solitary individuals who assisted Jews to organized groups sheltering those in need, rescue is a broad and diverse category. Often linked to rescue is the act of liberation itself. Across a spectrum of scholarly writing, the concept of rescue is frequently associated with "liberation" and "relief" efforts. Undoubtedly, these types of activities saved the lives of Jews during the Holocaust. For example, regarding the liberation of the Bergen-Belsen concentration camp in Germany, scholar Elly Trepman writes, "This rescue operation required the diverting of . . . units from the ongoing military campaign . . . [because] 'the dictates of humanity required quick action.'"[3] Likewise, Ulf Zander refers to the "British post-liberation rescue operation at Bergen-Belsen," while Ellen Ben-Sefer calls our attention to the "nurses involved in the rescue efforts" at the camp.[4] Meanwhile, Hagit Lavsky notes that Brigadier Glyn Hughes of the British Second Army "organized rescue operations in Bergen-Belsen upon liberation."[5] Lastly, Ben Shephard ponders how "rescuers," namely the liberators and aid workers alike, initially viewed the sick and starving survivors in the camps.[6] For many, the concept of rescue is closely tied to liberation and relief efforts.

Should liberation be viewed as simply another form of rescue? Is it problematic to equate rescue operations with the act of liberation itself? This essay argues that while liberation and rescue helped save the lives of Jews during the Holocaust, the two are not necessarily synonymous. Both the elements of choice and risk reveal stark differences between these two activities. Drawing distinctions between liberation and rescue can help us better appreciate the challenges and complexities faced by actors operating in either capacity.

Using the Bergen-Belsen concentration camp as a case study, this essay will compare the concepts of rescue and liberation in the context of the Holocaust. To begin, the topic of rescue will be placed in historical context, identifying how this category is typically defined by Holocaust researchers. Second, Bergen-Belsen will be introduced along with specific examples of the types of rescue operations that occurred at the camp. Third, the liberation of Bergen-Belsen will be examined. How and why was the camp liberated? What was the situation for the survivors in the immediate postwar period? Finally, this chapter concludes by contrasting liberation and rescue operations. How do the two activities compare and what might this reveal about the Holocaust?

Exclusivity of the Righteous Among the Nations

In 1953, the Knesset, Israel's Parliament, passed the Yad Vashem Law establishing the Martyrs' and Heroes' Remembrance Authority. Part of its function was to include "the Righteous Among the

Nations who risked their lives to save Jews."[7] The concept of the "righteous" has deep roots in ancient Jewish tradition. In biblical times the "nations" were the non-Israelite tribes. In short, any non-Jew who abided by the Seven Laws of Noah was considered a righteous gentile.[8] In 1962, Yad Vashem established the Commission for the Designation of the Righteous, which continues to be led by a Supreme Court judge, along with a panel of eminent Israelis that included Holocaust survivors.

Specific criteria must be met before one can qualify as Righteous Among the Nations. Actions must consist of "extending help in saving a life; endangering one's own life; absence of reward, monetary or otherwise; and similar considerations which make the rescuers' deeds stand out above and beyond what can be termed ordinary help."[9] Over the years the Commission for the Designation of the Righteous has made difficult and often controversial decisions in bestowing such an honour.[10]

Currently, more than twenty-six thousand people have been recognized as Righteous Among the Nations. However, does this mean that one should not be considered a Holocaust "rescuer" if unrecognized by Yad Vashem? Clearly, not all rescuers have been denoted by this honorific title. For example, since all Jews were targeted for destruction by the Nazi regime, escaping danger entirely was nearly impossible. For that reason, the choice to be a bystander was never an option for Jews. In contrast, bystanders could decide whether or not to intervene. Again, Jews had no such clear choice. Therefore, Yad Vashem does not recognize Jews as Righteous Among the Nations despite the fact that many clearly participated in the rescue of fellow Jews.

Moreover, Yad Vashem does not recognize those who gained financially from helping Jews. "Reward" rescuers do not meet their strict criteria. In other words, Righteous Among the Nations is an altruistic designation. Nevertheless, scholars have begun to challenge this type of categorization, arguing that it is far too simplistic as it ignores the complexity of certain situations.[11] Unquestionably, rescue efforts can fall into grey zones.

Lastly, Yad Vashem designates only individuals and never groups. For example, the Dutch resistance is not labeled as Righteous Among the Nations despite their successful rescue operations. While individual members of resistance organizations can be recognized, they cannot be nominated as a collective. Nevertheless, the rescue efforts of a number of organizations were highly effective.

It is clear that for many Holocaust scholars the criteria presented by Yad Vashem are both narrow and stringent. To be considered Righteous Among the Nations, motivations for rescue must be altruistic, with the individual putting his or her life, and the lives of those around them, in jeopardy. As a result, there are those who helped Jews but are not deemed rescuers by Yad Vashem.

Rescue in Historical Context

According to Christopher Browning, scholars of the Holocaust have generally studied four broad categories of rescue activities.[12] One category is international rescue, which relates to the role performed by global organizations and governments. For example, Œuvre de secours aux enfants (Children's Aid Society) rescued Jewish refugee children from France and across Western Europe during the Holocaust. Similarly, between 1938 and 1940 child refugees fleeing Nazi persecution were admitted into the United Kingdom. Known as the Kindertransport (Children's Transport), the operation rescued nearly ten thousand children, the majority Jews.

A second kind of recue activity operated at the national level. This involved governments protecting their Jewish populations during Nazi occupation. The most successful was the rescue of Jews in German-occupied Denmark. Danish authorities and citizens helped protect the vast majority of its Jewish population during the Holocaust, representing one of the highest survival rates in Europe.

A third type of rescue operation functioned at the group level. This involved small communities or underground organizations that worked together to help Jews escape maltreatment. In south-central France, for example, the commune of Le Chambon-sur-Lignon became a refuge for Jews fleeing the Nazi regime. Likewise, the underground organization Żegota in Poland provided financial support, forged identity documents, and offered hiding places for Jewish men, women, and children.[13]

A fourth type of rescue activity involved the individual. This generally consisted of the solitary person jeopardizing his or her personal well-being to save Jews. Perhaps the best-known example is Oskar Schindler, who sheltered more than one thousand Jews in his factories located in Nazi-occupied Poland and the Protectorate of Bohemia and Moravia.

The most ideal type of rescue operation during the Holocaust was helping Jews escape German-occupied Europe.[14] It was also the most difficult and the least likely form of rescue. Due to the dynamics of the war and Nazi occupation, there was a greater chance of emigration from Western Europe than in the East. Still, most European Jews found themselves trapped with no hope of escape.

If emigration was not an option, another possibility was for Jews to somehow evade their enemies within Nazi-occupied Europe.[15] In this type of rescue operation, Jews might obtain false papers, allowing them to assume the identities of gentiles. Forgers, clergymen, and foreign diplomats could thus become rescuers as Jews attempted to conceal their identities within occupied lands.

Often the last resort was to physically hide. For example, some Jewish children were accepted into convents. In other instances, neighbors allowed Jews to hide on farms, in bunkers or barns. The most famous example is Anne Frank and her family. During the German occupation of the Netherlands, the Frank family hid in concealed rooms in the building where Anne's father worked. Most Jews who hid from their persecutors, like Anne Frank, her sister, and mother, did not survive.

It is difficult to estimate the total number of rescuers during the Holocaust. While Yad Vashem has designated more than 26,000 individuals as rescuers, many have not and may never be identified. Some were killed during rescue operations and have never been recognized. For others, their stories have yet to be unearthed.

The total number of non-Jewish rescuers ranges from 50,000 to as high as 500,000 people.[16] Mordecai Paldiel, the former director of the Department of the Righteous at Yad Vashem, estimates that approximately 250,000 European Jews were rescued by gentiles during the Holocaust.[17] This figure, of course, pales in comparison to the 6 million Jews murdered by the Nazi regime and its collaborators. When considering courageous acts of rescue it is critical to keep this stark contrast in mind. Far more Jews were killed than rescued in the Holocaust.

Like many of the examples of rescue listed above, liberation and relief efforts unquestionably saved the lives of Jews during the Holocaust. Accordingly, liberators, like rescuers, are often viewed as moral counterweights to the brutality of the Holocaust. As the remainder of this chapter demonstrates, contrasting the challenges faced by rescuers and liberators can reveal essential differences. To uncover this complexity, let us turn to the example of Bergen-Belsen.

The "Horror Camp"

The Bergen-Belsen concentration camp was located on the Lüneburg Heath in northwest Germany. Originally built to house laborers, in 1940 the camp began accepting prisoners of war. By 1943 parts of the Bergen-Belsen complex were transformed into a concentration camp. Upon the directive of Reichsführer Heinrich Himmler, the Schutzstaffel (SS) set up an "exchange camp" inside Bergen-Belsen.[18] The German Foreign Office planned to exchange Jews for Germans interned by enemy nations or for much-needed foreign currency. As discussed below, the existence of the exchange camp in Bergen-Belsen became an opportunity for international rescue.

During its comparatively brief existence as a "concentration camp," Bergen-Belsen held approximately 120,000 men, women, and children. At the time of its liberation in April 1945, there were nearly 60,000 prisoners in the camp, and many were terribly ill. Of the prisoners still alive when the Allies reached Bergen-Belsen, approximately 60 percent were Jews. The prisoners included an assortment of nationalities, with Poles and Russians making up the largest ethnic groups, and women making up slightly more than half of the prisoner population.

In Bergen-Belsen the death rate was incredibly high. At the time of liberation, thousands of withered corpses were strewn around the camp's grounds as the crematorium was overtaxed by

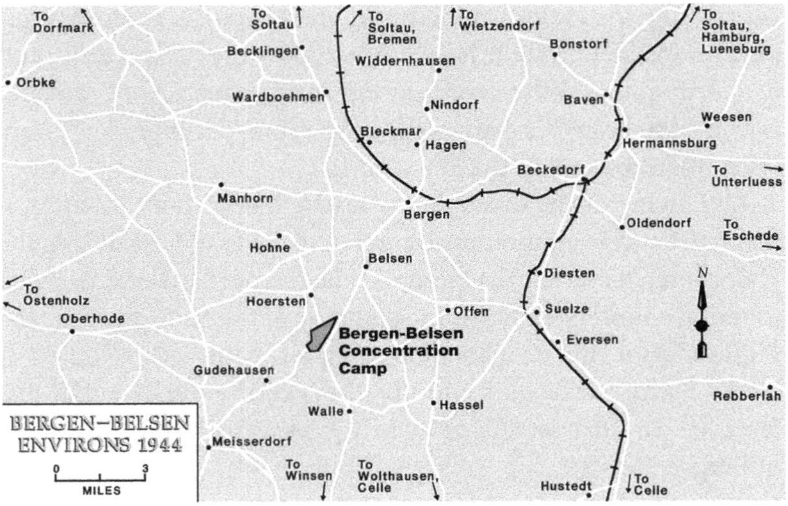

1. Bergen-Belsen environs, 1944. United States Holocaust Memorial Museum.

the number of dead. Between January and March 1945 approximately 35,000 people were killed at Bergen-Belsen.[19] The death rate continued to accelerate, and in the month of March 1945, another 18,000 people were murdered in the camp. In total, 50,000 people died in the Bergen-Belsen concentration camp prior to Allied personnel arriving at the camp. Starvation and disease were the principal reasons for death.

Bergen-Belsen and International Rescue Efforts

Prior to British forces and their Canadian counterparts arriving to liberate Bergen-Belsen, there was opportunity for international rescue by Allied governments. Between July 1943 and December 1944 approximately 15,000 Jewish prisoners were brought to the "exchange camp" at Bergen-Belsen, including nearly 3,000 children. These inmates were temporarily exempted from deportation to the extermination centers in order that they might eventually be exchanged for Germans held abroad.

According to Rainer Schulze, three categories of Jews held at Bergen-Belsen were available for exchange and rescue.[20] The categories consisted of the previously mentioned "exchange Jews," a second group of Jews from either neutral countries or those allied

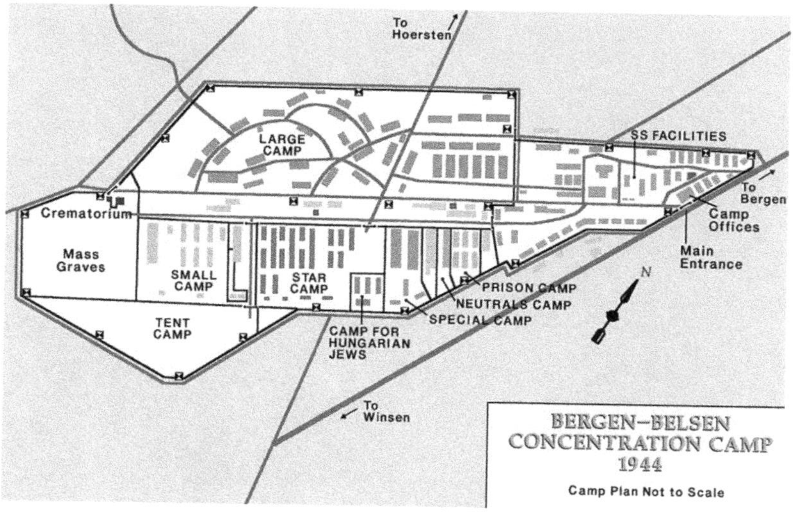

2. Bergen-Belsen concentration camp, 1944. United States Holocaust Memorial Museum.

with Nazi Germany, and, lastly, Hungarian Jews who arrived by transport and whose release was being negotiated by journalist and lawyer Rudolf Kastner. Ultimately, in late 1944, more than 1,600 Jews from the Kastner transport arrived safely in Switzerland.[21]

As for the other two groups available for exchange, few Jews were ever rescued. For several reasons, saving Jews from deportation to the extermination camps was not a priority for Allied governments. First, the Allies generally viewed such exchanges as blackmail or extortion. Second, the Allies feared that negotiating with the Nazi regime would undermine the war effort both at home and at the front.[22] Last, it was the belief of many that the best way to save as many Jews as possible was an outright victory over Nazi Germany. It was argued that anything that took focus away from the goal of winning the war was ultimately detrimental to the Allied cause.[23]

In the end, decisions made by the British Foreign Office, the U.S. State Department, and their respective intelligence agencies either delayed or thwarted the opportunity to save Jews at Bergen-Belsen.[24] Of the nearly 15,000 prisoners available for rescue between 1943 and 1945, the SS released approximately 2,560 exchange Jews.[25]

1. British soldiers accepting the surrender of a German officer in Bergen-Belsen. United States Holocaust Memorial Museum, courtesy of Hadassah Bimko Rosensaft.

Schulze suggests that had the Allies made it a priority, many more Jews could have been rescued from the exchange camp at Bergen-Belsen.[26] Due to this reluctance, the victims of Bergen-Belsen had to wait for Allied forces to liberate the camp.

The Liberation of Bergen-Belsen

Under the approval of Himmler, on April 12, 1945, Col. Hans Schmidt and other representatives from the First German Parachute Army crossed into British territory and revealed that inmates at a nearby camp were sick with typhus.[27] The Germans were concerned that if any inmates escaped due to the fighting they might infect the local population. German representatives were led to the headquarters of the British Army's VIII Corps at Winsen. Discussions regarding the handover of the camp were held between the VIII Corps chief of staff and the chief of staff of the First Parachute Army, Military Commandant Bergen. Signed on the morning of April 13, 1945, the agreement recognized a neutral area of forty-eight square kilometers around Bergen-Belsen and the nearby military training grounds. Subsequently, this led to the decision that the camp would come under the command of Lt. Col. R.I.G. Taylor of the British Army's Sixty-Third Anti-Tank Regiment. Due to fighting in the vicinity of Bergen-Belsen, the Allies were delayed from entering the camp by two days.

On April 15, 1945, the Sixty-Third Anti-Tank Regiment arrived in the neutral zone set aside in the agreement. At 1500 hours, the leading party of Taylor's regiment, the 249th (Oxfordshire Yeomanry) Battery, commanded by Maj. Benjamin Barnett, arrived at Bergen-Belsen. Lt. Col. Taylor instructed Capt. Derrick Sington and two other noncommissioned officers, Sgt. Eric Clyne and Lance Corporal Sidney Roberts, to enter the camp with an armored car equipped with a battery of loudspeakers. Entering the camp, Sington quickly announced that while the inmates were now free of Nazi tyranny, no one would be allowed to leave Bergen-Belsen.[28]

Motivations

Before examining British relief efforts at Bergen-Belsen, let us consider the impetus, if any, for coming to the aid of Jews during the war. According to Yad Vashem, motivations for rescue must be altruistic because they often place an individual's life, and those around them, in jeopardy. Did the fate of European Jews prompt the average British soldier to become involved in the war effort and subsequent liberation activities?

Prior to the outbreak of World War II, Britons could read in national newspapers about the crimes of Nazi Germany. However, properly evaluating the scale of terror was difficult. Alan Rose was born into a Jewish family in Dundee, Scotland. He was a sergeant in the Seventh Armored Division when he and his men from the Third/Fourth County of London Yeomanry entered Bergen-Belsen. Rose recalls that his decision to enlist was "prompted, first of all, because whilst nobody knew what Hitler was doing, we all knew what terrible things were happening in Europe."[29] Certainly, news about the treatment of Jews in German-occupied Europe was being followed by various communities in Britain, although much was still to be discovered.

Rose remembers that during the war military personnel gradually became aware of the deportations and murder. "I had heard on the radio," Rose explains, "on the BBC, that a concentration camp had been liberated in Eastern Europe. . . . One heard the horrors, but of course it was quite impossible to comprehend."[30] While news was being received by men at the front, grasping the enormity of devastation was a challenge. According to Rose,

> I mean, we had no idea in those days what deportation meant. I mean, it was inconceivable to us still in those days. And, you must remember, I lived in a very small world: I lived in a tank, and I heard the BBC news every night. . . . But, at that time, we had no knowledge of the gas chambers and the genocidal intention of the Nazis. At least, I didn't. I'm sure the Allied powers had. But, I'm the very lonely soldier sitting in a tank, with a very limited horizon.[31]

News of Nazi crimes certainly found its way to the men fighting at the front, albeit to a limited extent. For the average soldier in battle, securing victory as soon as possible was their priority. Additionally, surviving the war and returning home in one piece were often on most soldiers' minds.

For most other personnel, saving or rescuing Jews was never a reason for enlistment. At sixteen years old, John Gourlay Noble of Edinburgh lied about his age and enlisted in the Scots Greys.[32] In 1942 he joined the Special Air Service (SAS) as a driver. When the SAS stumbled upon Bergen-Belsen in April 1945, Noble admits to being oblivious about Hitler's camp system.[33] He was young, naïve, and when not busy with his military duties he was simply looking for a "good time."[34] Noble reveals that, unlike Rose, he rarely read the day's news, even while on leave. The horrors of the war were enough. Recognizing the scale of the Holocaust occurred only years after the war.

In short, information regarding the suffering in Europe certainly existed, and many military personnel knew that Jews and other groups were being ill treated by the Nazi regime. However, it is also clear that most British military personnel had no prior understanding of Nazi policy; they were unacquainted with the function of Hitler's camp system, and they were generally oblivious to the historical events that led to their formation. Therefore, it is fair to say that most British personnel did not enlist in the military to liberate Nazi camps or to save European Jews. "Nobody set out to liberate a concentration camp," Rose explains. "So the word 'liberator' is a misnomer, in a sense. Either we were all liberators or we were not liberators, but nobody specifically spent his or her time thinking, 'How am I going to liberate a concentration camp?' First of all, we hardly knew that they existed. I didn't."[35] In addition, the deliverance of inmates from Nazi camps in Europe was never an Allied military objective during the World War II.

Relief Efforts

Tending to the physical, mental, and spiritual needs of the survivors of Bergen-Belsen was largely the responsibility of the medical corps and chaplains of various denominations of the British Army. The tasks performed by army staff often went far beyond their typical duties. Military personnel found themselves facing conditions that they had not expected, and for which they were not prepared nor trained. As a result, chaplains often became involved in nonreligious activities, such as gathering clothes and medicine from the surrounding area, while medical personnel accepted jobs outside their typical obligations, such as the dispersal of food and water, as well as sanitation work.

The British were clearly ill prepared to handle the large number of survivors who needed urgent care. As the war in Europe continued, British Army staff at Bergen-Belsen were initially lacking personnel, supplies, equipment, facilities, and medications. Plans were soon devised to bury the dead in mass graves and to evacuate the living to the nearby Panzer Training School. Despite these efforts early on, headway was a constant struggle. Evacuation of the barracks was further complicated as healthier survivors intermingled with the ill and near dead.[36] Consequently, military

2. Feeding survivors in Bergen-Belsen after liberation. United States Holocaust Memorial Museum.

personnel were forced to make excruciating decisions regarding inmate prioritization.

Many of these problems were tackled by military authorities, such as Brigadier Glyn Hughes, deputy director of Medical Services. He arrived at Bergen-Belsen soon after the first Allied personnel entered the camp. Regarding which inmates would be given urgent treatment, Brigadier Hughes initiated a strategy of triage. He explains:

> Under the conditions which existed it was obvious that thorough diagnosis and elaborate treatment of individual patients . . . would take up so much time that only a small fraction of them could be dealt with and that to the exclusion of the elementary care of the remainder. The principle adopted was that the greatest number of lives would be saved by placing those who had a reasonable chance of survival under conditions in which their own tendency to recover could be aided by simple nursing and suitable feeding, and in which further infection could be prevented.[37]

Hughes made a judgment to offer a concerted form of assistance that would guarantee the highest numbers of people were saved. Survivors were separated into three categories: the first two included those who would likely survive and those who would likely die regardless of the care they received; the third were those for whom immediate care could mean the difference between life and death. Thus, the medical teams did not select those who needed the most urgent care. On the contrary, it was a calculated decision to select for evacuation only those who stood the best chance of surviving with only basic medical care. As a result, those who had suffered the most, and who were less likely to survive the next few hours or days, were not necessarily given priority.

Subsequently, stretcher-bearers were dispatched to bring selected survivors from the barracks to the nearby Panzer Training School for medical care. Again, knowing which of the inmates was to be removed from the barracks created yet another problem. In his moving account, Lt. Col. Mervin Willett Gonin, the officer commanding the Eleventh Light Field Ambulance revealed:

> The MO went into each hut and marked on the forehead of each patient a cross to indicate to the bearers that this patient would be moved. The MO made no attempt to fix a diagnosis—all he did was decide whether the patient had any chance of living if he or she were moved or what the chance of survival might be if the patient were left in the camp for another week. It was a heart-rending job and amounted to telling hundreds of poor wretches that they were being left to die. But, as I have said, the individual did not count.[38]

Lt. Col. Gonin, like Brigadier Hughes, experienced the agonizing decisions of prioritizing the sick based on which survivor had the best chance of surviving with limited care. Those barely clinging to life were left behind. The survivors who had the strength would cry out, desperate to be saved. It became an incredibly difficult situation for those making the decisions.

A relief worker with the British Red Cross observed some of these painful choices firsthand. "This was almost an impossible proposition," Myrtle Beardwell recalls about a doctor who had to make a number of these determinations. "Those whom he

3. Women and children, many of whom are suffering from typhus, typhoid, and dysentery, in a barracks at Bergen-Belsen after liberation. United States Holocaust Memorial Museum, courtesy of Hadassah Bimko Rosensaft.

knew had only a few hours to live he had to leave."[39] Survivors begged and clamored to get out in hopes of receiving medical attention. According to Beardwell, the situation became so difficult that "they had to have decoy stretchers at one door of the hut whilst the doctor went in at the other and quickly grabbed a sick person."[40] As these heart-wrenching scenes continued, the short-staffed British medical teams were also faced with issues involving their own health.

Indeed, medical personnel also had to be cognizant of the illnesses present in Bergen-Belsen. While precautions were adopted to guard against diseases in the camp, British medical personnel still caught various illnesses. Attached to the Thirty-Second Casualty Clearing Station, Lt. Col. F. M. Lipscomb revealed that at least ten Royal Army Medical Corps (RAMC) personnel contracted typhus while working at the camp. Furthermore, another twenty-three German nurses, ordered by the British to assist at the camp, also contracted typhus. And while none of the RAMC staff died, two of the German nurses succumbed to their illnesses.[41] Indeed, working in close proximity to the dead and diseased regularly put medical teams at risk.

Dr. D. T. Prescott of the Eleventh Light Field Ambulance similarly highlighted the danger of working near such illnesses in unsanitary surroundings. On a nightly basis, personnel from this unit visited the hospital at Bergen-Belsen to help in the removal of the dead. Prescott explains that typhus "took a toll, of our Unit 10% contracted the disease. . . . [T]hey were all seriously ill for about a week and then recovered only slowly after several debilitating weeks."[42] From his unit at least twenty men became sick, although all, fortunately, survived the ordeal.

British military personnel also had great difficulty relating to the people they were helping. The language used to describe the survivors often betrayed the life-saving work they were providing. "Human reactions to the unthinkable," scholars George M. Kren and Leon Rappoport remind us, "are inevitably primitive and visceral."[43] Those working in the camp were shocked and even disgusted by the gaunt, half-naked inmates in tattered prison uniforms. In addition, language barriers and glaring cultural differences made it challenging for many personnel to relate to and comprehend the survivors they were trying to help. Even when some of those barriers were removed, the encounter with survivors was still trying.

Leslie Hardman was born in 1913 in Glynneath, Wales, to a Polish father and a Russian mother. After a series of attacks on Jewish families by mineworkers in South Wales, the family moved to Liverpool. Hardman later became a chaplain in the British Army. Arriving at Bergen-Belsen two days after its liberation, he did as much as anyone to support the survivors. Reverend Hardman recalls his first encounter with a survivor at the camp. He writes:

> I shall always remember the first person I met. It was a girl, and I thought she was a negress. Her face was dark brown, and I afterwards learnt that this was because her skin was in the process of healing, after being burnt. When she saw me she made as though to throw her arms around me; but with the instinct of self-preservation, I jumped back.

> Instantly, I felt ashamed. . . . I looked at her; fear, compassion and shame were struggling for mastery within me; but she was the more composed of the two. We walked into the compound, keeping our voluntary "no-man's-land" between us.[44]

This might have been a moment for a Holocaust survivor to embrace her liberator. While many inmates had suffered for years in the camps and grown accustomed to seeing one another at their worst, this was clearly not the case for British personnel. Indeed, few had seen so many distressed people in such an enclosed area, surrounded by decomposing corpses. Hardman's reaction was an illustration of a natural defensive instinct. He spoke of the incident numerous times in interviews, always admitting embarrassment.[45]

British doctors, nurses, and other medical personnel completed a number of different tasks in Bergen-Belsen. They arrived at the camp unprepared, understaffed, and faced with conditions they had never before encountered. Their assignments were challenging, and some suffered mightily because of the work: dysentery, isolation, depression, and feelings of inadequacy were common. And yet, most accepted their tasks willingly, working with the resources they had around them.

Survivors in the Aftermath

For survivors in camps like Bergen-Belsen, liberation did not mean freedom in the way we normally use the term. Initially, the survivors were not given autonomy to leave the camp and go wherever they saw fit. Instead, in the weeks, and for some, in the months and even years that followed, they continued to live behind the barbed wire in the camps. When places like Bergen-Belsen became Displaced Persons (DP) camps, the survivors were still guarded—only by men in different uniforms.

Moreover, DP camps like Bergen-Belsen were often unpleasant places, especially for Jews who often discovered that they now lived alongside people who had collaborated with Nazi Germany or, in some rare instances, had even fought in German army uniforms. British officials at Bergen-Belsen also refused to recognize Jews as a distinct group, so Polish Jews were treated as Poles and Hungarian Jews as Hungarians. This led to serious tension, animosity, and in-fighting between the various groups. Consequently, since there was generally nowhere else to go, life could be rather grim, mainly for Jewish survivors of the camps.[46]

British forces were ill equipped to handle a camp of nearly sixty thousand people. Also, the war continued for another three weeks. For the British, the solution seemed obvious: retain as many camp staff as possible. While the SS were soon disarmed and arrested, soldiers from both the German and Hungarian armies remained on site to guard the camp.[47] In the days following liberation, several starving survivors were shot dead, mainly by Hungarian soldiers who guarded the kitchen and manned the watchtowers under British supervision. Later on, the Hungarians were employed for a variety of other roles. Therefore it was often difficult for survivors to feel secure following their liberation.

It was not only the use of German and Hungarian army personnel that so unnerved the survivors of Bergen-Belsen. It was also the employment of German doctors and nurses in the camp hospital.[48] To alleviate the overwhelming need for additional personnel, local German military doctors and nurses were used in the camp to assist the British medical teams.[49] The psychological impact on the survivors was profound. While the treatment they received was generally quite good, the effect of seeing doctors, some still in German army uniforms, was traumatic for many survivors.

If a survivor was healthy enough, why not simply allow him or her to leave the camp? Within weeks of their liberation, many non-Jews did return home. So, too, did Jews from Western Europe. The situation was quite different for Jews from Eastern Europe. For many of these survivors, returning home was generally unthinkable. The fear of antisemitic attacks and the haunting memories of what happened to their family and friends made this an unrealistic prospect. Many survivors wanted to leave Europe in pursuit of a life in a new Jewish state in Palestine. But, how was that possible? Britain had long maintained a policy of limiting Jewish immigration into Palestine, which they had done throughout the 1930s. The British had argued that the interests of the region would be better served by maintaining an Arab majority. Paradoxically,

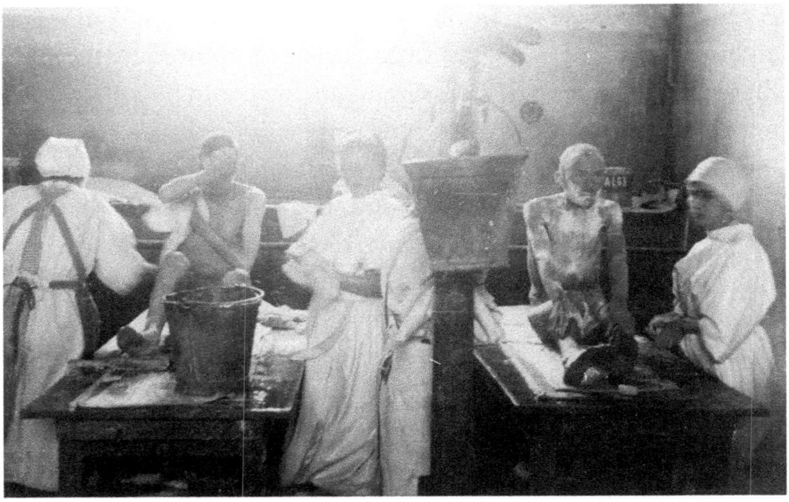

4. German nurses from nearby hospitals, who were conscripted to work in the camp, wash and disinfect survivors in Bergen-Belsen. United States Holocaust Memorial Museum, courtesy of Madalae Fraser.

the British helped save Jews by liberating them from the concentration camps but then turned around and basically re-imprisoned them in the immediate postwar period.

For many survivors, the way forward was Aliyah Bet, the code name given to illegal immigration by Jews to Mandatory Palestine. By 1948 more than one hundred thousand people had taken this route, including more than seventy thousand Holocaust survivors. However, the journey was not an easy one. Over 90 percent of the ships on their way to Palestine were intercepted by the Royal Navy. The refugees seized were moved to detention camps. By 1948, for example, the British held more than fifty thousand Jewish refugees in internment camps on Cyprus.

In rare instances, British liberators of Bergen-Belsen were later assigned to search these ships bearing Jewish Holocaust survivors in the postwar period. It was an astonishing turn of events. Men who a few years earlier had entered camps like Bergen-Belsen later searched ships to prevent those very same survivors—now refugees—from arriving in the only place they felt they could call home. While some of these soldiers merely

5. British soldiers transfer the refugees from the *Exodus 1947* to the deportation ships. United States Holocaust Memorial Museum, courtesy of Murray T. Aronoff.

claimed they were doing their jobs, for others it created a crisis of conscience.[50]

Conclusion

Should liberation be viewed as another type of rescue? As has been demonstrated above, there are commonalities between rescue and liberation. For example, both were attempts to aid Jews and alleviate some of their hardship. Indeed, upon liberation, relief teams rushed into camps like Bergen-Belsen to provide food and medicine. To the best of their ability, military personnel removed inmates from the squalor of the barracks and helped sanitize the facilities, with these efforts saving many lives. Likewise, Holocaust rescuers often provided food and shelter to Jews in a variety of situations. In times of distress, both liberators and rescuers attempted to make a positive impact on those in desperate need.

Furthermore, rescue and liberation activities loom large in the public imagination. The rescuer and the liberator, rightly or wrongly, have become moral counterweights in one of the darkest periods of human history. During the Holocaust, they were the ones who worked in constructive capacities, demonstrating hope and humanitarianism in an otherwise bleak time.

Still, liberation should not be conflated with rescue, for they are not synonymous.[51] Indeed, there are important distinctions to be made between the two activities. The threat of danger is frequently referenced when discussing the work of Holocaust rescuers. Many individuals clearly put themselves and their loved ones at risk while attempting acts of rescue. This is primarily why Yad Vashem places an emphasis on the degree to which an individual endangers his or her own life. However, as Agnes Grunwald-Spier has argued, some "rescuers did a great deal without doing anything so risky."[52] While this should not diminish their efforts, there were a range of activities during which the threat to the rescuer was somewhat limited. Moreover, as discussed above, British medical personnel also put themselves at risk while working in close proximity with survivors suffering from a variety of ailments.

Yet the question of danger is still an important one when distinguishing between rescue and liberation. Rather than focus on the rescuer and liberator, a better distinction can be made regarding the rescued and liberated. When a Jew was rescued during the Holocaust, the threat of Nazi persecution remained. In other words, rescue was always temporary. The danger did not evaporate; rather, it was a momentary reprieve. For example, a "rescued" Jew could later be revealed to be hiding on the property of a gentile, a false identity could one day be discovered, even those who emigrated could conceivably be sent back to a place of persecution. However, when a Jew was liberated by Allied forces, the danger, the direct threat posed by the Nazi regime, was typically removed. In short, rescue falls along a continuum, one where peril constantly waits, lingers, lurks. The act of liberation, in contrast, is an end in and of itself. While challenges still remained for those liberated at camps like Bergen-Belsen, their issues had little to do with any continued threat posed by Nazism. In camp after camp across Europe, Allied armies emerged victorious, effectively removing the danger posed by the Nazi regime.

Furthermore, when considering the agents of liberation and rescue, we can make another important distinction. Choice plays a significant role in Yad Vashem's decision to designate an individual as Righteous Among the Nations. A rescuer, like a bystander, has a choice to make—however difficult. While some operations were less risky, most acts made by rescuers put their lives and the lives of others in some degree of jeopardy. As David P. Gushee explains,

> Rescuers were those who chose to abandon relative safety and throw their lot with the Jews. Their decision to work for Jewish survival meant that their own survival was threatened. In the eyes of the Nazis, the rescuers' decision to help Jews reduced them to the status of Jews. . . . Once embarked on rescue, then, the Righteous were also forced to redirect their lives toward the quest for survival—both for themselves and their Jewish charges. . . . The fight for survival required that rescuers practice a most earthly ethic. They needed to learn how to be cunning and clever, how to lie and deceive, how to operate by stealth and by night, sometimes even to kill.[53]

Regardless of the level of risk, rescuers made the dangerous decision to become involved in the aiding of Jews.

Meanwhile, the majority of liberators made no such choice. We have already discussed that most British liberators did not enlist to help save Jews from Nazi persecution. As far as the liberation of Bergen-Belsen, military personnel received instructions from headquarters that a nearby camp had been surrendered, and they were instructed to take charge of it. As Ben Shephard reveals, Lt. Col. R.I.G. Taylor, who became commandant of Bergen-Belsen, was "less than overjoyed" at the assignment.[54] His desire was to continue to fight in the war. Indeed, military personnel often wanted no part of the liberation of Nazi camps. It was generally viewed as humanitarian work and not part of the war effort. As a result, the assignment at Bergen-Belsen was not something most soldiers requested. The majority of military personnel were stationed at the camp because of direct instructions from headquarters. Effectively, the decision had already been made for them.

Therefore, due to the threat posed to Jews even after rescue and the choices made by the rescuers themselves, liberation should not be conflated with acts of rescue. The elements of choice and motivation, along with the protracted threat of danger, clearly distinguishes rescue from liberation. While both activities belong to the category of helping Jews during the Holocaust, significant differences remain.

Still, for many Holocaust survivors, liberation did not mean absolute freedom but a protracted experience of internment. In the Bergen-Belsen DP camp, months after liberation, conditions were still lacking. A U.S. Army lieutenant perhaps put it most succinctly. Lt. Abraham Klausner was the first Jewish chaplain to enter the Dachau concentration camp after its liberation. He was instrumental in establishing services for survivors and bringing their problems to the attention of the wider world.

After the war in Europe ended, Klausner visited fourteen displaced persons camps in Germany. In June 1945 he submitted a report concerning the state of the survivors in the DP camps. He wrote, "Liberated but not free, that is the paradox of the Jew. In the concentration camp, his whole being was consumed with the hope of salvation. That hope was his life, for that he was willing to suffer. . . . [But] no new source of hope has been given him. Suffering continues to be his badge."[55] Indeed, by liberating Europe, Allied armies put an end to Nazi tyranny, but were unable to bring an end to Jewish suffering.

Questions for Further Discussion

- What might be some differences between rescue *during* wartime and rescue immediately *after* wartime?
- Traditional ideas of Holocaust rescue involve a friend, neighbor, or perhaps stranger providing relief or protection—despite a danger to themselves. How is this similar/different to military victors providing aid?
- What challenges would survivors of the Holocaust have been facing immediately after liberation? What needs did they have? (Think about physical, emotional, psychological, and other types of needs.)

- Consider these factors for determining if a rescuer is "righteous": extending help to save a life, risking one's own life, absence of a reward, and verifiable proof of the events. Do these requirements seem reasonable? Would you add others?
- You can learn more (including reading featured stories and exploring the database of Righteous Rescuers) at: http://www.yadvashem.org/righteous.html. A sad fact is that most rescue attempts were unsuccessful. Even with help, the circumstances working against Jews and other persecuted individuals and groups were, most often, simply insurmountable. While Yad Vashem also recognizes rescue attempts that were unsuccessful, there is frequently no one to testify to these efforts. What does this information add to our understanding of Holocaust rescue?
- What other Holocaust rescuers have you heard about? What category would you place them in?
- Because British military personnel and "liberators" were unaware of what they would encounter in the concentration camps, they were also unprepared for it. Discuss the ways in which liberators were likely unprepared (supply-wise, emotionally, and so on). Consider contemporary disaster relief efforts. What kind of training and supplies do today's relief workers have that the military liberators did not?
- The example of medical teams choosing not to treat those who were least likely to survive is an example of a moral dilemma posed by the Holocaust. Lessons and materials regarding "choiceless choices" in the Holocaust can be found at www.facinghistory.org.
- Communication and transportation resources were limited at this time. Discuss how the British troops would have gone about requesting needed supplies, and how long these would take to reach them. Due to the urgency of the situation, the troops often "liberated" supplies from nearby German towns. The townspeople were required to bring food, linens, clothing, and other items. How do you think the liberators justified these actions? Do you believe these actions were justified? Why/why not?

- One of the reasons survivors were "re-imprisoned" was because they had no place else to go. As explained in the text, they could not or would not return to their prewar homes. Immigration to Palestine was severely limited. What were the immigration policies of other nations at this time? Research the refugee and immigration policies in the post–World War II period (1945–48) in the United States, Australia, South American countries, and others.
- The years spent by liberated Jews in the DP camps are a fascinating period. Learn more by visiting the United States Holocaust Memorial Museum website (ushmm.org) and searching terms such as "displaced persons," "displaced persons oral history," "DP camp vocational schools," "DP camp weddings," "DP camp births." Yad Vashem has an online exhibition with stunning photographs of the DP experience: http://www.yadvashem.org/yv/en/exhibitions/dp_camps/index.asp.

Notes

1. For recent studies, see Dan Stone, *The Liberation of the Camps: The End of the Holocaust and Its Aftermath* (New Haven CT: Yale University Press, 2015); John J. Michalczyk, *Filming the End of the Holocaust: Allied Documentaries, Nuremberg and the Liberation of the Concentration Camps* (New York: Bloomsbury Academic, 2014); and Mark Celinscak, *Distance from the Belsen Heap: Allied Forces and the Liberation of a Nazi Concentration Camp* (Toronto: University of Toronto Press, 2015).

2. Raul Hilberg, *The Destruction of the European Jews* (Chicago: Quadrangle Books, 1961) and *Perpetrators, Victims, Bystanders: The Jewish Catastrophe 1933–1945* (New York: HarperPerennial, 1993).

3. Elly Trepman, "Rescue of the Remnants: The British Emergency Medical Relief Operation in Belsen Camp, 1945," *Journal of the Royal Army Medical Corps* 147 (2001): 282.

4. Ulf Zander, "To Rescue or Be Rescued: The Liberation of Bergen-Belsen and the White Buses in British and Swedish Historical Cultures," in *The Holocaust on Post-war Battlefields: Genocide as Historical Culture*, ed. Klas-Göran Karlsson and Ulf Zander (Malmö: Sekel, 2006), 353; and Ellen Ben-Sefer, "Surviving Survival: Nursing Care at Bergen-Belsen, 1945," *Australian Journal of Advanced Nursing* 26, no. 3 (March–May 2009): 102.

5. Hagit Lavsky, *New Beginnings: Holocaust Survivors in Bergen-Belsen and the British Zone in Germany, 1945–1950* (Detroit MI: Wayne State University Press, 2002), 97.

6. Ben Shephard, *The Long Road Home: The Aftermath of the Second World War* (New York: Alfred A. Knopf, 2011), 101.

7. Mordecai Paldiel, *The Righteous Among the Nations* (Jerusalem: Yad Vashem, 2007), xi.

8. The Seven Laws of Noah are as follows: 1) Do not deny God; 2) Do not blaspheme God; 3) Do not murder; 4) Do not engage in illicit sexual relations; 5) Do not steal; 6) Do not eat of a live animal; 7) Establish courts/legal system to ensure law obedience, https://www.jewishvirtuallibrary.org/the-seven-noachide-laws.

9. Moshe Bejski, "The Righteous Among the Nations and Their Part in the Rescue of Jews," in *The Catastrophe of European Jews*, ed. Yisrael Gutman and Livia Rothkirchen (Jerusalem: Yad Vashem, 1976), 584.

10. For example, Richard L. Rubenstein, "Was Dietrich Bonhoeffer a 'Righteous Gentile'?," *International Journal on World Peace* 17, no. 2 (June 2000): 33–46.

11. For example, see Istvan Pal Adam, "Tipping the Rescuer? The Financial Aspects of the Budapest Building Managers' Helping Activity during the Last Phase of the Second World War," *S:I.M.O.N.–Shoah: Intervention. Methods. Documentation* 2 (2015): 4–14. Also see Adam's *Budapest Building Managers and the Holocaust in Hungary* (Cham, Switzerland: Palgrave 2016), esp. chap. 5.

12. Christopher R. Browning, "From Humanitarian Relief to Holocaust Rescue: Tracy Strong Jr., Vichy Internment Camps, and the Maison des Roches in Le Chambon," *Holocaust and Genocide Studies* 30, no. 2 (Fall 2016): 211.

13. Browning, "From Humanitarian Relief to Holocaust Rescue," 212.

14. David P. Gushee, *The Righteous Gentiles of the Holocaust: A Christian Interpretation* (Minneapolis MN: Fortress Press, 1994), 76.

15. Gushee, *The Righteous Gentiles of the Holocaust*, 76.

16. Gushee, *The Righteous Gentiles of the Holocaust*, 9.

17. Mordecai Paldiel, *Saving the Jews: Amazing Stories of Men and Women who Defied the Final Solution* (Rockville MD: Schreiber, 2000), 9.

18. More can be learned about the various camps within Bergen-Belsen here: https://www.ushmm.org/wlc/en/article.php?ModuleId=10007778.

19. Paul Weindling, "Belsenitis: Liberating Belsen, Its Hospitals, UNRRA, and Selection for Re-emigration, 1945–1948," *Science in Context* 19, no. 3 (2006): 403.

20. Rainer Schulze, "'Keeping Very Clear of Any 'Kuh-Handel': The British Foreign Office and the Rescue of Jews from Bergen-Belsen," *Holocaust and Genocide Studies* 19, no. 2 (Fall 2005): 229.

21. Randolph L. Braham, "Rescue Operations in Hungary: Myths and Realities," *East European Quarterly* 38, no. 2 (2004): 175.

22. Schulze, "'Keeping Very Clear of Any 'Kuh-Handel,'" 231.

23. *Hansard Parliamentary Debates*, 5th Series 389 (May 19, 1943), col. 1120. In particular, see the remarks by Osbert Peake, undersecretary of state.

24. Max Paul Friedman, "The U.S. State Department and the Failure to Rescue: New Evidence on the Missed Opportunity at Bergen-Belsen," *Holocaust and Genocide Studies* 19, No. 1 (Spring 2005): 27; Schulze, "'Keeping Very Clear of Any 'Kuh-Handel,'" 243.

25. Lower Saxony Memorials Foundation, *Bergen-Belsen: Wehrmacht POW Camp, 1940–1945-Concentration Camp, 1943–1945-Displaced Persons Camp, 1945–1950*, project coordinator, Marlis Buchholz (Göttingen: Wallstein, 2010), 185.

26. Schulze, "'Keeping Very Clear of Any 'Kuh-Handel,'" 244.

27. Paul Kemp, "The Liberation of Bergen-Belsen Concentration Camp in April 1945: The Testimony of Those Involved," *Imperial War Museum Review* 5 (1991): 30–31.

28. Derrick Sington, *Belsen Uncovered* (London: Duckworth, 1946), 7–11.

29. Alan Rose, "Transcript of Interview with the Holocaust Documentation Project," SV257-SV259, March 17, 1982, Canadian Jewish Congress Records, Alex Dworkin Canadian Jewish Archives, Montreal, 2.

30. Rose, "Transcript of Interview with the Holocaust Documentation Project," 5.

31. Rose, "Transcript of Interview with the Holocaust Documentation Project," 5–6.

32. Gavin Mortimer, *Stirling's Men* (London: Cassell, 2004), 101.

33. Interview with John Gourlay Noble, March 7, 1987, Imperial War Museum (hereafter, IWM), London, UK, 18175.

34. Interview with John Gourlay Noble.

35. Rose, "Transcript of Interview with the Holocaust Documentation Project," xx.

36. Ben Shephard, *After Daybreak: The Liberation of Bergen-Belsen, 1945* (New York: Schocken, 2005), 53–6.

37. Brigadier Glyn Hughes, "Report on Medical Aspects of Belsen," 10, Contemporary Medical Archives Collection, Wellcome Library, Royal Army Medical Corps (hereafter, RAMC), London, UK, 1218/2/13.

38. Private papers of Lieutenant Colonel M. W. Gonin DSO, IWM, Department of Documents, 3713.

39. Myrtle F. Beardwell, *Aftermath* (Ilfracombe, UK: A. H. Stockwell, 1945), 39.

40. Beardwell, *Aftermath*, 39.

41. Account given to Royal Society of Medicine by Col. Lipscomb, June 4, 1945, National Archives, War Office, London, UK, 222/201.

42. D. T. Prescott, "Reflections of 40 Years Ago—Belsen, 1945," Contemporary Medical Archives Collection, Wellcome Library, RAMC 1790.

43. George M. Kren and Leon Rappoport, *The Holocaust and the Crisis of Human Behavior* (New York: Holmes & Meier, 1980), 125.

44. Leslie H. Hardman and Cecily Goodman, *The Survivors: The Story of the Belsen Remnant* (1958; London: Vallentine Mitchell, 2009), 2.

45. Interview with Leslie Hardman, September 22, 1997, IWM, Sound Archive, 17636.

46. Hadassah Rosensaft, *Yesterday: My Story* (New York: Yad Vashem and the Holocaust Survivors' Memoirs Project, 2005), 58.

47. Private Papers of E. Fisher, February 1, 1995, IWM, Department of Documents, 3056.

48. For a more detailed discussion of these debates, see Susan Armstrong-Reid and David Murray, *Armies of Peace: Canada and the UNRRA Years* (Toronto: University of Toronto Press, 2008), 249–86.

49. Lyle M. Creelman, "With the UNRRA in Germany," *Canadian Nurse* 43, no. 7 (January 1947): 556.

50. Arieh O'Sullivan, "Dad's Army: John Burrows' Search for His Non-Jewish Father's Machal Exploits," *Jerusalem Post Magazine*, May 18, 2001, 10.

51. My thanks to Paul Morrow and Istvan Pal Adam for their input.

52. Agnes Grunwald-Spier, *The Other Schindlers: Why Some People Chose to Save Jews in the Holocaust* (Stroud, UK: History Press, 2010), 152.

53. Gushee, *The Righteous Gentiles of the Holocaust*, 89–90.

54. Shephard, *After Daybreak*, 34.

55. Abraham J. Klausner, "A Detailed Report on the Liberated Jew," June 24, 1945, Central Archives for the History of the Jewish People, Hebrew University, Jerusalem, RP068.

4

The War Refugee Board

Formulating Rescue from Washington

REBECCA ERBELDING

On January 22, 1944, President Franklin Roosevelt issued Executive Order 9417, announcing a new American policy of the proactive rescue and relief of Jews and other persecuted minorities, so long as this work did not interfere with the "successful prosecution of the war."[1] Most of the staff of the newly formed War Refugee Board (WRB), responsible for carrying out the order, lived in and around Washington DC, more than three thousand miles from continental Europe—a place some, including the WRB's first director, John Pehle, had never visited—and they were now responsible with disrupting a mass murder campaign they could not see and barely understood.

The WRB staff learned quickly, soliciting information from American embassies abroad and suggestions from more than one hundred relief organizations in the United States. Over the sixteen months between the WRB's establishment and the end of the war, the staff explored every idea and opportunity that arose. Though the WRB staff did not explicitly think of their rescue and relief work in these terms (or at least, did not record it if they did), their projects can be split into three categories: moving refugees away from the margins of Axis-occupied territory to safety, convincing would-be perpetrators not to commit crimes, and keeping those trapped in Nazi territory alive for as long as possible.

In what follows I describe briefly the creation of the WRB and explain that the United States found little international cooperation for their efforts beyond the neutral nations (Spain, Portugal, Sweden, Switzerland, and Turkey), which sought to curry American favor. Subsequently I present examples of the WRB's efforts within the three categories, showcasing their extraordinary attempts to rescue and provide relief for the victims of Nazism, all within the context of military and political realities, bureaucracy, a lack of influence or power over Nazi perpetrators, and little prompt communication or reliable information.[2] From Washington, rescue was never easy.

The Creation of the War Refugee Board

Roosevelt's establishment of an American agency tasked with saving the lives of noncitizens being persecuted and murdered by a wartime enemy was, and is, unprecedented. It is important to examine how and why the War Refugee Board came into being, particularly since it is so unique in American history and played such an important role in the 1944–45 rescue efforts.

In 1943, as Americans read more information in newspapers and magazines about the Nazi mass murder of Jews, the idea that the United States should take direct steps to rescue the victims became more popular. The loudest voice for rescue, Peter Bergson, a Palestinian-Jewish activist and radical Zionist, convinced sympathetic congressmen to introduce joint resolutions, together nicknamed the "Rescue Resolution," on November 9, 1943 (the fifth anniversary of the Kristallnacht attacks). The resolutions urged Roosevelt to create a "commission of diplomatic, economic, and military experts to formulate and effectuate a plan of immediate action designed to save the surviving Jewish people of Europe from extinction at the hands of Nazi Germany."[3] The Committee on Foreign Relations approved the resolution unanimously and scheduled a full Senate vote for late January 1944. The House Foreign Affairs Committee held hearings in November, during which Assistant Secretary of State Breckinridge Long testified in secret session, touting the (supposed) positive work the State Department and international community was already doing to aid refugees. (At the time, "refugee" was a catchall term, used for both immigrants escaping persecution and those trapped in Nazi territory; the WRB even used "refugee" when referring to concentration camp prisoners. There were no international legal protections for refugees prior to or during World War II.) When Long released his testimony to the public in December, Congressman Emanuel

Celler criticized it immediately. He seized upon Long's claim that the United States had already welcomed 580,000 refugees from Nazism, a vast overestimation, demonstrating that Long had either been lying or was ignorant of the much-lower reality. Newspapers picked up the story; Long was vulnerable.[4]

The Foreign Funds Control staff in the Treasury Department ultimately involved themselves in rescue work by accident. Among other duties, they were responsible, along with State Department officials, for issuing licenses for the (rather few) financial transfers allowed between the United States and either neutral or Axis-controlled areas, including relief aid. By November 1943, the State Department had already delayed for seven months a World Jewish Congress request to send humanitarian relief money to Romania and France. While investigating, the Treasury staff discovered that, in addition to impeding the request, Long's staff had, months earlier, temporarily ordered the American legation in Bern, Switzerland, to cease sending reports about Nazi mass murder to the United States.[5] Shocked and angered, the Treasury Department staff drafted a seventeen-page memo, "Report to the Secretary on the Acquiescence of this Government in the Murder of the Jews." The report provided forceful talking points for Secretary of the Treasury Henry Morgenthau Jr., which his staff hoped he could use to convince Roosevelt to transfer refugee matters out of the State Department entirely.

On January 16, 1944, Morgenthau, Foreign Funds Control director John Pehle, and Treasury general counsel Randolph Paul met with the president, presenting both a shorter version of their report (now titled "Personal Report to the President," though Roosevelt never read it) and a draft executive order creating a group responsible for aiding the victims of Nazi persecution.[6] After listening to their evidence, Roosevelt, who was clearly also responding to the mounting public and congressional pressure, issued the executive order creating a War Refugee Board. Nominally headed by the secretaries of War, State, and Treasury, this new agency assumed the State Department's duties related to refugees. For all practical purposes, however, the WRB was a Treasury creation, comprising largely Treasury staff, and located within the main Treasury building, not far from Morgenthau's office.

Formulating Rescue Plans

The WRB's first director, John Pehle, a thirty-five-year-old lawyer, had joined the Treasury Department immediately after graduation from Yale Law School and, since 1940, had been the director of Foreign Funds Control, responsible for overseeing billions of dollars of frozen assets. Like most of the other members of the War Refugee Board staff, he had no experience in refugee work. Even before Pehle and his team presented Morgenthau with the "Acquiescence" report, Pehle had summoned Moses Leavitt, the director of the American Jewish Joint Distribution Committee ("the Joint," an international humanitarian organization founded in 1914), to Washington to explain the basics of relief work, just in case their efforts to form a new agency were successful. Leavitt gave a clear-eyed account of how the immigration visa process worked, the possibility of establishing refugee camps in the United States, and the likelihood that neutral countries would agree to admit refugees if the Allies promised they would soon be evacuated.[7] Once formed, the new WRB immediately began turning some of Leavitt's suggestions into reality.

From Washington, Europe had been as if in fog for several years. Confirmation of a Nazi mass murder plan reached American newspapers in November 1942, just a few weeks after the first Allied troops landed in North Africa. Even as Americans learned more about the atrocities, they were not seeing visual evidence of the crimes, nor were they (or government officials) receiving consistent or reliable information. American and British forces, mired in southern Italian mud, were hundreds of miles from the scenes of the worst crimes. The WRB received little additional intelligence beyond press reports and sometimes learned of new developments (such as the end of the Joel Brand ransom negotiation and the Horthy offer to release certain categories of Hungarian Jews)[8] by reading the newspaper.

Without their own stream of secret information, the WRB staff knew they needed suggestions to maximize the efficacy of their work beyond Leavitt's ideas. Pehle surveyed all the State Department consulates abroad to investigate the refugee situation in their area and report on the willingness of the other countries to assist in the WRB's humanitarian goals. Since Washington DC was so far from Nazi territory, the WRB's rescue efforts needed partners but found few countries eager to participate.

Responses from embassies and consulates trickled in throughout February 1944. Most were negative. The Foreign Service staff largely reported that "their" countries could not take increased immigration, especially if the immigrants were Jewish. From Tegucigalpa, Honduras, the WRB staff was informed that there were 185 Jewish refugees there, and that they had no desire for any more: "It is unlikely that the immigration of other races incompatible with the mass of the present population (Spanish-Indian) would be permitted."[9]

This response was typical of most Central and South American countries. In North Africa and the Middle East—the most obvious destination for the evacuation of refugees due to its proximity to Europe—responses ranged from caution to dismissal. Ambassador James Moose in Saudi Arabia reported that "in the past two years one Jew is known to have come to Saudi Arabia. . . . That he ever came to Arabia is believed to have been due to a misconception of where Jidda is on his part, and to ignorance on the part of the Saudi officials that he was a Jew."[10] Baghdad was unwilling to let Jews cross Iraqi territory.[11]

In Europe and elsewhere, nations affiliated with the Allied cause—including members of the newly reconstituted Intergovernmental Committee on Refugees (IGC), a largely ineffective body formed after the Evian Conference in 1938 initially to find an international solution to the German Jewish refugee crisis—expressed their opinions in sharply negative terms. Australia, reported Ambassador Johnson, "is not interested in taking any initiative looking toward admittance of refugees, or in rescuing or assisting them." Moreover, their membership in the IGC was "partly a matter of prestige and partly a fear of appearing to be disinterested in the humanitarian side of the question."[12] In Calcutta, recent epidemics and a 1943 famine meant that there was no way to support refugees.[13] Afghanistan had a similar problem: "The willingness of the Afghan Government to admit qualified

Europeans is probably exceeded by the reluctance of such persons to come. . . . [L]iving conditions . . . are hard."[14] The embassy in Yunnan, China, reported a growing scorn for Jews, though there were only about twenty German Jews in the province and most Chinese had never met one.[15]

Ireland thought scarcity of food and transportation might prove an obstacle, though they agreed to accept five hundred Jewish refugee children if those issues could be overcome.[16] Iceland had no restrictions on Jewish immigration and had no visa requirements, but "since Iceland has never been approached . . . it has not been in a position to 'cooperate' in their entry."[17]

Although the responses from the American embassies, consulates, and legations were informative, they also showed the staff of the WRB that there would be no easy solutions, and the United States would be largely operating unilaterally.

As their meeting with Leavitt showed, the WRB staff recognized they had little experience in rescue activities but were willing to seek out those who did. On February 8, Pehle sent letters to ninety-four organizations based in the United States asking for ideas. After detailing the purpose of the WRB, the form letter explained that "the WRB is not unmindful of the fact that private agencies, including yourselves, have for some time been active in seeking means to effect the relief and rescue of Jews and other minority groups . . . the WRB would appreciate . . . a detailed statement in writing of such specific action as you believe the WRB should take."[18]

Some of the relief agencies were large and well known—the Joint received a letter, as did the World Jewish Congress—but Pehle also wrote to the Legion of Young Polish Women in Chicago, and to the Camp Little Norway Association in Minneapolis.[19] The WRB issued a press release about the request for recommendations, adding that any organization that did not get a letter should write in. Many more did, and the total number of groups solicited was well over one hundred. As with the embassy information requests, the responses from relief agencies arrived throughout February and March.

Even though many of these organizations had been thinking about rescue and relief problems for years, they had no magic bullets—no ideas that, had they been implemented earlier, would have halted the Nazi mass murder campaign. But many similar themes and actionable ideas emerged out of the responses. One popular suggestion involved merely appealing to Germany and requesting the release and evacuation of Jews, though details of how this should work varied. Agudas Israel, an Orthodox group, suggested offering an exchange for German prisoners in the United States, while the Union of Orthodox Rabbis wanted to ensure that any potential exchange included rabbis and scholars. They felt that those refugees who could not be evacuated should be protected in other ways—through material aid, with protective papers identifying them as under the protection of Allied governments, or with formal identification papers similar to the Nansen passes issued by the League of Nations, which permitted otherwise stateless persons to cross borders. Whether or not the Germans agreed to release prisoners, those who could be evacuated should be smuggled out through underground networks, or by paying bribes. The Balkans were the most logical area for this work, with multiple organizations pointing out the need for ships to transport refugees and for Turkish visas.

The use of psychological warfare—direct appeals to the German people and to those in satellite nations—was also widely recommended. Whether through leaflets dropped from the sky or radio broadcasts, the WRB was encouraged to make American policy clear to the populations of these countries and remind them that the Allied governments had already pledged to bring those who participated in persecutions to justice after the war.

Though finding areas of temporary refuge was explicitly listed in the executive order as one of the WRB's stated purposes, many organizations reiterated this idea. Of the larger organizations polled, seven suggested that if the WRB could remove refugees from neutral nations to designated safe havens, there would likely be more opportunities for refugees to escape from occupied countries to the neutrals. Ideas as to where the safe havens should be located ranged from large camps within the neutral nations (Jewish Labor Committee) to southern Italy (Joint) to Iraq (American Friends Service Committee, which clearly had not asked the American ambassador whether Jews were allowed in Iraq).[20] The United States, lacking its own refugee policy, was exhorted to move to open its own doors to refugees, and the British exhorted to open Palestine.

Armed with these suggestions and the depressing lack of intergovernmental cooperation, the WRB began its work. Historians who summarize the WRB as "too little and too late" also tend to argue that the WRB was "understaffed and underfunded." Though the WRB faced many challenges, staffing and funding were not among them. Roosevelt initially granted the WRB a budget of one million dollars meant to cover administrative costs and confidential rescue operations. Ultimately, between additional money from Roosevelt, private donations, and congressional appropriations, the WRB spent nearly $1.4 million dollars and returned more than $640,000 to the federal government. The WRB's staff, officially capped at between twenty-five and thirty, in reality swelled to nearly seventy in the summer of 1944, as employees throughout the government worked "on loan" with the agency.[21]

The WRB placed representatives in most of the neutral nations (Portugal, Sweden, Switzerland, and Turkey, but, due to the obstinate American ambassador, not Spain) as well as in North Africa and later in London. With the help of the State Department in those areas, WRB staff used the leverage of near-certain Allied victory to gain support for their mission. These representatives not only initiated their own rescue projects, they acted as facilitators and liaisons, assisting the multitude of private relief organizations already on the ground in these countries so they could receive increased funding, streamline communications and regulations, and eventually reach and assist more people. Over the course of 1944, WRB staff purchased ships to rescue people from the Baltic nations, fought through myriad bureaucracies to bring thousands of refugees from Romania to Palestine, warned would-be perpetrators of postwar justice through radio broadcasts and leaflets dropped from the sky over German-occupied territory, participated in ransom negotiations with the Nazis, and sent hundreds of thousands of food packages into concentration camps in the final days of World War II.

Historian David Wyman credits the WRB with saving two hundred thousand lives, including the surviving Jews of Budapest and of Transnistria. Although these claims have been intrinsically linked to descriptions of the WRB ever since, they run contrary to the WRB's own claims (and the available evidence), which were more modest.[22] In the WRB's final report in September 1945, staff wrote, "The accomplishments of the Board cannot be evaluated in terms of exact statistics, but it is clear, however, that hundreds of thousands of persons as well as the tens of thousands who were rescued through activities organized by the WRB, continued to live and resist as a result of its vigorous and unremitting efforts, until the might of the Allied armies finally saved them and the millions of others who survived the Nazi holocaust."[23]

The WRB's assertion—that they rescued tens of thousands but assisted hundreds of thousands more—still represents an extraordinary success in light of the many challenges they faced formulating rescue plans from Washington. In the remainder of this chapter I detail three specific projects within the three major categories of their work: moving refugees away from the margins of enemy territory (the establishment of the Fedhala refugee camp near Casablanca), deterring crimes by warning would-be perpetrators (the WRB's failed attempt to rescue Jews in Slovakia), and keeping refugees alive deep inside Nazi Germany (the WRB's relationship with Swedish rescuer Raoul Wallenberg).

Moving Refugees to Fedhala

The Fedhala refugee camp outside of Casablanca, alternatively known as Camp Maréchal Lyautey, had been a bureaucratic nightmare long before the WRB was created. In the wake of the April 1943 conference in Bermuda that was called to address public pressure for action to rescue Jews, British and American officials looked for a refugee camp in North Africa to populate with refugees currently in Spain. Such a camp, the Allies hoped, would serve as an inducement for Spain to allow additional escape over the French border. They chose an army base, Fedhala, but, nearly immediately, the camp was mired in red tape: the State Department, the Foreign Economic Administration, the Joint Chiefs of Staff, the United Nations Relief and Rehabilitation Administration (UNRRA), the Intergovernmental Committee on Refugees, the French Committee of National Liberation, the British government, and, after January 1944, the WRB, were all negotiating over security, logistics, and funding.

When Moses Beckelman, the UNRRA director of the still-empty Fedhala camp, went to Spain to interview potential residents in January 1945, he quickly learned that there were likely fewer than one thousand Jewish refugees still in Spain. Out of the eighty-one he interviewed, only twenty-five were interested in leaving for Fedhala, while fifteen were indifferent and forty-one were actively opposed to the idea. Of those opposed, many disliked the idea of being in territory under control of the Free French, wanted to see if other immigration opportunities (like Palestine) would arise, or thought they would have more freedom in Spain.[24] They had already escaped French territory and had no intention of going back, even in North Africa, particularly since Beckelman could not guarantee the residents would be able to leave the camp or work.

Leonard Ackermann, the WRB's representative in North Africa, became deeply involved in the attempt to populate the camp. By March 1944, the French had approved 454 refugees and were preparing to review a second set of 415 applications, many of which were from a group of Sephardic Jews who had been released from the Nazi concentration camp Bergen-Belsen to Spain after the United States promised they would be removed quickly from Spanish soil.[25]

The British promised to provide the ship carrying the passengers from Cádiz to Casablanca; in March, however, they announced a vessel would not be available until the end of April.[26] The end of April came and went. On May 1, Beckelman suggested the next French convoy include a small group of skilled refugees—mechanics, cooks, and carpenters—who could help prepare the camp for the arrival of the others; the first thirty-eight refugees arrived in the second week of May. Though Beckelman hoped the rest of the refugees could leave Spain on May 17, no ship appeared. On May 23, the British announced that the ship would leave Spain on June 7. Six days later, Ackermann reported to the WRB that it would be delayed yet a fourth time, sailing no earlier than June 20.[27] Although the American embassy in Madrid complained that the Spanish would soon threaten to imprison the refugees, the British would not reveal the real reason why the ship could not sail from Spain on June 7.[28] Ackermann received a cable that while the Joint's representative [likely a reference to Beckelman, who had long worked for the Joint] was angry about the delay, "it was impossible to mention operational requirements, he was told that ship needed repair and could not be available until about June 20th."[29] The refugees remained in Spain, and on June 6, the "operational requirements" necessitating a ship were made clear when Allied forces landed on the Normandy beaches.

After fifteen months of preparation and seemingly endless negotiations between the United States, the British, the Free French, UNRRA, the WRB, and the Intergovernmental Committee of Refugees, 573 refugees arrived in Fedhala. David Blickenstaff, a twenty-seven-year-old relief worker in Madrid, was responsible for gathering the refugees in Spain. The delays gave a representative of the Jewish Agency time to try removing 64 Sephardic Jews from the group so they could wait for transport to Palestine instead. In response, Spain threatened to hold up the entire evacuation unless everyone left as soon as possible, and Blickenstaff had to convince the Jewish Agency that refugees could also leave for Palestine from Fedhala.[30] In a letter to the American Friends Service Committee, Blickenstaff complained:

> It often seemed that complications and difficulties were purposely put in the way to retard the whole process from beginning to end—from the filing of applications; preparation and dispatch to the various authorities of the applications; screening of the lists; preparation and processing of exit visa requests; preparation of identity documents; synchronization of rail transport, lodging of such a large group in such a small town as Cádiz; medical, customs, and police control in Cádiz; to the mechanics of getting everyone on board in a minimum time.[31]

His frustration had not ended on June 21, when the group finally sailed on a boat that the WRB had arranged with assistance from the War Shipping Administration. Twenty-two of the refugees were found to have lice and were left behind in Spain, leaving Blickenstaff to frantically contact local police and bureaucrats to adjust their papers, find them housing—which resulted in a fourteen-hour trip to another town only to be turned back because the mayor of the town would only allow them to remain for twenty-four hours—and finally arrange for passage on a French convoy leaving a week later.[32]

Within three weeks, Beckelman wrote to his UNRRA superiors suggesting that Fedhala be closed, since it would be more cost effective to transfer the refugees to larger UNRRA camps in North Africa.[33] Though many did depart for the other camps, the WRB insisted Fedhala remain open to serve as a possible haven for anyone else they might be able to rescue from enemy territory. The entire Fedhala story has largely been forgotten; it is barely mentioned in any of the major books on American response that cover the WRB, though the negotiations over the camp required a great deal of the WRB's time and attention for months. The story is complicated, and since the camp did not open until after D-Day, made little impact on the ability of Jews to escape into Spain. The reality of war and politics delayed the opening of Fedhala for nearly a year after the camp was first proposed. The WRB simply did not have the ability to unilaterally open havens and move refugees.

Warning Perpetrators in Slovakia

In late August 1944, as Romania was joining the Allies and just before Bulgaria realigned as well, the Slovak underground rose up against the regime of Jozef Tiso. Nominally independent, although allied with Germany, Slovakia had deported approximately fifty-seven thousand Jews in 1942, but Tiso halted the operation in the fall of that year. By 1944, more than twenty thousand Jews remained in the country. The uprising in 1944 was quickly squashed by the Einsatzgruppe H, which moved in at the Slovak government's request to capture the partisans and deport the remaining Jews. Information about the uprising—and the German threat against the Jews—reached the United States almost immediately; the World Jewish Congress was alerted the morning after the uprising began by the chief of the Slovakia desk at the Office of War Information (OWI), a cartoonist originally from Prague named Adolf Hoffmeister.[34] The *New York Times* reported it on the front page the next day.[35] Within a week, the WRB's representative in Switzerland, a thirty-year-old American Friends Service Committee relief worker named Roswell McClelland, contacted Gerhart Riegner of the World Jewish Congress and Nathan Schwalb of the Jewish youth movement Hechaluz for information and to increase aid to the partisans. On September 11, just two weeks after the uprising began, McClelland's notes from a conversation with Joint representative Saly Mayer read, "Deportation 18–20,000 Jews in Slovakia; Vatican should intervene; Bring Slovakia into Kasztner 'vertrag' [contract]."[36] McClelland considered adding a demand for the cessation of deportations from Slovakia to the ongoing ransom negotiations over the fate of Hungarian Jewry.

With general information about the threat to Jews in Slovakia readily available, the WRB hoped to prevent the inevitable deportations. Having dealt with a similar situation after Hungary had been invaded in the spring, the WRB hoped to employ the same tactics. They encouraged the Swiss, Swedish, and Red Cross to send strong warnings into Slovakia of postwar punishment to all who participated in deportations. They urged the Vatican to intervene, particularly reminding the Pope that Slovakia was a Catholic country and Tiso a Catholic priest. McClelland authorized sending 950,000 Swiss francs into Slovakia for relief and rescue, and the Joint applied for and received a license to send $178,000 dollars so Joint representative Saly Mayer could send more.[37] But nothing seemed to help, and they did not have someone on the ground in Slovakia. The WRB asked Raoul Wallenberg, the Swedish attaché in Hungary secretly working for the WRB, if he could find out any information, but the Swedish Foreign Office informed them that Sweden had only one honorary consul in Slovakia, with no cipher or pouch communications. There was no way to communicate with him.[38]

In mid-October the WRB learned that the majority of the Jews of Bratislava had been deported. At the same time, they heard that all those holding protective papers—a document claiming the bearer was under the protection of an Allied or neutral nation—had been gathered at a castle in Marianka. The WRB, protesting through the Swiss, tried to have Switzerland (as the protecting power for the United States and most of Latin America) and Spain

6. Meeting of the War Refugee Board in the office of John Pehle. Pictured: Albert Abrahamson, J. E. Dubois, and John Pehle. United States Holocaust Memorial Museum.

(Paraguay's protecting power) request information from the Slovak and German authorities about the group, and tried to get the group included in a Red Cross relief program. Nothing worked. The Germans rejected any warnings the United States sent through the Swiss. In November McClelland reported that the Marianka camp was almost certainly abandoned, with the inhabitants likely deported to Auschwitz.

Although the WRB staff tried everything they could think of to keep the remaining Jews in Slovakia alive, they were unsuccessful. The Allied armies were fighting elsewhere, the neutrals were unable to assist, and, as always, the Nazi will to murder the Jews remained greater than the possibility of Allied rescue.

Raoul Wallenberg's Efforts to Keep Jews Alive in Budapest

Following the Nazi invasion of Hungary in March 1944, the WRB approached the governments of five neutral nations (Sweden, Switzerland, Portugal, Spain, and Turkey), asking them to increase their

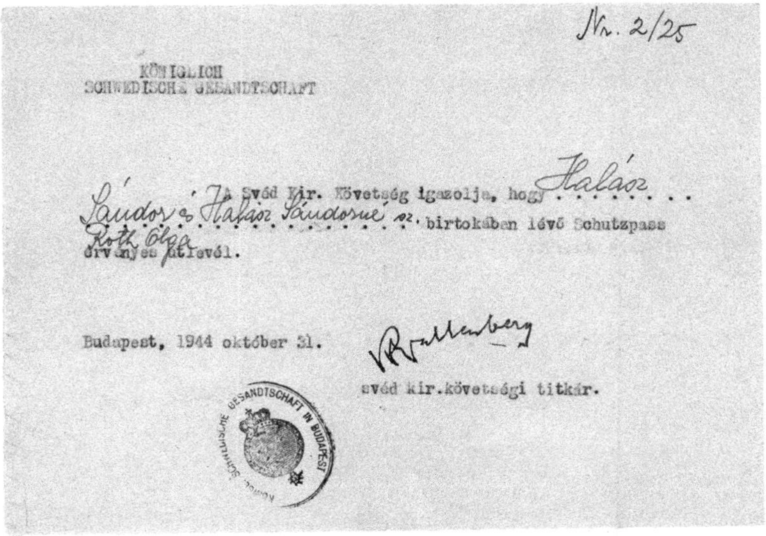

Nr. 2/25

KÖNIGLICH
SCHWEDISCHE GESANDTSCHAFT

A Svéd Kir. Követség igazolja, hogy Halász Sándor és Halász Sándorné sz. Roth Olga birtokában lévő Schutzpass érvényes útlevél.

Budapest, 1944 október 31.

Wallenberg

svéd kir. követségi titkár.

Königliche Schwedische Gesandtschaft in Budapest

7. *Schutzpass* (protection paper) issued and signed by Raoul Wallenberg in Budapest. United States Holocaust Memorial Museum.

diplomatic representation in Hungary in order to act as a source of information, be witnesses to the persecution of Hungarian Jewry, and to assist with humanitarian aid. On June 9, Sweden became the only neutral nation to agree. Minister Herschel Johnson sent a cable three days later: "Have found a Swede who is going to Hungary in very near future on business trip and who appears willing to lend every possible assistance on Hungarian problem. Am having dinner with him . . . for the purpose of exploring possibilities and to obtain in some measure his capabilities along those lines."[39] Johnson did not send the WRB any details about this meeting but announced on June 21 that Raoul Wallenberg had severed his business connections and was planning to devote his full attention to relief and rescue activities in Hungary. The Swedish government appointed him as an attaché to their Budapest delegation and were unconcerned about securing the necessary visas because they planned to refuse to recognize the newly arrived Hungarian chargé d'affaires if the Hungarians did not recognize Wallenberg. At the end of the cable, Johnson requested the WRB consider sending a list of proposed activities and look into financing for the operation. Likely due to delays in cable traffic, he made this request four times—on June 21, 27, 29, and July 1—before the WRB finally sent instructions for Wallenberg on July 4, which the State Department transmitted to Stockholm three days later.[40]

When the WRB's instructions for Wallenberg finally arrived, they reflected the fact that he was not an official American representative and would have much more freedom of action as a citizen of neutral Sweden. The WRB was clear on his position, explicitly stating, "While he cannot, of course, act as the WRB's representative, nor purport to act in its name, he can, whenever advisable, indicate that as a Swede he is free to communicate with Stockholm where a representative of the WRB is stationed."[41] The first suggestion involved bribes: "Since money and favorable post-war conditions might motivate action . . . it should be ascertained in what quarters such inducements may be effective." The WRB transferred $50,000 to Iver Olsen (the WRB representative in Stockholm) to hold for any projects Wallenberg might propose. The WRB supplied Wallenberg with a list of names they had gathered of politically and economically important Hungarians who might be sympathetic to his program and willing to give advice. The WRB was "confident . . . that further lives will be saved."[42] Wallenberg was already in Budapest by the time Stockholm received his instructions.

The WRB in Washington never had direct communication with Raoul Wallenberg and knew no details about the man personally save for a mention from Johnson that Wallenberg was half-Jewish (which was erroneous, but apparently a detail Wallenberg frequently told people).[43] They sent messages to Stockholm, where either Olsen or Johnson passed them to the Swedish Foreign Office for transmission to Wallenberg in Budapest. The cable delays inherent in each stage of this process meant that it took a month, on average, to receive replies to messages. The WRB relied mainly on the periodic reports of activities Wallenberg sent through Olsen.

Due to the complications of communication with Budapest, the WRB received only three reports on Raoul Wallenberg's activities between mid-August and the end of November: two via Olsen and a letter directly from Wallenberg. Wallenberg confirmed in Sep-

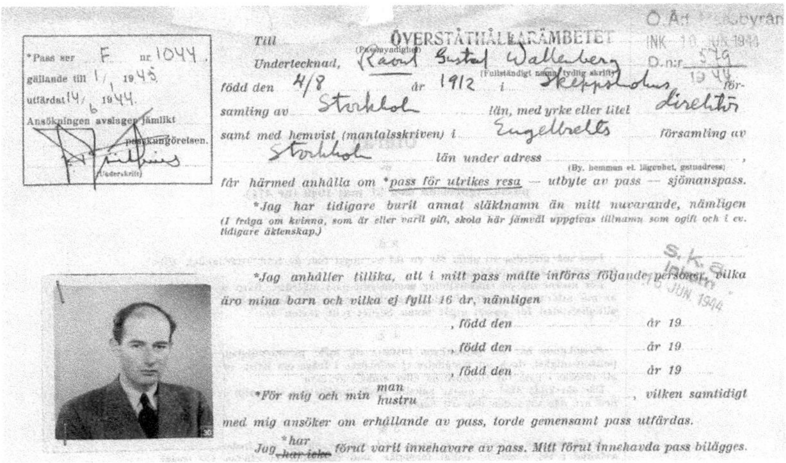
*Pass ser F nr 1044
gällande till 1/1 1945
utfärdat 14/6 1944
Ansökningen avslagen jämlikt passkungörelsen.

Till ÖVERSTÅTHÅLLARÄMBETET
Undertecknad, Raoul Gustaf Wallenberg
född den 4/8 år 1912 i Skeppsholms församling av Stockholm län, med yrke eller titel direktör
samt med hemvist (mantalsskriven) i Engelbrekts församling av Stockholm län under adress
får härmed anhålla om *pass för utrikes resa — utbyte av pass — sjömanspass.
*Jag har tidigare burit annat släktnamn än mitt nuvarande, nämligen
(I fråga om kvinna, som är eller varit gift, skola här jämväl uppgivas tillnamn som ogift och i ev. tidigare äktenskap.)
*Jag anhåller tillika, att i mitt pass måtte införas följande personer, vilka äro mina barn och vilka ej fyllt 16 år, nämligen
, född den år 19
, född den år 19
, född den år 19
*För mig och min man / hustru , vilken samtidigt med mig ansöker om erhållande av pass, torde gemensamt pass utfärdas.
Jag *har / har icke förut varit innehavare av pass. Mitt förut innehavda pass bilägges.

8. Raoul Wallenberg's travel paperwork from June 1944 with his photo. Courtesy of the Riksarkivet, Stockholm, Sweden.

tember that while deportations had ceased, concentration camps still remained in the rural districts. Jews in Budapest were reasonably safe. The WRB attempted to make several requests through Wallenberg—to find out information about the situation in Slovakia, to extend assistance to individuals with family members in the United States, and to investigate a ransom scheme involving Leopold Aschner, the managing director of a General Electric subsidiary in Hungary who was being held at Mauthausen and offered for release in exchange for one million Swiss francs. The lag time between question and answer rendered the requests useless; Wallenberg did not respond to any of them.[44]

Wallenberg's two reports from October described the drastic change in Budapest after October 15, following the takeover of Hungary by the pro-Nazi Arrow Cross. Just three days earlier, Wallenberg had reason to be optimistic. Jews with Swedish papers were exempted from building military fortifications outside the city, but those who were subjected to labor were treated relatively humanely. A report from October 22, by contrast, was much more frantic: Wallenberg's Jewish staff had disappeared on October 17. He had managed to find most of them and brought them to safer areas, but ten were still missing. A few thousand Jews had already been murdered, and it seemed likely that any privileges enjoyed by Jews holding protective papers would be stripped away.[45] As the situation deteriorated in Hungary, the WRB took many of the same actions they had in Slovakia and that they had taken when the Nazis had invaded Hungary in March. They asked the Vatican to broadcast an appeal to Hungary, called public attention to the threat against the Jews of Budapest, and challenged the German refusal to accept protests transmitted through the Swiss.[46] But, for the most part, the WRB waited; with the Arrow Cross and Nazis in control, there was not much more they could do. By November 1, the *New York Times* reported that the Red Army was only twenty-four miles from Budapest, and the WRB hoped and assumed the residents of Budapest would be liberated soon.[47]

On December 6, the WRB sent their last communication to Raoul Wallenberg. In a letter, rather than a cable, Pehle wrote that the WRB had been kept informed of the difficult and important work Wallenberg had done and had followed his efforts with keen interest. Before he closed the letter with his deep appreciation, Pehle added: "I think that no one who has participated in this great task can escape some feeling of frustration in that, because of circumstances beyond our control, our efforts have not met with complete success. On the other hand, there have been measurable achievements in the face of obstacles which had to be encountered, and it is our conviction that you have made a very great personal contribution to the success which has been realized in these endeavors."[48]

Wallenberg likely never received this letter. On December 22, the WRB received a report from Wallenberg written two weeks earlier. The situation for Jews in Budapest had deteriorated even further since his previous report in November. More than forty thousand people were sent on a forced march toward Germany, and twenty thousand labor battalion men were sent to the border. Jews had been forced into a ghetto, where dysentery broke out. The seven thousand Jews in Swedish houses were being vaccinated to prevent disease. Through Wallenberg's intervention, the Honvéd Minister commanded that Jews holding foreign documents were exempted from labor service and more than fifteen thousand people were able to return to Budapest. Wallenberg rescued two thousand people from deportation, but German threats of force curbed his activities.[49] By the time the WRB received this information, the Red Army had almost completely surrounded the city. The Spanish diplomatic corps had fled, leaving the Swedish legation in charge of the nearly three thousand Jews under Spanish protection.[50] On December 29, Minister Johnson in Stockholm informed the WRB that the Swedish Foreign Office could no longer communicate with Budapest.[51] The WRB heard no news from Budapest for more than three weeks. The first cable they received was reassuring: "Wallenberg is safe and sound in that part of Budapest occupied by Russians."[52]

The WRB did not realize that Raoul Wallenberg had disappeared until early April 1945.[53] In June, Olsen donated 10,000 kronor (about US$2,500) on behalf of the WRB to the newly formed "Raoul Wallenberg Committee for Hungarian Refugee Relief."[54] The American legation in Stockholm also requested Moscow investigate Wallenberg's fate; they never received a reply.[55]

Conclusion

The WRB's activities were complicated by bureaucracy, by the sporadic support of allies, by the reality of wartime communications, and by constantly changing realities on the ground. *Arrows in the Dark*, the title of Tuvia Friling's book on the Yishuv during the Holocaust, also provides an apt description of the work of the WRB: They constantly shot arrows into a darkened Europe, hoping to find something that would work.[56] When the timeline of the Holocaust (which would only come to be understood in retrospect as a separate phenomenon from the war) is merged with World War II, the argument that the WRB's work was "too little" becomes difficult to sustain. The three examples provided, of Fedhala, Slovakia, and Budapest, illustrate some of the challenges they faced. That the WRB did not or could not save more lives is not so much because they were "little and late" but because, after the war began, mass rescue was an impossibility without delaying military victory. The Nazis were determined to murder as many Jews as possible, for as long as possible—far more determined, we must be clear, than any Allied government, including the United States, was to save them.

Questions for Further Discussion

- On June 12, 1944, President Roosevelt informed Congress that the United States would establish a refugee center at Ft. Ontario in Oswego, New York, where 982 refugees were welcomed as "guests" of Roosevelt. The stipulations were: returning to Europe when conditions permitted, the inability to leave the fort for work or visiting family located nearby, and having no legal standing. Considering date, location, and restrictions, how would you evaluate the attractiveness of the offer to go to New York? What are some positive aspects of such a plan?
- When did the United States have significant information about the Nazi plan to exterminate the Jews of Europe?
- Conduct an Internet search and examine the August 8, 1942, cablegram of Gerhart Riegner, secretary of the World Jewish Congress. Create a timeline of events from the date the cablegram was sent to the establishment of the War Refugee Board and any subsequent actions taken by the War Refugee Board.
- The use of the word "race" in formal Foreign Service communications seems to buy into Nazi propaganda that Jews are a race of people. Nazis used pseudo-science to attempt to prove that Jews were an inferior race of people. How did the Nazis define who was Jewish? Did they use religious information to make the determination? How does the response to the War Refugee Board from Honduras support Nazi racial ideology?
- In 1942 the Allies declared and pledged that it would bring the perpetrators of genocide to justice after the war. What impact would this pledge have on Nazis who were certain of victory and believed they were acting in the best interest of Germany?
- Bureaucracy was a deliberate tool that hindered the escape of Jews from Nazi control in the late 1930s. Those in Nazi Germany were faced with almost impossible requirements to obtain a visa. The obstacles encountered by the War Refugee Board in

their rescue efforts proved to be very similar. How do contemporary immigration laws impede escape from dangerous situations? How does balancing national security with humanitarian needs impact a nation's decisions on immigration?

- Look at the circumstances outlined in the opening paragraph of this chapter: The staff of the newly formed War Refugee Board was charged with "disrupting a mass murder campaign" taking place more than three thousand miles away while ensuring that rescue and aid "did not interfere with the 'successful prosecution of the war.'" How might all of these factors impede progress? What other factors caused the frustration mentioned in the letter to Wallenberg? Despite these obstacles, what surprises you most about what was accomplished?
- What does the concluding paragraph of this chapter say to heads of state and to citizens around the world today about responsibility for humanitarian crises, be they natural or political?

Notes

1. Text of Executive Order 9417. The WRB staff did not have a solid definition of what they meant by "relief" and "rescue," and few historians have attempted to provide working definitions for these terms. I accept Dan Michman's definition of "rescue" as "an action taken to extricate Jews from an immediate Nazi menace or total removal of Jews from an area that the Nazis' tentacles reached." Michman does not provide a definition of "relief" but describes it as activities that could be performed without creating extraordinary agencies or adopting unusual approaches; it "created maneuvering room for use in developing rescue actions." Dan Michman, *Holocaust Historiography: A Jewish Perspective: Conceptualizations, Terminology, Approaches, and Fundamental Issues* (London: Vallentine Mitchell, 2003), 181.

2. For a more thorough examination of the entirety of the WRB's work, please see Rebecca Erbelding, "About Time: The History of the War Refugee Board" (PhD diss., George Mason University, 2015).

3. Text of S. Res 203, as printed in the *Congressional Record*, November 9, 1943.

4. Long's testimony is reproduced in *Problems of World War II and Its Aftermath, Part 2: The Palestine Question, Problems of Postwar Europe, Selected Executive Session Hearings of the Committee, 1943–50* (U.S. House of Representatives, Washington DC: U.S. Government Printing Office, 1976). For an example of newspaper criticism, see the "Bunk Because" column in *PM*, December 14, 1943.

5. Cordell Hull, Cable 354 from Washington to Bern, February 10, 1943, RG-84, General Records, Box 13, Folder "Jews," National Archives, College Park MD.

6. The executive order was drafted by Oscar Cox, the Lend-Lease administrator, who had been working on various proposals for such an organization since June 1943. Draft Executive Order, January 15, 1944, the Morgenthau Diaries, vol. 694, FDR Library, Hyde Park NY.

7. Transcript, Conference Memorandum, January 10, 1944, 2014.300.1, Florence Hodel Papers, Folder 2, United States Holocaust Memorial Museum Archives (hereafter, USHMM), Washington DC.

8. For more information on these cases, see Rebecca Erbelding, *Rescue Board: The Untold Story of America's Efforts to Save the Jews of Europe* (New York: Doubleday, 2018), chaps. 11 and 14.

9. John Faust, Cable from Tegucigalpa, February 4, 1944, Papers of the War Refugee Board (hereafter, PWRB), Microfilm LM0305, Reel 23, 385–386, USHMM.

10. James Moose, Cable from Jidda, February 16, 1944, PWRB, LM0306, Reel 4, 442, USHMM.

11. Loy Henderson, Cable from Baghdad, February 28, 1944, PWRB, LM0306, Reel 2, 155–157, USHMM.

12. Nelson Johnson, Cable from Canberra, February 24, 1944, PWRB, LM0306, Reel 1, 739–742, USHMM.

13. Kenneth Patton, Cable from Calcutta, February 23, 1944, PWRB, LM0306, Reel 2, 151, USHMM.

14. Cornelius Van Engert, Cable from Kabul, March 5, 1944, PWRB, LM0306, Reel 4, 368–369, USHMM.

15. C. E. Gauss, Cable from Chungking, March 22, 1944, PWRB, LM0306, Reel 1, 786–796, USHMM.

16. David Gray, Cable from Dublin, February 10, 1944, PWRB, LM0306, Reel 2, 400–402, USHMM.

17. Leland Morris, Cable from Reykjavik, February 19, 1944, PWRB, LM0306, Reel 4, 426–427, USHMM.

18. John Pehle, WRB asks Agudas Israel for suggestions, February 8, 1944, PWRB, LM0305, Reel 1, Folder 4, 333–334, USHMM.

19. Lawrence Lesser, List of organizations solicited for suggestions, February 10, 1944, PWRB, LM0306, Reel 24, Folder 7, 448–468, USHMM.

20. WRB staff, Digest of Suggestions Submitted to the War Refugee Board by Various Private Organizations in Response to Circular Letter, undated, PWRB, LM0306, Reel 24, Folder 7, 427–446, USHMM.

21. Erbelding, "About Time," appendix B.

22. David Wyman, *The Abandonment of the Jews: America and the Holocaust, 1941–1945* (New York: Pantheon Books, 1984), xiv, 405n129.

23. Note the use of the word "holocaust" at a time before it became the most common word used to label the Nazi crimes. WRB staff, "History of the War Refugee Board," vol. 1, 1945, PWRB, LM0305, Reel 27, 575, USHMM.

24. Moses Beckelman, Report from Spain to UNRRA, January 23, 1944, PWRB, LM0305, Reel 1, 248–254, USHMM.

25. Leonard Ackermann, Letter to Pehle, March 21, 1944, PWRB, LM0305, Reel 1, 218–222, USHMM.

26. Selden Chapin, Cable to WRB, March 31, 1944, PWRB, LM0306, Reel 11, 300, USHMM.

27. Selden Chapin, Cable to WRB, May 29, 1944, PWRB, LM0306, Reel 11, 176, USHMM.

28. Carlton Hayes, Cable to State Department, May 31, 1944, PWRB, LM0306, Reel 11, 171, USHMM.

29. British representative in Algiers, Memo to Ackermann, June 1, 1944, PWRB, LM0306, Reel 11, 541–42, USHMM.

30. Selden Chapin, Ackermann asks Blickenstaff to intervene with Jewish Agency, June 16, 1944, PWRB, LM0306, Reel 11, 525, USHMM.

31. Lois Kellogg Jessup, Jessup shares letter from David Blickenstaff, August 11, 1944, American Friends Service Committee Refugee Section, Box 5, Folder "Spanish Refugees," American Friends Service Committee Archives, Philadelphia PA.

32. Jessup, Jessup shares letter from David Blickenstaff.

33. UNRRA staff in Casablanca, Cable listing reasons why Fedhala should be closed, 1944 July 22, PWRB. LM0306, Reel 20, 846–848, USHMM.

34. Kurt Grossman, Memo on OWI report on Slovakia, August 30, 1944, World Jewish Congress New York Office, D-Series (Rescue and Relief), Digital collection, Folder 109–3, USHMM.

35. John MacCormac, "Slovaks in Rising Seize Rail Center," *New York Times*, late city ed., 1.

36. Roswell McClelland, Notes on conversation with Mayer, September 11, 1944, PWRB, Box 65, Folder 7, FDR Library, Hyde Park NY.

37. The 950,000 Swiss francs were broken down as follows: 95,000 to Czech resistance for Slovakia by Riegner and McClelland; 50,000 through Hechaluz to Bratislava; 500,000 to Bratislava by Saly Mayer; 305,000 to Neutra by Sternbuch. Leland Harrison, Cable from McClelland reporting on meeting with Sternbuch, September 21, 1944, PWRB, LM0306, Reel 27, 552–53, USHMM.

38. Herschel Johnson, Cable to WRB, October 14, 1944, PWRB, LM0305, Reel 29, 296, USHMM.

39. Herschel Johnson, Cable from Stockholm to WRB, June 9, 1944, PWRB, LM0306, Reel 5, 673, USHMM; Herschel Johnson, Cable from Stockholm to WRB, June 12, 1944, PWRB, LM0305, Reel 29, 251–52, USHMM.

40. In fact, Stockholm did not know if the WRB had received any of their cables about Wallenberg until July 6, when the WRB staff sent Johnson and Iver Olsen, the WRB's representative in Sweden, a copy of a cable from Roswell McClelland about the situation in Hungary, advising them they could share the cable with Wallenberg at their discretion. The more controversial the cable, the longer it took to pass through Censorship and the State Department; it is likely that discussions about using a Swedish citizen to unofficially work on behalf of the WRB may have raised some red flags at one or both of these departments that may have delayed the WRB's receipt of the cables. The WRB was typically very quick to respond to cables, usually within a day of receipt. Delays occurred due to clearance with the State Department and Office of Censorship. Cordell Hull, Cable to Stockholm with possible plan for Wallenberg, July 7, 1944, PWRB, Microfilm LM0306, Reel 5, 617–620, USHMM.

41. Hull, Cable to Stockholm.

42. Hull, Cable to Stockholm.

43. Ingrid Carlberg, *Raoul Wallenberg: The Heroic Life and Mysterious Disappearance of the Man Who Saved Thousands of Hungarian Jews from the Holocaust* (New York: MacLehose Press, 2015), 110.

44. The WRB's requests for Wallenberg are located in PWRB, LM0305, Reel 29.

45. Herschel Johnson, Cable from Stockholm with report from Wallenberg, October 30, 1944, PWRB, LM0305, Reel 29, 297–299, USHMM.

46. John Pehle, Letter to Cicogniani, October 20, 1944, PWRB, LM0306, Reel 6, 946, USHMM.

47. "War News Summarized," *New York Times*, November 1, 1944, 1.

48. John Pehle, Letters of thanks to Johnson and Wallenberg, December 6, 1944, PWRB, LM0305, Reel 29, 399–400, USHMM.

49. Herschel Johnson, Cable from Stockholm with report from Wallenberg, December 22, 1944, PWRB, LM0306, Reel 5, 537–541, USHMM.

50. Edward Stettinius, Cable to Stockholm about representing Spanish interests, December 21, 1944, PWRB, LM0306, Reel 5, 534–536, USHMM.

51. Herschel Johnson, Cable from Stockholm that communications with Budapest legation cut off, December 29, 1944, PWRB, LM0306, Reel 5, 533, USHMM.

52. Herschel Johnson, Cable from Stockholm that Wallenberg is safe in Sweden, January 20, 1945, PWRB, LM0305, Reel 29, 307, USHMM.

53. Herschel Johnson, Cable from Stockholm about Wallenberg's disappearance, April 4, 1945, PWRB, LM0305, Reel 29, 334, USHMM.

54. Iver Olsen, Letter to Sven Salen, June 6, 1945, PWRB, LM0305, Reel 29, 320, USHMM.

55. Johnson, Cable to State Department, June 7, 1945, PWRB, LM0305, Reel 29, 319, USHMM.

56. Tuvia Friling, *Arrows in the Dark: David Ben-Gurion, the Yishuv Leadership, and Rescue Attempts during the Holocaust* (Madison: University of Wisconsin Press, 2005).

5

Raoul Wallenberg

The Making of an American Hero

MICHAEL DICK

Walking down the Lincoln Memorial steps to the right of the reflecting pool, then past the Washington Monument and the World War II Memorial, you come to the former Fifteenth Street SW as it bisects the National Mall. Bearing right just one block across Independence Avenue, you find the United States Holocaust Memorial Museum, which broke ground for construction in 1985. In that same year, an act of Congress renamed Fifteenth Street SW Raoul Wallenberg Place SW, which today remains the only street on the National Mall named after someone born outside of the United States. Raoul Wallenberg's name literally occupies a prominent address in U.S. national memory, as if he was an adopted son. The National Mall in Washington DC is the U.S. centerpiece of art, architecture, museums, and memorialization. The Mall symbolizes history, identity, and national consciousness, and the National Park Service reports, "Each year, millions visit the National Mall and Memorial Parks to recreate, to commemorate presidential legacies, to honor our nation's veterans, to make their voices heard, and to celebrate our nation's commitment to freedom and equality."[1]

Raoul Wallenberg, Swedish businessman and novice diplomat, saved thousands of Jews during the 1944–45 Nazi occupation of Hungary. Recruited and financed by the United States, Wallenberg left a life of luxury to manage rescue operations in chaotic Budapest during the latter phases of World War II. With the Soviet Red Army closing in, and the German and Hungarian Nazis persecuting and murdering Jews to the last minute, Wallenberg kept working to save lives. In the midst of the danger, Wallenberg disappeared under Soviet custody in January 1945. His fate to this day remains inconclusive.

Wallenberg was not the first Holocaust rescuer, nor was he, *initially*, the most famous. Yet Wallenberg's historic legacy has been adopted by the United States, and he has been transformed into an American hero. In 1994, Congress adopted a resolution to have a bust of Wallenberg placed in the U.S. Capitol building. In 1981, he became just the second person in history to be honored with American citizenship by an act of Congress, British wartime prime minister Winston Churchill being the first.

This chapter aims to show how and why, despite his Swedish nationality, Wallenberg's historical memory has been Americanized. This investigation into post-1945 newspapers, letters, diplomatic speeches, and government documents suggests that the U.S. memorialization of Wallenberg both honored a Holocaust humanitarian and served an American political schedule. The American memorialization of Wallenberg, while duly informing of his humanitarian rescue work, reminds us that the politics of public memory can and does utilize the past to promote a contemporary agenda.

This chapter is informed by, and sits at the intersection of, Peter Novick's *The Holocaust in American Life* (1999), Paul A. Levine's *Raoul Wallenberg in Budapest: Myth, History and Holocaust* (2010), and Tanja Schult's dissertation-turned-book, *A Hero's Many Faces: Raoul Wallenberg in Contemporary Monuments* (2009). Novick is critical of America's increasing fixation on the Holocaust, while Levine, one of the world's leading Wallenberg scholars, narrows that lens to Budapest and questions why Wallenberg's "lives saved" number continued to rise dramatically long after the event itself. Schult's public memory study has a global focus, looking at monuments spread out over twelve countries. Schult notes that the first Wallenberg memorial was erected, understandably, in Hungary shortly after the war, but then she examines questions such as "why it took [until 2002] to erect a Raoul Wallenberg monument in Stockholm."[2]

What follows are the developments, major factors, and turning points that led to Raoul Wallenberg, famed Holocaust rescuer from Sweden, being made into an "American hero."

From Privilege to "Citizen of the World"

On August 4, 1912, in Kappsta, Sweden, Raoul Wallenberg was born into a family of high finance and worldly connections. Owning Sweden's first private bank and employing forty-five thousand Swedes in various firms, the Wallenbergs were the "Swedish Rockefellers." Raoul's great-grandfather Andre Oscar Wallenberg founded Sweden's first private bank, Enskilada Banken, in 1856. Raoul's uncles, Jacob and Marcus Wallenberg, navigated the family business through the difficult years of World War II. The Wallenbergs had very close ties with German businesses, and with the armament industry.[3] These ties also continued well into the war, which is not surprising, given Sweden's neutrality. Wallenberg's family money as well as his family's contacts with high society would later prove beneficial to countless others.

Raoul's father died three months before the future Holocaust rescuer was born, and the male influence in his life shifted to his paternal grandfather, Gustav Oscar Wallenberg. Raoul was groomed early on to have a kinship with the United States. Grandfather Wallenberg told Raoul "only if you go [to America], you will develop your character in the right way."[4] Encouraged to be educated in the United States, Raoul entered the University of Michigan in 1931. His letters home to his grandfather confirmed he both caught the American spirit and learned from it. In November 1931, Raoul wrote, "I read the *New York Times* every day. It's the best paper I've ever read."[5] Gustaf Wallenberg had hoped his grandson would become a "citizen of the world," and he was certainly beginning to play the part. Soaking in the American culture, he hitchhiked one summer to Mexico wearing blue jeans and tennis shoes. Depression-era Michigan further shaped his sympathies for people struggling with forces out of their control. Per Anger, his fellow Swedish diplomat in Budapest, reflected, "It came as no surprise, from what he learned in Ann Arbor, what he did for humanity later in the war."[6]

Raoul's classmate Dr. Sol King, who in 1972 inaugurated a University of Michigan lecture series in Wallenberg's honor, recalled Wallenberg as "warm, friendly, not in the least snobbish, with an

9. Per Anger poses in front of a portrait of Raoul Wallenberg in his office. United States Holocaust Memorial Museum, courtesy of Per and Ellena Anger, 1985.

Americanized predilection for hot dogs and sneakers."[7] As Raoul graduated with honors in less than four years, Adolf Hitler seized power in Germany. The world held different designs for both of them, one to help save what the other sought to destroy.

Wallenberg's American experience was not limited to scholastics. At the 1933 "Century of Progress" World's Fair in Chicago, he worked as a rickshaw driver and in various jobs at the Swedish exhibition. Here, Wallenberg first met Swedish Count Folke Bernadotte, himself later involved with Holocaust rescue. Wallenberg wrote, "As visitors and supervisors [at the exhibition] we sometimes had . . . the royal emissary Folke Bernadotte the polite and decent, and his good-looking Estelle."[8] Bernadotte was of Swedish royalty but had married an American, Estelle Ekstrand of Pleasantville, New York. Bernadotte became involved in humanitarian work through the Swedish Red Cross well before Wallenberg went to Budapest, but, despite the American connection through his wife, he never received the American memorialization bestowed on Wallenberg. In May 1948, the United Nations enlisted Bernadotte to broker a peace deal between Arabs and Israelis.[9] In September 1948, Bernadotte was assassinated by Lohamei Herut Israel (Lehi),[10] a radical group whose military operations were directed by future Israeli prime minister Yitzhak Shamir.[11] Bernadotte and Wallenberg biographer Kati Marton wrote, "For Israel, Sweden, and the United States, the murder of Folke Bernadotte was something to forget about as soon as possible."[12] In the years immediately following the war, Count Bernadotte was highly acclaimed for his humanitarian work, but today he is largely forgotten, at least in part because he did not fit the emerging Cold War narrative.[13] Wallenberg's story, on the other hand, contained useful elements for a role model in the new political climate: He opposed the Nazis and became a victim of the communists.

Following graduation and some travel in the United States, Wallenberg returned home and, in 1936, with Grandfather Gustav's influence, Wallenberg next headed to Haifa in Mandatory Palestine, employed in an import-export position with the Holland Bank. In Haifa, Wallenberg first encountered Jews who had fled Germany's 1935 Nuremberg Laws. Wallenberg wrote, "[the

Jewish refugees from Germany] have no choice except to settle here."[14] In Haifa, Wallenberg realized that the situation for Jews in Europe was dire, and National Socialism was responsible. Returning to Stockholm and the family business in 1937, he understood the Nazis to be the world's menace.

Before he left Palestine, Wallenberg committed to helping victims of persecution should an opportunity present itself. However, when his grandfather died in 1937, Uncle Jacob arranged the next position for Raoul with the Central European Trading Company (CETC). Wallenberg engaged the position in hopes of travel, certain he did not want to be stuck in Stockholm as a banker. The principle owner of the CETC, Hungarian-Jewish businessman Koloman Lauer, had moved his headquarters to a Stockholm office building but could no longer travel freely through Europe under the newly enacted Nuremberg Laws. Wallenberg, not being Jewish, could move about as a citizen from a neutral country. In this new position, Wallenberg made at least two trips to Budapest, where he honed his language (he spoke Swedish, English, German, Hungarian, and Russian), management, and organizational skills. When war broke out in 1939, Wallenberg had been traveling through Europe with the CETC for two years. Now, as a junior partner, he would spend the next five years dealing with Nazi bureaucracy in Germany, France, and Hungary, looking more and more like "a citizen of the world."[15]

Hungary Becomes a Battleground

Fascist-leaning Admiral Miklós Horthy had ruled Hungary since 1919. Bounded by potential enemies and having lost much of its territory, resources, and population following World War I, Hungary's authoritarian government under Horthy formed an alliance with Mussolini's Italy and Hitler's Germany.[16] Between 1938 and 1942, Hungarian versions of the Nuremberg Laws were implemented, codifying an already antisemitic convention in the country. For the Jews of Hungary in 1942, things were bad and getting worse, but in no way similar to the annihilation already underway in Nazi-occupied Poland. Hungary was the last national Jewish community in Nazi-controlled Europe with any degree of relative safety. Of course, this depended on Hungary's alliance with Germany, and as historian Andrew Handler wrote, "By the fall of 1943 even to the casual visitor it was apparent that Budapest was nothing like the capital of a nation in alliance with the Third Reich."[17] When the Soviets defeated Hitler's armies at Stalingrad in February of 1943, Horthy slowly began to reconsider Hungary's allegiance to Nazi Germany, furthering a political environment of suspicion and mistrust.

Horthy was set to announce Hungary's surrender to the Soviets at a parliamentary session on March 20, 1944.[18] The proposed March 20 speech never occurred, as the German army marched in on March 19, 1944, and occupied Hungary. Horthy, while antisemitic, had never given over "his" Jews to the Nazis. With the German invasion of Hungary, Horthy's "protection" was worthless. Washington DC was aware of this growing menace—the Nazis would escalate their atrocities as the German war effort failed. On March 24, 1944, President Roosevelt made sure his radio broadcast could be heard throughout Hungary. His message was clear: the Hungarians and Admiral Horthy, under threat of postwar trial of war crimes, were not to participate in Nazi offenses against the Jews.[19]

Before Roosevelt's radio warning to Hungary, belated humanitarian aid from the United States to Europe's Jews had begun by the end of 1943. Secretary of the Treasury Henry Morgenthau pleaded to President Roosevelt concerning the urgency of helping Europe's Jews when he wrote, "Only a fervent will to accomplish, backed by persistent and untiring effort, can succeed where time is so precious."[20] Roosevelt acted, establishing the War Refugee Board (WRB) with most financial resources obtained through U.S. Jewish nongovernment organizations. Of utmost concern was how to get help to the Jews in Hungary and, more specifically, *who* was going to help them. The WRB knew its candidate must be from a neutral nation and that the United States, currently at war with Hungary, could not be seen as the engine of the mission. The operative would have to be innovative, multilingual, organized, and above all have "a fervent will to accomplish."

Raoul Wallenberg had been to Budapest before, for a sum total of eight weeks. The Danube River still bisected Budapest, with

A' SVÉD KIRÁLYI KÖVETSÉG
SZÜKSÉGKÓRHÁZA
BUDAPEST, V., TÁTRA-UTCA 14–16

Budapest, 1944. december 15.
TELEFON

IGAZOLVÁNY

Fenti kórház vezetősége igazolja, hogy
Galambos Istvánné
született Debrecen, 1892.
szakácsnő minőségben
állandó szolgálatot teljesít.
Érvényes: 1944. december 31-ig.
Meghosszabbitás: 1945. jan. 31-ig
Meghosszabbitás: 1945.
Meghosszabbitás: 1945.

A Svéd Kir. Köv. KÓRHÁZA

igazgató főorvos.
svéd kir. követségi megbizott.

10. A Wallenberg *Schutzpass* issued for in December 1944. United States Holocaust Memorial Museum, courtesy of John Gerrard.

Buda to the west, and Pest to the east, but this time the city was different. The effects of war were obvious, and yellow stars marked Jews for death. Wallenberg immediately combined his design talents with the clout of the Swedish Foreign Ministry and drew up a protective passport that would fool the authority-loving Nazis. Full of crowns and blue and yellow, the dubious passports worked. This *Schutzpass* was given to all members of his staff. The wording on the document was clear: the holder of this document is under the protection of the Swedish government until arrangement for emigration could be made.[21] When Wallenberg ran out of authorized passports, he just made more. For Wallenberg, saving lives by any means necessary took precedence over following diplomatic protocol.[22]

Within six months of his July 1944 arrival in Budapest, Wallenberg exhibited a combination of leadership expertise and sheer bravery. He continually frustrated the Nazis, particularly the SS "deportation logistics expert" and future fugitive Adolf Eichmann. Wallenberg spoke German and Hungarian, and often quite forcefully with an authoritarian tone to which the Nazis and Hungarian fascists themselves were accustomed. Wallenberg established "safe houses" under the Swedish flag for Budapest's Jews. With WRB funds, Wallenberg purchased thirty-two houses, mostly on the Pest side, where Jews could live and receive food and medical care. He bought off police officers and soldiers to either ignore the Jews or bring them to safe houses. Lists he obtained of bribable Hungarian officials began to bear fruit.[23] Wallenberg remained aware of the potential for unfulfilled promises, but he committed to using any methods at his disposal. For example, Swedish diplomat Anger reports on Eichmann and Wallenberg's first meeting, which resulted in the irate Nazi being calmed by Wallenberg's gifts of cigarettes and whiskey.[24] But these devices would have consequences. For all his notable work saving the Jews of Budapest at the crucial moment, his payoffs to Nazis and Hungarian officials could later be considered by the Soviets as aid to the enemy and by the Swedes as overstepping the bounds of his authority.

The Soviets liberated the Pest side of the city, the area where Wallenberg operated, between January 13 and 17, 1945. Despite the more dangerous conditions, Wallenberg stayed on the Pest side, closer to his work. Anger recalled, "I remember how I pleaded with him to suspend his operation and stay with us on the Buda side."[25] Raoul declined, and focused on seeking jobs and housing to revive the bombed-out city. If the Soviets would be disinterested in or could not assist the Jews, Wallenberg figured he would take his proposal to the WRB at the war's conclusion.[26] As it happened, the Soviets were not at all interested in Wallenberg's plans to bring humanitarian relief to Budapest, but they were quite interested in why he was there in the first place. As a result, Wallenberg never made it back to either Sweden or the United States, but the preconditions for his symbolic return to the United States as an American hero were laid. What remained necessary for him to become adoptable into American historical memory was his partial abandonment by Sweden.

On January 17, 1945, with the Red Army surrounding Budapest, Wallenberg rode east from his Pest side office to meet the Soviets and discuss his rescue efforts. Swedish Legation ambassadors counseled him against the trip, suggesting he let the Soviets come to him. Wallenberg, having successfully negotiated with Nazis for six months and having had friendly encounters with the frontline Red Army for five days, disregarded their advice and headed under "courteous escort" deeper into Soviet lines. Wallenberg may have been anxious to advise the Soviets on the Jewish ghetto's location in hopes of avoiding shelling. Perhaps he was looking for assistance to improve conditions for the Jews. However, before he left for his mission in July 1944, Stockholm diplomats in neutral Sweden warned him that if arrested he was on his own. Perhaps Wallenberg thought this warning referred only to detention by Nazi functionaries. That was not to be the case. Wallenberg's precise fate remains inconclusive to this day, though it is likely he died in Soviet custody.

The Selection of a Swede

Wallenberg's Swedish citizenship is central to understanding both his being selected for the Hungarian rescue mission and his later memorialization in the United States. On the brink of World War I, Raoul was born into a neutral nation, a fortunate occurrence that would later save thousands of lives. Officially impartial during World War II, Sweden stretched its definition of neutrality to fit immediate needs. Sweden aligned itself subject to the fortunes of war at any given moment—a survival strategy often employed by neutrals to offset the disruption of peacetime trade. While Winston Churchill understood the plight of fickle neutrals, he warned unsympathetically, "Neutrals who have played a selfish part throughout ought to be made to suffer in the post-war world."[27] Sensing the momentum of the war, by 1944 Sweden began to seek Allied favor as the outcome of the war became ever more obvious.

Family associations with prominent figures in the intelligence world contributed to the selection of Wallenberg. In 1944, with Raoul's uncles heavily scrutinized for German connections, the Wallenberg family sought out their former lawyer for their American businesses, Allen Dulles, for advice. Dulles, now working in the Swiss capital, Bern, as the director of the Office of Strategic Services (OSS, a wartime predecessor of the CIA) in Switzerland, suggested Raoul help the Hungarian Jews in order to "deflect criticism" away from Wallenberg family dealings with Nazi Germany.[28] Dulles later became a major player during the Cold War. As top official of the U.S. wartime intelligence service in Europe, he brokered the secret surrender of German forces in northern Italy in 1945, a move that showed clear signs of an anticommunist maneuver to keep the Soviets out of Italy. From 1953 to 1961, Dulles served as CIA director, while his brother John Foster Dulles served as President Eisenhower's secretary of state from 1953 to 1959.[29] That the Wallenbergs had business dealings with the Nazis and with a U.S. intelligence operative that conspired to circumvent established arrangements could have raised suspicions from the Soviet point of view. High-level connections and the family name paved the way for Wallenberg's selection to the rescue mission, but these associations could prove risky if a World War II ally became a Cold War enemy.

The immediate concern, however, was the Jews of Budapest. A Swedish committee that included Wallenberg's boss, Koloman Lauer, initially designated Count Bernadotte for the mission, but his application for travel to Hungary was denied by Hungarian authorities, possibly on the grounds of his wife being an American. OSS accountant Iver Olsen, now handling funds for the WRB in Stockholm, had an office down the hall from Lauer. Upon Bernadotte's rejection, Lauer nominated his young business partner for the post.[30] Sweden threatened to remove Hungarian diplomats if their second choice of Wallenberg was refused. Hungary, considering German defeat likely, acquiesced in hopes of maintaining good relations with neutrals that might help them in complicated postwar negotiations with the Allies.

In 1944, Wallenberg's selection as Budapest envoy fit the needs of Sweden, the United States, and the Budapest Jews. Ironically, his appointment suited Hungary as well in that Bernadotte was not acceptable and good relations with Sweden had to be maintained. Sweden, already having supplied war materials that killed Allied soldiers, had to focus on humanitarian efforts, and neutrals such as Switzerland were already competing for postwar Allied favor. The United States could assuage some of its belated rescue efforts, and it is possible the Americans wanted an agent on the ground in Budapest that could provide ongoing useful information. For the Jews in Budapest, the Wallenberg selection was fortunate. An energetic, clever, and committed idealist seeking his life's calling was on the way to Hungary.

Sweden, however, was quick to return to its neutral tradition in the coming Cold War, and Wallenberg would be caught between these new front lines. After World War II, Sweden failed to aggressively seek answers to Wallenberg's fate. While Wallenberg's mother and half-siblings pressured the Swedish government to get answers from the Soviets, the Wallenberg business elite toed the official Swedish line of neutrality in hopes of maintaining some semblance of private business in the postwar Soviet sphere, where the nationalization of capital was beginning to be realized.

Sweden's abandonment of Raoul Wallenberg must be understood in the context of its neutrality in both World War II and the Cold War. Historiography identifying Sweden as an "innocent bystander" regarding its involvement with Germany in World War II has been termed "small-state realism."[31] As the "small-state" thesis goes, Sweden, by nature of its size, geographical location, and military readiness had to concede to German demands. By not antagonizing the Germans, the Swedes hoped to make it through the war without starving, being occupied, or worse. The small-state realism argument is convincing, but it muted for several years after the war any Swedish self-reflection concerning neutral profiteering, the Holocaust, or Wallenberg's fate.

Nevertheless, during the closing years of the war, with the Red Army's victory at Stalingrad and the Allies coming up the Italian peninsula, Sweden saw a need to momentarily rethink its small-state logic. Swedish trade with Germany officially stopped by November 1944.[32] The Allies, particularly the Americans, expected the Swedes to seek redemption from the postwar world for having supplied, among other products and services, the iron ore for German bullets. From a humanitarian perspective, however, both the United States and Sweden had seen prosecuting the war as having priority over the fate of the Jews. The Swedes had vowed to stay out of the war, and the Americans, led by President Roosevelt, focused exclusively on winning it, all the way up to Morgenthau's plea and the subsequent creation of the WRB.

In the immediate postwar years, Swedish economic success placed a positive spin on their neutral identity during the war. Any inclination for Sweden to reevaluate its wartime behavior was correspondingly reduced. Recently declassified files also illustrate the Soviet Union's immediate interest into improving postwar relations with Sweden. To that end, "the Soviet demand for the total extradition of approximately 30,000 Baltic refugees in Sweden was suddenly dropped (in March 1946)."[33] Improving relations with the Soviet Union meant taking the Wallenberg disappearance off the Soviet-Sweden agenda. In addition, questions of whether Wallenberg had overstepped his authority or had passed on information to the Americans began to surface. Nevertheless, Wallenberg's mother, Maria ("Maj") Sofia Wising, and his half-sister, Nina Lagergren, led efforts for years to find Raoul, while his powerful uncles, running in Swedish aristocratic circles, disregarded the issue. The independent Eliasson Commission, assembled in 2003, "confirmed what everyone has known for decades: That the Swedish government mishandled the Wallenberg case, especially through its disturbing lack of initiative during the critical early years 1945–47."[34] The Swedish Holocaust hero immediately following World War II was Count Bernadotte, though his memorialization was also cut short in the interest of neutrality. While Wallenberg and Sweden had been highly invested in saving Jews, the assassination of Bernadotte led Sweden to believe his murder, if not actually endorsed by Israel, was investigated with "astonishing negligence" by Israeli authorities.[35] Relations between the countries improved throughout the 1960s and 1970s, but chilled during the Yom Kippur war. In 2014, when the Swedish Social Democratic Party took power, they announced recognition of the state of Palestine. In turn, Israel recalled its diplomats, and, in response to the recall, the Swedish government boycotted a 2016 Israeli honoring of Wallenberg.[36]

The longtime Swedish ambivalence about Wallenberg was confirmed just six months after the diplomatic incident with Israel when Swedish foreign minister Carl Bildt, speaking before members of Congress at a luncheon honoring Wallenberg, said, "There was a fairly long period where, I wouldn't say Raoul Wallenberg and his fate was entirely forgotten, that would be to exaggerate slightly, but it was neglected."[37] Sweden initially approached its memory of World War II, the Holocaust, and Wallenberg waving the neutrality flag. They chose to not press the Soviets on the Wallenberg disappearance, should his being in Hungary be considered a violation of previous agreements at Yalta concerning postwar spheres of influence. This left Wallenberg symbolically orphaned and likely already physically dead in the Soviet Union. Thus, his memory was readily available for adoption by the United States when the Cold War reengaged in the early 1980s, at precisely the same time when Holocaust awareness in the United States grew.

Mass Media Discovers Wallenberg

Following V-E Day, Sweden showed far more interest in getting on with postwar business, and the Wallenberg elites were certainly not going to be blackmailed with ransom demands from anyone. Wallenberg's uncles were far more interested in salvaging their soon-to-be nationalized holdings in Eastern Europe. The United States, where Holocaust rescue was never the first priority, remained engaged with Japan. Upon the conclusion of World War II, American attention shifted to the Marshall Plan and the containment of communism. It was not until Wallenberg's story crept back into the emerging Cold War narrative during the late-1970s spike in Holocaust interest that even a small fraction of Americans knew who Wallenberg was. By this time he had been missing for more than thirty years.

Mass media belatedly became the American vehicle of Holocaust education, memory, and heroization. Despite its soft approach, or maybe because of it, *The Diary of Anne Frank* has been the entry point to the Holocaust for Americans since 1952.[38] American schoolchildren know of the German-Jewish girl and establish a peer-like bond with her, imagining themselves in her shoes.

The radio-broadcasted trial of Hitler henchman and Wallenberg antagonist Adolf Eichmann from Jerusalem in 1961–62 brought the starker reality of the Holocaust to American homes, if they chose to listen. Overall, Americans did not, but Eichmann's trial then became part of the public record. Sixteen years later, in

April 1978, U.S. Holocaust awareness was rejuvenated when NBC's *Holocaust* ran for four nights to 120 million American viewers. American television concerning oppression, racism, and persecution had been primed a year before by *Roots*, Alex Haley's book turned into a mini-series that won nine Emmy awards. Both films were directed by Marvin Chomsky, cousin of American philosopher Noam Chomsky. Also watching *Holocaust* was President Jimmy Carter, who "was so moved that a mere two weeks later he announced the creation of the 'President's Commission on the Holocaust,' whose final report suggested the building of the United States Holocaust Memorial Museum."[39]

On July 15, 1979, President Carter delivered his nationally televised "Crisis of Confidence" speech in which he said, "We can see this crisis in the growing doubt about the meaning of our own lives and in the loss of a unity of purpose for our Nation."[40] Clearly, Carter was looking for inspiration for himself and his country. Ironically, inspiration had found Carter a few months before, from a Jewish Hungarian-American woman, even if nobody knew it yet. As a teenager, Annette Lantos, who founded the International Free Wallenberg committee in 1977, had used a Wallenberg-issued *Schutzpass* in 1944 to escape from Hungary. Her childhood sweetheart, Tom Lantos, also a Hungarian Jew, was captured and worked repairing Danube bridges bombed nightly by the Allies during the German occupation. Most of their family members dead, the two reunited after the war and immigrated to the United States, where Tom taught economics at the University of San Francisco and later became the Berkeley district's representative to Congress. In October 1978, Annette Lantos's postcard was randomly drawn from entries to the CBS radio call-in show *Ask President Carter*. She seized the moment to bring Wallenberg to the president's attention. Carter followed up with a letter to Mrs. Lantos, explaining that the Soviets refused to deal with the United States concerning Wallenberg as he was a Swedish, not American, citizen. Annette Lantos was undeterred, but she realized Wallenberg's story had to get out.

Prior to 1979, American newspaper coverage of Raoul Wallenberg was scarce. The first American article, in the April 26,

1945, *New York Times*, summarized Wallenberg's life and activities in Budapest. The article cites Raoul's aunt, Mrs. William Calvin of Greenwich, Connecticut, the wife of former U.S. military attaché to Stockholm, Col. William Calvin. Mrs. Calvin is quoted as saying President Roosevelt "effected" Wallenberg's activities, resulting in twenty thousand Hungarian Jews being saved before Wallenberg "disappeared."[41] The brief article covers basic facts undisputed to this day, an indication that the essence of Wallenberg's story was available before the close of the war in Europe. In 1947, Wallenberg's half-brother, Guy von Dardel, residing in Ithaca, New York, and frustrated with "official Swedish channels," wrote a letter to the *Washington Post* in which he identified OSS operative Olsen as having direct involvement in Wallenberg's mission. In his effort to raise American awareness about Wallenberg, von Dardel pointed out that Raoul "was strongly bound to [the USA] where he received his education and carried out his dangerous mission as an unofficial representative of the War Refugee Board."[42] Albeit limited, by 1947 American newspaper coverage had at least opened the door on Wallenberg, with his half-brother expounding on two of the solid connections Wallenberg had with the United States—his education at Michigan and the use of American money in Budapest.

American officials did not respond to von Dardel's letter. Despite Wallenberg's having connections to and family in America, reports concerning any U.S. government involvement with Wallenberg were not forthcoming. On April 30, 1961, the *Washington Post* gave Wallenberg just one sentence in its Eichmann trial coverage, noting that Wallenberg "single-handedly saved tens of thousands."[43] It would be almost eighteen years later when Annette Lantos, unsatisfied with the "noncitizen" answer from the Carter administration, teamed up with famed Austrian Nazi-hunter Simon Wiesenthal. The pair assisted Pulitzer Prize–winning columnist Jack Anderson in writing Wallenberg's story for American mass-media consumption. In "The Man in the Iron-Curtain Mask," set right between *Peanuts* and the crossword on one of the *Washington Post*'s most popular pages, Anderson leads off with "The Kremlin lied about a heroic Swedish diplomat."[44] Cold War rhetoric was already paramount and seen as the hook in the emerging Wallenberg story. Reports about his actual work in Hungary did begin to come in but with reckless escalation in the numbers of "lives saved." The *Guinness World Records* book reported Wallenberg's numbers at one hundred thousand for "most lives saved" in history.[45] With the passage of time, Wallenberg began to be perceived in American consciousness as having saved more and more lives. Wallenberg's American adoption was underway, complete with a moral scoreboard increasingly tracking "lives saved" as both a representation of Cold War anti-Soviet sentiment and a lessening of American feeling of guilt for being late to Holocaust rescue.

On April 27, 1981, *Missing Hero*, a BBC television documentary based on Kati Marton's book of the same name, was broadcast in the New York area just as plans for a film starring Academy Award–winner Jon Voight (*The Deer Hunter*, 1979) as Wallenberg became public. Wallenberg's life-saving numbers were now reported at "20,000, perhaps indirectly 100,000."[46] Hollywood would not be outdone by New York broadcasts. With the number of lives saved now "at least 30,000" people, the *Los Angeles Times* reported a November 1981 Wallenberg black-tie event at the Simon Wiesenthal Center previously unparalleled for fund-raising. Elizabeth Taylor, Barbara Streisand, Jon Voight, Carroll O'Connor, and Milton Berle joined at least "seven or eight persons [who] had known Wallenberg" at the $500-per-plate gala. California governor Jerry Brown, already politicizing Wallenberg's memory, questioned President Reagan's "divergence of our foreign policy in the Middle East."[47] Representative Lantos and his wife watched the evening's performance with 1,200 others.

Numerous cultural events, local dances, fund-raisers, and speeches began to occur in local communities in honor of Wallenberg. High schools across America now bear his name, and the effects reach far into Americana. For example, today, at the Wallenberg Traditional High School in San Francisco, "The Wallenberg Four" skateboarding stair jump has become legendary, with a consistent presence on social media, blogs, and YouTube. Skateboarding journalist Leigh Roche noted, "In March 2010,

Nike issued a 'Wallenberg' shoe to commemorate 20 years of the Wallenberg skate spot." Skateboarding came to life off the California coast in the late 1970s and early 1980s when surfers looked for winter activities, precisely when Holocaust awareness was rising. As an example of cultural connection, the "Holy Grail" of skateboarding in the United States bears the name of Wallenberg.[48]

With the efforts of Annette Lantos and others, the slow start to Wallenberg awareness quickly increased in the early 1980s. The mass media in the United States had "found" Raoul Wallenberg at the same time that attention to the history of the Holocaust in the United States was growing.

Citizen Wallenberg

Disappointed with official Swedish efforts, Nina Lagergren became aware of Annette Lantos's efforts in the summer of 1979 and came to the United States to join her. Wallenberg's story had been relayed by the White House to Senator Patrick Moynihan's office, and Moynihan formed the Free Wallenberg Committee, with the help of three other senators. On August 4, 1979, the *New York Times* bested Anderson's *Washington Post* column with a profound shift in content and urgency. Occupying almost all of page 5, the article featured a photo of Annette Lantos and Nina Lagergren, together with a picture of Wallenberg and commentary on Moynihan's Senate committee. The two women had just completed a meeting with Secretary of State Cyrus Vance and a New York City news conference sponsored by the American Jewish Committee. Vance advised the women that the administration had brought the matter up with the Soviets and "we are awaiting a Soviet reply." Clearly, the United States did not intend to drop the matter. For the first time since 1945 there was a sense of America's role in Wallenberg's assignment, as "Wallenberg answered a request made to the American Ambassador to Sweden by President Roosevelt to help save the Jews of Hungary."[49] Further, speculation grew that Wallenberg might still be alive, and, regardless, the Soviets needed to answer as they were the last reported to see him alive.

Following Joseph Stalin's death and the Cuban Missile Crisis of 1962, there was a period of relative quiet in the Cold War—the era of détente—until the late 1970s. The Iranian hostage situation consumed the Carter administration and American foreign policy, distracting Washington from Soviet advances in several countries, most notably Afghanistan. The United States responded on the cultural front by declining to participate in the 1980 Moscow Olympic Games, a favor the Soviets were to return by bowing out of Los Angeles in 1984. In July 1980, the Republicans nominated devoted anticommunist Ronald Reagan for the presidency, and he picked Texan George Bush, the former head of the CIA, as his vice-presidential running mate. George's father, Prescott Bush, had married the daughter of George Herbert Walker, the founder of Harriman and Company, whose "Union Banking Corporation" had reportedly managed some Nazi business ventures in the United States.[50] The Cold War began to heat up again.

Annette's husband, Dr. Thomas (Tom) Lantos, would soon play a major role in lobbying for Wallenberg as a congressman. Lantos was a professor at the University of California–San Francisco when, in November 1978, California Eleventh District U.S. congressman and former Nebraska history teacher Leo Ryan was killed in Guyana while investigating complaints from parents about Jim Jones's Peoples Temple. Ryan was replaced in a run-off election by Republican Bill Royer. Encouraged to run despite expected Republican victories in 1980, Democrat Lantos defeated Royer by a narrow 3 percent.[51] For the next twenty-seven years, Lantos's humanitarian commitment cultivated votes in his Berkeley-dominated district, and he retained his seat by landslides. Beginning in January of 1981, Wallenberg's memorialization, or even potential rescue, for he would have been sixty-eight at the time, had a powerful proponent on Capitol Hill in U.S. representative and Holocaust survivor Tom Lantos.

President Carter had informed Annette Lantos that the Soviet Union insisted the Americans take no role in uncovering Wallenberg's fate, as he was not a citizen of the United States. Annette's husband eliminated that problem with his first piece of legislation as a congressman. Newly inaugurated Representative Lantos introduced Joint Resolution 220 of the Ninety-Seventh Congress, offering U.S. citizenship to Wallenberg on March 26, 1981.[52] In the same week as Lantos proposed his bill, President Reagan, likewise just inaugurated, was among several million Americans who watched television's No. 1 show, CBS's *60 Minutes*, lead off their March 22 program with a twenty-minute segment on Wallenberg. On March 26, Lantos, making the social circuit in Washington meet-and-greets, met Alexander Haig, the secretary of state in Reagan's new cabinet. Haig informed Lantos that the president had seen *60 Minutes* and told the State Department to "get behind the effort to help free him." In the same *New York Times* report, Senator Moynihan is quoted as saying, "[Wallenberg] was an American agent." Lantos, for his part, suggests, "The Congress . . . and the American people will not only have honored this man, but we will have honored ourselves."[53] The resolution passed Congress by a vote of 396–2 and was signed into law by President Reagan, who declared Wallenberg's work to being of "biblical proportions."[54] Wallenberg followed Winston Churchill as being only the second person to have U.S. citizenship confirmed by an act of Congress. The specific law has two sections: the citizenship confirmation and the directive for the president "to take all possible steps to ascertain from the Soviet Union the whereabouts of Raoul Wallenberg and to secure his return to freedom."[55] In short, he's ours, you have him, and we want him back. America in 1980 was looking for heroes. Reagan and Wallenberg appeared to share some characteristics: handsome and charming, the "good guy come to save the day." Reagan would indeed "rescue" the Iranian hostages through threat of war, but his role as a symbol of peace was highly questionable. With the U.S. tradition of focusing on the individual, the rising interest in the Holocaust demanded a sympathetic, outstanding person, and the Cold War setting provided one.

In 1984, Wallenberg's U.S. citizenship demonstrated itself legally, albeit with little effect. Just prior to Mikhail Gorbachev's rise to power and sensing little progress from the Reagan administration, the Wallenberg family employed lawyer Morris Wolff, who filed *Wallenberg vs. USSR* in a Washington DC Federal Court.

U.S. District Judge Barrington Parker found in favor of the Wallenberg family for $1 million for each year of Raoul's detainment—a total of $39 million.[56] While the Soviets ignored the suit, Wolff continued his public mission. In an interview with *The Crossover Project* for the Jewish Television Network, Wolff stressed his continuing work, "We are going to make it our mission to find his remains and arrange for a burial in the United States at the appropriate place with a garden and a marker."[57] The attorney for the Wallenberg family made it clear that when Wallenberg's remains were discovered, he would be laid to rest in the United States.

The watershed year for Wallenberg public memorialization was 1985. Henry Kissinger, despite having rejected Raoul's mother's appeal during the Nixon administration in 1973, could not avoid the American adoption of citizen Wallenberg and attended a March 13, 1985, black-tie tribute in New York City. Narrating the tribute's program was Peter Jennings, longtime ABC *News* anchorman and husband of Wallenberg biographer Kati Marton, whose parents had survived World War II in Hungary.[58] Jennings previewed a clip from the soon-to-be-released mini-series *Wallenberg*, starring Richard Chamberlain, which would run April 8–9 on NBC. Millions of Americans watched the series dramatize Wallenberg's playboy and bravado persona, and the production served as the zenith of U.S. media attention on Wallenberg. The New York City Government was certainly aware of the moment. During lunch hour on April 9, in between the two parts of the Wallenberg mini-series, the city of New York dedicated a mile-long sidewalk directly across the street from the United Nations complex as "Raoul Wallenberg Way."[59] International visitors walking out of the front door of the United Nations were instantly greeted with an American memorialization of Wallenberg.

In late 1985, an act of Congress rededicated the former Fifteenth Street SW in Washington DC as "Raoul Wallenberg Place."[60] Extending from Jefferson Drive at the Washington Monument south to the end of the U.S. Bureau of Engraving and Printing building, Raoul Wallenberg Place brings visitors to the west entrance of the United States Holocaust Memorial Museum, which opened its doors in 1993. At that entrance is a plaque honoring Wallenberg and his "mission of mercy on behalf of the United States."

On April 18, 1994, the U.S. Congress authorized the placement of a bust of Raoul Wallenberg in the U.S. Capitol Building.[61] The bust acknowledges Wallenberg as saving "100,000 lives during 1944–45" and commemorates the fiftieth anniversary of his disappearance at the hands of "the Red Army." The bronze statue by sculptor Miri Margolin, the aunt of Israeli prime minister Benjamin Netanyahu, stands in Emancipation Hall of the Capitol Visitor Center. In 2005, Nebraska governor Dave Heineman put his state's seal on a proclamation that highlights "Wallenberg's courage and . . . Stalin's directives."[62] By 2016, thirty states and three local jurisdictions had joined Nebraska in annually honoring their hero by observing October 5 as Raoul Wallenberg Day. The specific day was chosen not for his birthday, work, or disappearance but to honor his U.S. citizenship, which had been signed into law on October 5, 1981.

Numerous speeches honored Wallenberg's one hundredth birthday in 2012, and there was a general upsurge in attention in 2014. Most notably, on July 17, 2014, seventy years to the day from Wallenberg's arrival in Budapest, nine senators and eleven representatives jostled for position on the podium at a congressional luncheon honoring the International Raoul Wallenberg Foundation. Speaking were politicians as disparate as 2016 presidential hopeful Senator Ted Cruz (R-TX) and Senator Al Franken (D-MN), who had recently mentioned Wallenberg as "the person I would have liked to learn more about in High School." The Wallenberg family, Swedish officials, and members of President Obama's cabinet joined Annette Lantos, widow of the recently deceased congressman, at the luncheon. Amid speeches filled with honor and praise came the most telling moment. Senator Lindsey Graham (R-SC) brought the politicization of Wallenberg into the post–Cold War era when he said, "Will we be the Raoul Wallenberg's of the 2014 period? Will we speak up and say no to the Iranians desire to get a nuclear weapon? Are we going to stand by Israel as the rockets fly?"[63] To be sure, humanitarian efforts are rarely, if ever, entirely altruistic, but the memory of Wallenberg appears to be forever wrapped in politics. In this light, the United States utilized Raoul Wallenberg *twice*—once in rescue, a second time in memory. Senator Graham is going for a third.

Conclusion

Exiting out of the United States Holocaust Memorial Museum on a midsummer evening, past the Wallenberg plaque on the museum's exterior and walking north up Raoul Wallenberg Place, you find yourself in the shadow of the Washington Monument, right next to a Wallenberg street sign. The museum was built adjacent to the National Mall so museum visitors who had just been through a haunting historical recreation could, upon exiting, be immediately comforted by the familiar landmarks and institutions of Washington DC. The American museum initiative created the first Holocaust museum outside of Israel, which was not even in Europe, where the Holocaust took place. The United States, born with the spirit of individualism, needed more than a building to enhance its standing in Holocaust rescue and remembrance; America needed a face. With Wallenberg's name and likeness now in such prominent positions, he has become an important face. While Anne Frank remains the person with whom most Americans first engaged the Holocaust, it is Raoul Wallenberg's association with the United States and humanitarian rescue that commands the attention of the more mature visitor to the National Mall.

This chapter began by arguing that there is a need for a discussion of Wallenberg within the larger context of the Americanization of the Holocaust. Schult notes that there are more public memorials to Wallenberg in the United States than any other nation, even as several countries around the world honor him. Peter Novick warns of the pitfalls of overhyping the American connection to the Holocaust, and Paul Levine insists that the number of lives saved by Wallenberg has been distorted upward to build up his myth. His unsolved disappearance, then, makes a martyr of Wallenberg at the hands of the Soviet Union. Thus Wallenberg became an effective Cold War weapon, but this utilization runs the risk of becoming the essence of Wallenberg's story, which in turn shifts focus off the victims of the Holocaust. Nevertheless, Wallenberg's ascent to becoming the American image of Holocaust rescue conveys to a mass audience "that one person who has the courage to care can make a difference," just as Wallenberg's plaque outside the United States Holocaust Memorial Museum declares. Therefore, it is important to Holocaust education to maintain a balance that serves to honor Wallenberg without misrepresenting him. Wallenberg was certainly a hero to all he helped, no matter what his exact "numbers," no matter whom he was working for.

From Annette Lantos's lucky postcard being pulled on Jimmy Carter's radio show to the critical career change of her husband Tom Lantos to U.S. congressman, from Wallenberg's life of privilege to his selection for a rescue mission, the chance of this Swede becoming an American hero might seem unlikely. However, the findings presented here show that Wallenberg's name did not just happen to appear on American street corners or museum plaques; the timing of the placement of these memorials coincided with both a surge in overall Holocaust awareness in the United States and a reescalation of the Cold War from the late 1970s through the mid-1980s. This making of an American hero was not an accident. Wallenberg met the required political trappings to become an American hero, including having a love for hot dogs, sneakers, and the *New York Times*. It is past likely that Wallenberg is alive today—he would be 105. His epic rescue work deserves to be recognized, and the American connection appreciated, but, in the larger picture of the Americanization of the Holocaust, the making of Raoul Wallenberg into an American hero serves as an example of how the makers of public memory often have motivations aside from simply honoring a Holocaust rescuer for his life-saving work.

Questions for Further Discussion

- A common trait among rescuers is their level of awareness of the suffering of others—the difficulty of putting the faces of the victims out of their mind. How might Wallenberg's experiences in "depression-era Michigan" have contributed to his actions in Hungary?

- Two Nuremberg Laws, called race laws, were passed in 1935: The Law for the Protection of German Blood and German Honour and the Reich Citizenship Law. Were these laws based on religious identity? What examples of Nazi pseudo-science helped support these laws?
- Roosevelt established the War Refugee Board in January 1944 amid pressure from within the government. Create a timeline that includes not only the establishment of the WRB but also Hitler's rise to power, the establishment of the Auschwitz complex of concentration camps, and the beginning of the use of poison gas to exterminate Jews. How does this timeline give rise to the efforts of the American government being called "Too little, too late"?
- By the time Wallenberg arrived in Hungary, the Jewish population there had been greatly impacted. Between May 14 and July 8, 1944, 148 freight trains had carried Jews out of Hungary. What was the percentage/number of Jews already deported by the time Wallenberg arrived?
- Wallenberg was originally given permission to issue 1,500 passes. Why do you think he continued to issue *Schutzpasses* beyond that number? How many did he reportedly issue?
- How did Wallenberg aid those already on trains and death marches?
- Wallenberg was not the only diplomat to defy the orders of his government. Research Chiune Sugihara of Japan and Carl Lutz of Switzerland through the websites of the Jewish Virtual Library or Yad Vashem. How were the actions of the three men similar? How did Japan look upon Sugihara's actions? How did the Swiss government treat Lutz? What is your reaction to each man's treatment by his government?
- How is neutrality defined? Does it surprise you that neutral countries "played the system"? How did the Swedish government aid the Nazis?

- In 1963, Raoul Wallenberg was named one of the Righteous Among the Nations. This honor is bestowed by Israel's Holocaust Memorial and Museum, Yad Vashem. What are the requirements for such a prestigious honor?
- Discuss the phrase "One person can make a difference" in reference to Wallenberg. The United States Holocaust Memorial Museum uses a similar phrase—"What you do matters"—as a call to action. How can each of us today take a stand or make a choice that will make a difference?

Notes

1. "National Mall and Memorial Parks," National Park Service, accessed December 3, 2014, https://www.nps.gov/nama/index.htm.

2. Tanja Schult, *A Hero's Many Faces: Raoul Wallenberg in Contemporary Monuments* (New York: Palgrave Macmillan, 2009).

3. Andrew Handler, *A Man for all Connections: Raoul Wallenberg and the Hungarian State Apparatus, 1944–1945* (Westport CT: Praeger Publishers, 1996), 7–8.

4. Per Anger, "1995 Wallenberg Lecture," Raoul Wallenberg Medal and Lecture, University of Michigan, YouTube, posted April 13, 2014, https://www.youtube.com/watch?v=GReOBV5kHQY.

5. Raoul Wallenberg, *Letters and Dispatches 1924–1944*, trans. Kjersti Board (New York: Arcade Publishing, 1995), 41.

6. Anger, "1995 Wallenberg Lecture."

7. Sol King, quoted in Elenore Lester, "The Lost Hero of the Holocaust," *New York Times*, March 30, 1980.

8. Wallenberg, *Letters and Dispatches*, 90.

9. Gerald Steinacher, *Humanitarians at War: The Red Cross in the Shadow of the Holocaust* (New York: Oxford University Press, 2017), 219.

10. Joanna Saidel, "Yitzhak Shamir: Why We Killed Lord Moyne," *Times of Israel*, July 5, 2012, https://www.timesofisrael.com/yitzhak-shamir-why-we-killed-lord-moyne/.

11. Cary David Stanger, "A Haunting Legacy: The Assassination of Count Bernadotte," *Middle East Journal* 42, no. 2 (Spring 1988): 265.

12. Kati Marton, *A Death in Jerusalem* (New York: Pantheon Books, 1994), 260.

13. "Folke Bernadotte," in "Glossary," in *Israel in the Middle East: Documents and Readings on Society, Politics, and Foreign Relations, pre-1948 to the Present*, ed. Itamar Rabinovich and Jehuda Reinharz (Waltham MA: Brandeis University Press, 2008), 588.

14. Wallenberg, *Letters and Dispatches*, 173.

15. Paul Levine, *Raoul Wallenberg in Budapest: Myth, History and Holocaust* (London: Vallentine Mitchell, 2010), 55.

16. Handler, *A Man for All Connections*, 11.

17. Handler, *A Man for All Connections*, 16.

18. Robert Rozett. "International Intervention," in *The Nazis' Last Victims: The Holocaust in Hungary*, ed. Randolph L. Braham and Scott Miller, (Detroit MI: Wayne State University Press, 1998), 138.

19. Martin Lorenz-Mayer, *Safehaven: The Allied Pursuit of Nazi Assets Abroad* (Columbia: University of Missouri Press, 2007), 232.

20. "U.S. Policy during World War II: Morgenthau Documents State Department Inaction (January 16, 1944)," Jewish Virtual Library, accessed March 2, 2015, http://www.jewishvirtuallibrary.org/morgenthau-documents-state-department-inaction-january-1944.

21. Wallenberg, *Letters and Dispatches*, 220–22.

22. Bengt Jangfeldt, *The Hero of Budapest: The Triumph and Tragedy of Raoul Wallenberg* (London: I. B. Tauris, 2014), 380–82.

23. Thomas Streissguth, *Raoul Wallenberg: Swedish Diplomat and Humanitarian* (New York: Rosen Publishing, 2001), 80–82.

24. Alex Kershaw, *The Envoy* (Cambridge MA: Da Capo Press, 2010), 71.

25. Wallenberg, *Letters and Dispatches*, 229.

26. Kershaw, *The Envoy*, 151.

27. Levine, *Raoul Wallenberg in Budapest*, 67.

28. Kershaw, *The Envoy*, 65.

29. Kerstin von Lingen, "Conspiracy of Silence: How the 'Old Boys' of American Intelligence Shielded SS General Karl Wolff from Prosecution," *Holocaust and Genocide Studies*, 22, no. 1 (Spring 2008): 80–81.

30. Levine, *Raoul Wallenberg in Budapest*, 137.

31. Johan Östling, "The Rise and Fall of Small-State Realism: Sweden and the Second World War," in *Nordic Narratives of the Second World War: National Historiographies Revisited*, ed. Henrik Österberg Stenius and Johan Mirja Östling (Lund, Sweden: Nordic Academic Press, 2011), 127–47.

32. U.S. National Archives and Records Administration, "RG: 84, Sweden: Records of the Foreign Service," accessed April 2016, https://www.archives.gov/research/holocaust/finding-aid/civilian/rg-84-sweden.html.

33. Johan Matz, "Sweden, the USSR and the Early Cold War 1944–47," *Cold War History* 15 no.1 (2015): 27.

34. Susanne Berger, "Stuck in Neutral," *Searching for Raoul Wallenberg*, August 2005, Raoul Wallenberg Honorary Citizen Committee, https://www.raoul-wallenberg.eu/.

35. Stanley Meisler, *The United Nations: The First Fifty Years* (New York: Atlantic Monthly Press, 1995), 51.

36. Adam Taylor, "Sweden's Relations with Israel Were Already Bad. They Just Got Worse," *Washington Post*, January 14, 2016.

37. FriedlanderGroup, "Congressional Luncheon Honoring International Raoul Wallenberg Foundation," July 9, 2014, video by Shmuel/Dov Lenchevsky, YouTube, published July 17, 2014.

38. Helene Flanzbaum, ed., *The Americanization of the Holocaust* (Baltimore MD: Johns Hopkins University Press, 1999), 1.

39. Jan Taubitz, "35 Years after the Miniseries 'Holocaust,' 35 Years after 'The Deer Hunter': How Meryl Streep Spurred the Memory Boom," *Commemorative Culture*, accessed June 22, 2013, http://fyg.hypotheses.org/74.

40. Jimmy Carter, "Crisis of Confidence" speech, Oval Office, July 15, 1979, accessed December 27, 2017, http://www.americanrhetoric.com/speeches/jimmycartercrisisofconfidence.htm.

41. "Jews in Hungary Helped by Swede," *New York Times*, April 26, 1945.

42. Guy von Dardel, "Raoul Wallenberg's Secret Mission," *Washington Post*, April 25, 1947.

43. Eleanor Templeton, "Trial Spreads Guilt to Merely Apathetic: A Cunning Exploitation," *Washington Post*, April 30, 1961.

44. Jack Anderson, "The Man in the Iron-Curtain Mask," *Washington Post*, February 20, 1979.

45. Joshua Prager, "The Wallenberg Curse," *Wall Street Journal*, February 28, 2009, https://www.wsj.com/articles/SB123207264405288683.

46. John O'Connor, "TV: The Swede Who Saved Jews," *New York Times*, April 27, 1981.

47. Mary Lou Roper, "Salute to a Hero: Wiesenthal Center Fetes Wallenberg," *Los Angeles Times*, November 24, 1981.

48. Stephen Oliveria, "The Best Tricks Done Down Wallenberg," *Ride*, May 13, 2015.

49. Nadine Brozan, "Mystery Surrounds Fate of Swede Who Saved Jews," *New York Times*, August 4, 1979.

50. Edwin Viera, "Allen Dulles: Secrecy in Statecraft," *Elias Alias*, January 16, 2015, https://thementalmilitia.net/2015/09/29/allen-dulles-secrecy-in-statecraft/.

51. Staff report, "Poll Sparks Talk of Speier vs. Lantos," *San Francisco Examiner*, February 7, 2007.

52. House of Representatives, "Calendars of the US House, 97th Congress," 1982.

53. A. O. Sulzberger Jr., "Congressman Acts to Repay His Wartime Rescuer," *New York Times*, March 29, 1981.

54. UPI, "Swedish Hero Is Declared U.S. Citizen," *New York Times*, October 6, 1981.

55. Public Law 97–54, 97th Congress, October 5, 1981, accessed September 2, 2014, https://www.gpo.gov/fdsys/pkg/STATUTE-95/pdf/STATUTE-95-Pg971.pdf.

56. Ruth Marcus, "Soviets Lose Wallenberg Ruling," *Washington Post*, October 17, 1985.

57. Rozalie Jerome, "Morris Wolff: Rescuing the Rescuer," *The Crossover Project*, published January 15, 2013, accessed September 11, 2018, https://www.youtube.com/watch?v=k7PtMMGkEEY.

58. Ann Gerhart, review of "Paris, A Love Story" by Kati Marton, *Washington Post*, August 31, 2012.

59. Susan Heller Anderson, "New York: Day by Day," *New York Times*, April 10, 1985.

60. Historical Marker Project, "Raoul Wallenberg Place," accessed April 21, 2015, http://www.historicalmarkerproject.com/markers/hmqp8_raoul-wallenberg-place_Washington-dc.html.

61. U.S. Government Publishing Office, "Raoul Wallenberg Bust Placement in the U.S. Capitol," Congressional Record, 103rd Congress, 1993–94, accessed March 29, 2015, https://www.gpo.gov/fdsys/pkg/CREC-1994-04-18/html/CREC-1994-04-18-pt1-PgS22.htm.

62. "Raoul Wallenberg Day in Nebraska," International Raoul Wallenberg Foundation, accessed September 24, 2017, http://www.raoulwallenberg.net/wallenberg/tributes/wallenday/usa/nebraska/.

63. FriedlanderGroup, "Congressional Luncheon."

6

The University in Exile and the Garden of Eden

Alvin Johnson and His Rescue Efforts for European Jews and Intellectuals

GERALD J. STEINACHER AND BRIAN BARMETTLER

Alvin Johnson was born in Homer, Nebraska, in 1874. The son of Danish immigrants, Johnson grew up in Nebraska a typical country boy whose values and work ethic came from farm life. He always "considered himself a bona fide pioneer and a Midwesterner to the core."[1] His father was a strong believer in social justice and racial and social equality, and his mother was a first-wave feminist. About his father, Johnson once wrote that "pro-semitism was so firmly fixed in his blood . . . that it became, apparently, a transmissible acquired characteristic, which runs undiluted into the fourth generation."[2] This upbringing shaped him. According to U.S. sociologist Lewis A. Coser, Johnson "was imbued with the populist and progressive traditions of the Middle West."[3] German author Monika Plessner adds: "With his youthful creativity and his fighting dignity [Alvin Johnson] personified . . . typical American culture. In his eventful life he always sided with the weaker ones, fought against majorities for minorities, and stood up against oppression in the name of the persecuted ones."[4]

As a boy, Johnson attended Nebraska public schools. When he was eighteen, he enrolled at the University of Nebraska in Lincoln, where he studied economics as well as classical and German literature. Several years later, he served in the U.S. Army during the Spanish-American War (1898).[5] He was always proud of his midwestern roots, as illustrated by the dedication to his autobiography: "To my wife Edith Henry Johnson, pioneer's daughter, bearer of the spirit that thrust resolutely westward from the New England coast and won a continent for the mightiest republic in history."[6]

When Johnson was older and living in New York, he liked to say that he had experienced the best of two worlds—both his humble

11. Portrait of Alvin Johnson, undated. University of Nebraska–Lincoln, University Archives, Alvin Johnson Collection 150813-00004.

rural background and urban life in a big cosmopolitan city. He was known to reminisce at one moment about farm life in Nebraska, and a moment later to quote the German poet Friedrich Schiller in fluent German.[7] American journalist and educator Max Lerner saw in Johnson "a multifarious man who is not by that fact a split man."[8] Like so many Americans and Europeans in the nineteenth century, Johnson admired German science and culture. Many U.S. scholars earned doctorates from German universities or had at least spent some time in Germany. Likewise, the faculty and students at the University of Nebraska, as well as the local population, had strong ties to Germany. German-speaking settlers from all over Europe (even Germans from Russia) were common in the state, and German was widely spoken prior to 1917.[9] Although Johnson acknowledged the many good qualities of the university system in German-speaking Europe, he also criticized certain negative characteristics—for example, the elitist attitude that was widespread among German-speaking professors. In his autobiography, Johnson hinted at his admiration for Germany's liberal and open-minded traditions. He admired the revolutionaries of 1848 and the Schleswiger (immigrants from the Danish-German Schleswig region), who had made a new home in the Midwest: "There was a Little Deutschland [Germany] of Germans who hated Bismarck but loved beer and high voltage cheese."[10]

After receiving his master's degree, Johnson was accepted to Columbia University, where he earned a PhD in economics in 1902. After graduation, he held academic positions at Columbia; the universities of Nebraska, Chicago, and Texas; and Cornell and Stanford. In 1916, he took a yearlong leave of absence from Cornell in order to work for the *New Republic*, which was at the time one of the most influential liberal magazines in the United States. Johnson returned to Cornell, but when the United States entered World War I in 1917, he resigned from his post to return to the *New Republic* as an assistant editor. According to Plessner, the "driving force" in Johnson's life was "to fight for a better world" and to make that world "materialize . . . here and now."[11] During and after the war he tried—unsuccessfully—to sway public opinion in favor of a fair peace settlement for Germany. In the end, however, U.S. president Woodrow Wilson gave in to the demands of Great Britain and France to harshly punish the defeated enemy.

Part 1: Intellectuals in Exile

The New School

In 1922, Johnson became director of the New School for Social Research in New York, which would soon become a haven for a generation of scholars who had fled from Hitler and Mussolini. In the 1930s, Johnson's New School became a major center for social research, almost unmatched in the United States.

The New School started from humble beginnings. It was first organized in 1918 and began as a project of dissident academics. In 1917, historian Charles A. Beard resigned from Columbia University together with his colleague and close friend James Harvey Robinson. Columbia's president wanted to make the faculty duty bound to support the war politics of the U.S. Congress and President Wilson. Not only did Beard disagree with the official U.S. stance on the war, he saw this forced support as a threat to academic freedom.

So he and Robinson gathered together a group of friends and fellow scholars, all of whom were associated with the *New Republic*, where Johnson was working. Johnson began taking part, along with Beard, Robinson, and others, in weekly sessions planning for a new school. Based on European traditions and the ideas of American educational reformer John Dewey, the New School for Social Research in New York pioneered a new model for adult education in America. Inspired by the German *Abendvolkshochschule*—a type of secondary schools for adults—Johnson wanted to make the New School a center for research and adult learning with a popular teaching program that would not only educate but also critically analyze U.S. society and politics and "educate the educated."[12] The New School was also meant to be a home for liberal and radical thinkers. As Claus-Dieter Krohn puts it: "One of [Johnson's] convictions was that only a teacher with a mission could be a good teacher."[13] Fostering research was another part of the New School's mission. As early as 1915, Johnson was arguing the merits of research requirements for professors. In his essay "In Defence of the Professor Who Publishes," Johnson wrote,

> If I were a university president, loving harmony, but forced by financial straits to pay my professors, in part, with promises, I should take pains to make the proportion of mere promise large in the case of men who are writing books. Those who never write at all I should endeavour [*sic*] to pay in hard cash. Thus could I

barter justice, a great good, for peace, the greatest good of all. Or better, I should try to man the institution entirely with writers of books. Thus could I dispense altogether with justice—excellent, but expensive commodity![14]

In 1922, Johnson got his chance to helm a university. He was elected director of the New School and remained in that position for the next eighteen years. Historians Peter Rutkoff and William Scott write: "When [Johnson] accepted the directorship of the New School, he immersed himself in its spirit and activities. Johnson expanded adult education, worked to reestablish the research division, and organized numerous programs to train business executives, labor leaders, educators, and civic leaders. Similarly, he reaffirmed the New School's policy to act as a forum to address contemporary issues and propose solutions for social problems. And like the earlier founders, Johnson fervently believed in the possibility of human progress."[15]

By 1924, Johnson was basically making all the key decisions that shaped the institution in its formative years. Sitting on the New School's advisory board at this time were Nebraska-born Pulitzer Prize–winning author Willa Cather; jurists Felix Frankfurter, Roscoe Pound, and Learned Hand; journalist Walter Lippmann; *New Republic* editor Bruce Bliven; Eleanor Roosevelt; Sidney Hillman of the Amalgamated Clothing Workers; and a former president of the U.S. Chamber of Commerce, Julius Barnes.[16]

The University in Exile

In 1927, Johnson became the associate editor of the *Encyclopedia of the Social Sciences*, an ambitious project with hundreds of contributors from the United States and Europe. Johnson was very impressed by German scholarship and thus made an effort to include many entries written by Germans scholars in the *Encyclopedia*. From this experience, he became personally acquainted with a number of German academics and was able to establish networks in Europe.

Soon after Hitler came to power in Germany in 1933, the Nazis purged the country's universities. In that year alone, 1,200 Jewish and socialist intellectuals lost their jobs. Some of these victims of Nazi persecution had been contributors to the *Encyclopedia*. Ultimately, the number of intellectuals barred from working as well as from participating in cultural and social life in Germany reached 12,000. Thus began the massive "brain drain" from the Reich. Some scholars went to Great Britain, some to Switzerland, and others to France. Thousands of intellectuals made their way from Europe to the United States, leaving a legacy that can be traced to this day.

Assistance for the refugee scholars was often left up to private organizations. The Notgemeinschaft Deutscher Wissenschaftler im Ausland, a German self-help organization based in Switzerland, was able to find jobs for thirty professors at the University of Istanbul. Across the Atlantic, meanwhile, Johnson was thinking about bringing such scholars—particularly those whom he knew from the *Encyclopedia*—to the United States. Initially he seemed to have in mind only the Marxist economist Emil Lederer. Soon, however, he came up with the idea of establishing a "University in Exile" based at the New School and formed around a whole group of exiled scholars. He was especially interested in German sociologists and political scientists who worked in the tradition of Max Weber.

The Nazi expulsion of Jewish, socialist, and other antifascist scholars from universities and public service had made it clear to Johnson that protests in the form of letters or public demonstrations would not be enough: "I, therefore, propose a protest which will arrest the attention of every person interested in scholarship, namely, the prompt establishment of an institution to be known as 'The University in Exile,'" wrote Johnson. "The world is quick to forgive invasions of academic liberty by a forceful government. It long ago forgave Mussolini. It will never forgive Hitler as long as we have a working University in Exile."[17]

Moreover, the University in Exile was Johnson's means of protest not only against Nazi barbarism but also against antisemitism and ignorance in his own country. And it was through Johnson's personal commitment that the first twelve scholars were invited to New York. As president of the New School, Johnson also had a secondary agenda. Up to that point, the New School had been a small experimental academy for adult education, but with the European brain drain, that could change.[18] In a bold bid to bring top European scholars to the New School, Johnson aimed to relocate an entire academic community. He was particularly interested in scholars from the Hochschule für Politik in Berlin. Founded in 1920, the Berlin institution had a guiding philosophy similar to that of the New School.[19] Rutkoff and Scott point out how remarkable Johnson's project was: "In a single stroke, Johnson transplanted a school of German social science to the United States and fulfilled his own pledge, made more than ten years earlier, to make the New School a center for social science research."[20] Krohn points out the deliberate naming of Johnson's project: "In choosing the name 'University in Exile' . . . he wanted to demonstrate publicly that the university tradition now suppressed in Germany was to be preserved for an indefinite period."[21] "For," as Alvin Johnson wrote, "it was the university itself that was being exiled from Germany."[22]

But there were many obstacles to overcome. It was difficult to arrange visas for some scholars, as American quota regulations remained unchanged even during the war. The U.S. State Department often opposed the entry of certain émigrés on the grounds that they were Jewish or "radical thinkers." And the economic hardship and high unemployment caused by the Great Depression made it even harder to secure entry for exiles. President Roosevelt sympathized with Johnson's efforts but was unable to break the often xenophobic resistance of immigration authorities at the time. To make matters worse, antisemitism was also widespread on U.S. campuses. As Krohn writes: "When Alvin Johnson first broached his plan of setting up a university in exile for displaced scholars, many of his colleagues thought he could not possibly succeed in placing Jews in an American university."[23] For this and other reasons, many universities sabotaged rescue efforts. The Austrian economist Joseph A. Schumpeter, who was by invitation teaching at Harvard University, attempted to create a committee to help fellow academics trapped in Nazi Germany. According to Krohn, Schumpeter learned firsthand the difficulties of bringing scholars with Jewish backgrounds to the United States in the face of pervasive antisemitism.[24]

Luckily for Johnson and the scholars he was trying to help, New York was a more open-minded and diverse destination. The city remained very connected to Europe—little Italy was still Italian at the time, and immigrants from all over Europe preserved elements of their ethnic identities and kept close ties to their homelands. In 1933, New Yorkers elected as their new mayor the progressive politician Fiorello La Guardia, making him not only the city's first Italian American mayor but also the first person with a Jewish background to hold the position.[25] La Guardia and other like-minded New Yorkers championed immigrants and ethnic minorities, and opposed fascism. Johnson could therefore rely on some support and sympathy from local politicians.

Money was always a problem for the University in Exile. Johnson wrote endless appeals, but money trickled in very slowly. After the *New York Times* published an article about the project, however, things began to change. The Rockefeller Foundation donated a large share of the necessary funds, but a number of other foundations and industrialists also made generous contributions. Meanwhile, the faculty grew from twelve in 1933 to twenty-six by 1941, and continued to grow during the war years. The student body was expanding as well: By the fall of 1940, students numbered 520.[26] What Johnson accomplished with the University in Exile was no small achievement:

> Almost every exiled scholar who can be counted among the reform economists found a haven at the New School for Social Research in New York. The importance of this institution for German scholarship in exile lies not just in its having accepted the largest group of expelled university faculty but also in its offering a place where the German tradition in the social sciences, having just being eradicated in its country of origin, could be carried on. The school's division of social sciences, staffed by an international faculty unique among American institutions of higher learning, would soon become the most significant center of its kind in the United States.[27]

The "University in Exile" contributed to a fruitful dialogue between continental and American thought. Krohn lists 184 émigré scholars who were affiliated with the New School. Among them were Hans Kelsen, Claude Levi-Strauss, Gaetano Salvemini, and Max Wertheimer. For the New School's twenty-fifth anniversary, the renowned German writer Thomas Mann, who occasionally guest lectured at the institution, delivered the laudation "Alvin Johnson—World Citizen."[28] Other prominent scholars including theologian Paul Tillich and philosopher Ernst Bloch also taught general seminars at the New School.[29] Johnson was not always successful in his attempts to bring scholars over, however. He tried to get Marc Bloch out of Nazi-occupied France, but State Department hurdles stymied Johnson's efforts. Bloch stayed in France, joined the Resistance, and in 1944 was executed by the Gestapo.

Still, Johnson managed to save hundreds of others. With Hitler's annexation of Austria in 1938 came the next big wave of refugee scholars. The Austrian Marxist Paul F. Lazarsfeld made his way to the United States and became one of the founding fathers of social research in the United States. Other Austrians included Erich Hula, a former assistant to legal scholar Hans Kelsen, and Felix Kaufmann, an epistemologist and Husserl student who was initially a jurist of the Kelsen school.[30] The work of these scholars from Austria—where most of the contemporary economic theory had originated—made a huge impact on research in the United States.[31]

Soon, Germans and Austrians were joined by other nationals from a long list of countries, including Algeria, Belgium, Czechoslovakia, France, Hungary, Italy, Poland, Russia, Spain, and Switzerland. At this point, the New School might easily have developed into a broadly European university. But French and Belgian scholars, joined by Paris-based Czechoslovakian, Hungarian, and Polish academics, formed the École Libre des Hautes Études in New York—a project that was supported by Johnson in many ways. Classes at the École were taught in French, while lectures at the University in Exile were in English (although sometimes with a strong foreign accent). Because of the École Libre des Hautes Études, the faculty at the University in Exile remained mostly German and Austrian. The Graduate Faculty at the New School constituted "a little piece of Germany in New York," as one émigré recalled.[32] Coser stresses this aspect:

> Almost all of them came from Germany and Austria, even though somewhat later a few scholars from other countries were added to the . . . Faculty roster. Most of them had held prestigious academic positions in their native country; some of them had been academic Marxists, more of them had been fairly close to German social democracy, and several had been highly placed civil servants in the Social Democratic administration of Prussia. Their homogeneity of background and of age as well fostered a tendency among the refugees to seek out the companionship of like-minded men and women and to create what I have called a gilded ghetto in New York.[33]

The Graduate Faculty

Johnson realized that rescue would be a long-term project. The Nazis would not disappear overnight, and the permanent integration of scholars and other refugees into U.S. society was the logical consequence. The refugee scholars shared this view and saw themselves more as immigrants than as exiles. The sociologist Louis Wirth—himself a Jewish American who had emigrated with his family from Germany to Omaha, Nebraska, as a boy—called the idea of "intellectual emigrants" a contradiction in terms because intellectuals are lifelong nomads in the universe of the mind.[34] According to Coser, "The term 'University in Exile' had been appealing as a fund-raising device during the formative period, but a number of the new faculty members resented the term 'exile' and pressed for a name that would clearly indicate that the new institution was an integral branch of the New School and a permanent part of the American educational system."[35] Thus in 1935 the University in Exile became the Graduate Faculty—a permanent research division of the New School that offered fully developed doctoral programs in philosophy and the social sciences.

Refugee scholars were dispersed widely across the United States. But some groups of scholars formed and maintained a collective identity, as was the case with the New School cohort as well as a group of social science researchers at Columbia University

12. Alvin Johnson attending the testimonial dinner tendered by the members of the New York State Temporary Commission against Discrimination, New York City, April 28, 1945. University of Nebraska–Lincoln, University Archives, Alvin Johnson Collection 150813-00012.

that formed around the German scholars Max Horkheimer and Theodor W. Adorno.[36] "Indeed," writes Krohn, "the New School acquired university status only through the 'University in Exile,' staffed entirely by immigrants, and through the Graduate Faculty that grew out of it. In terms both of institutional structure and of personnel, the New York School more closely resembled the Institute of Social Research in Frankfurt, which found a home as a body at Columbia University; and there were many personal and intellectual connections between these two émigré centers."[37]

And there existed also a certain rivalry between the scholars of the New School and the relocated Frankfurt School, which was now based at Columbia. The Frankfurt School had its own financial resources, whereas the New School's Graduate Faculty "was and always remained dependent on outside funding."[38]

During the first years of their tenure, the New School refugee scholars focused their research on the most important problem of their era: the rise of German and Italian fascism. As sociologists and political scientists, they worked hard to understand the causes and the nature of these regimes. During World War II, their knowledge and research was highly sought after by military and political decision makers in the United States. The Graduate Faculty included international affairs experts and was considered "the academic group most frequently consulted by US government officials" on all aspects of German leadership as well as Germany's military and economy.[39] The Office of Strategic Services, the U.S. wartime intelligence service, recognized that the most capable German intellectuals were based at the New School.[40]

Under Johnson's leadership, the Graduate Faculty started its own publication, called *Social Research*. The new journal was to be published in English for an American audience, whereas the Frankfurt School's *Zeitschrift für Sozialwissenschaft* continued to be published in German until the outbreak of the war—perhaps a sign that its editors "chose to continue in splendid isolation"[41] and resisted adapting to U.S. life. While this may have been true, they likely were also more at ease writing and expressing their ideas in their native tongue rather than in English. Many articles in *Social Research*, however, were translations from German and could be identified as such by native English speakers.[42] The European backgrounds of the refugee scholars was both an asset and a potential problem. Their fresh foreign perspectives probably helped to "deprovincialize" the academic world in the United States, but the "splendid isolation" of the recent emigrants on their intellectual island made the exchange of ideas harder. According to Coser, "All indicators point to the fact that the Graduate Faculty, even though functioning as an accredited American academic institution, was nevertheless not fully part of American cultural and intellectual life."[43] Hoping to change that, in 1943 Johnson proposed establishing a bachelor of arts program at the New School and lobbied the New York Board of Regents for its approval.

After the war ended, most of the refugee scholars stayed in the United States. Early hopes for a better world now rid of Hitler and Mussolini eventually gave way to harsh reality. Cooperation with German universities was sometimes uneasy, as many Nazi scholars remained on the faculties and continued their academic careers after 1945. (In the 1950s, Cold War politics would

13. "The University in Exile opens its work in New York: Dismissed or furloughed German professors ready to begin their teaching at the New School for Social Research." Johnson is seated in the center, wearing glasses. This newspaper article is from October 1933. University of Nebraska–Lincoln, University Archives, Alvin Johnson Collection 150813-00011.

cover up their fascist pasts.) Moreover, plans to establish a school for democratic leadership at the New School were never realized, even as threats to American democracy, notably in the form of Senator Joseph McCarthy's anticommunist crusade—would not disappear. Alvin Johnson was very much opposed to McCarthy's search for "communists" and "communist sympathizers"—a witch hunt that was poisoning the country's intellectual, political, and cultural climate. Johnson officially retired in December 1945, and his departure left the future of the New School and its graduate faculty uncertain. The New School, of course, survived, and Johnson witnessed its ongoing success as a professor emeritus at the school, with his own office and secretary.

What is the legacy in the United States of the New School refugee scholars? Opinions on this question vary widely. According to Coser, more than the émigrés themselves, it was their students who made the greatest impact on U.S. academia and contributed most to the "de-provincialization of the American mind."[44] The intellectual significance of the New School for both the American and European social sciences, although difficult to measure, should not be underestimated. Nearly seventy years after the New School's founding, Rutkoff and Scott described it this way:

> Anchoring the northern edge of Greenwich Village at 66 West Twelfth Street, the New School for Social Research has become an established feature of New York's cultural life. New Yorkers from all five boroughs and the various suburbs gather here each evening to take courses on virtually every subject imaginable from Confucian philosophy to urban gardening. The adult education program has no admissions requirements and only modest course fees; its instructors are freelance intellectuals and artists. The students come to learn, drawn by what they have heard about the school: that it is a free place and an eclectic place, a place where one is bound to meet interesting people. This reputation has enabled the New School to grow and thrive.[45]

Part 2: The Garden of Eeden

Alvin Johnson's ideals, together with his love for farming, which he developed as a child in Nebraska, led him to establish a farm settlement for refugees in near Wilmington, North Carolina, in 1939. Johnson hoped that the settlement could offer those who had suffered the chaos and persecution in Europe a new home where they could make a living for themselves and their families. Unfortunately, the refugee farm, named Van Eeden, did not fulfill Johnson's high expectations, and none of the refugees found a permanent home there.

Johnson's academic work focused heavily on theory, but the Nebraskan never gave up his love and admiration for the soil. At his home in Nyack, a suburb of New York City, he had a small vegetable garden that continued to become more fertile under the professor's delicate care.[46] Johnson did not sanction all types of farming: His heart lay with the small farmer and the peasant. In his autobiography, *A Pioneer's Progress*, Johnson wrote, "The one growth of the soil I most cherish is the independent small farmer . . . He is my brother and his historic fate is mine."[47] It was this belief that largely informed his decision to start the settlement.

As the situation in Europe continued to darken, many refugees who had escaped persecution now faced material struggles in the United States. The situation was precarious. Johnson states: "New York was filling with Jewish refugees from Germany. There was no employment for them, and more and more of our 'humane' Congressmen were urging that we close our doors."[48] On top of that, ordinary citizens adopted an even more hostile attitude toward the refugees.[49] Johnson decided to watch no longer and started planning his second refugee project—this one based on his love of the land and located in North Carolina.

In Johnson's eyes, a farm settlement seemed most practical. His friend Hugh MacRae, who was born and raised in Wilmington, North Carolina, had already experimented with small farm settlements in and around Wilmington. MacRae had recruited farmers from Germany, Italy, the Netherlands, and Poland.[50] Castle Hayne, a MacRae settlement where mostly Dutch settlers worked and resided, soon became a thriving business.[51] So when Johnson decided to launch his own farm colony, he chose one of Hugh MacRae's old farms, Van Eeden.

Van Eeden was named for Herr Van Eeden, the leader of the property's earlier Dutch settlement. Herr Van Eeden had moved to North Carolina in the early twentieth century and tried his luck at farming under the supervision of Hugh MacRae. Unfortunately, wrote Johnson, "Van Eeden was a gentleman, not a farmer, and the colony petered out."[52] There also seemed to be a drainage problem on the property, but Johnson, the confident Nebraskan, was undaunted. He visited Van Eeden himself and found a ditch that could be used to drain the land.[53] The property otherwise appealed to Johnson, who appreciated the fact that there were already three-room cottages there (though they were in need of some repair). Johnson also had a few new four-room houses built to accommodate larger families.[54] Indeed, he thought that he had found the ideal location.

In 1939, Johnson began reaching out to potential sponsors for Van Eeden and selecting refugee families whom he thought would be suitable for his settlement. The Alvin Corporation was founded that summer to finalize the project and raise the necessary funding.[55] The Refugee Economic Corporation, which was run by Johnson's friends Charles Liebman and Bernard Flexner, invested $32,500 of the $65,000 needed to run the settlement for a year and supply the new farmers with the necessary equipment.[56] Individual investors donated the remaining funds. By the end of the summer of 1939, the Alvin Corporation had purchased 150 acres of farmland and 100 acres of woodland from the Hugh MacRae Corporation. The entire Van Eeden contract, including the 150 acres that the Alvin Corporation had already purchased, consisted of 1,080 acres, which MacRae was willing to sell for $50,000.[57]

The Alvin Corporation had ambitious plans for the settlement. Van Eeden (also referred to as Eden, which is what the settlement's small train station was called, for example) was to provide a home for fifty to a hundred families; each family would be entitled to one ten-acre plot.[58] The settler families were given a credit, which they were to pay back at a small interest rate. Johnson had strict ideas when it came to whom he wanted to join the farm colony. Most important, the potential settlers needed to have experience in farming. Johnson was, however, willing to make exceptions: "I never believed that one has to come directly off the soil if he is to know the soil and love it. We are all sons of Adam: his hoe is on our shoulders."[59] But Johnson was realistic and knew that previous farm experience would make life easier for him and for the settler. He expressed additional preferences in a letter to Ernst Elias, a potential unmarried settler who was turned down by Johnson, who explained: "We prefer as settlers married men with children. On a farm a man needs a wife to help him, and children to make life in the country pleasant and worthwhile."[60]

The settlers were not chosen randomly from the arriving refugee boats, but rather were recruited by Johnson himself, who made use of his international network in order to get the best potential settlers. It is important to note here that Johnson did not plan to restrict Van Eeden only to German Jewish refugees. But he knew that until he managed to get non-Jewish funding, he would mostly have to settle Jewish refugees.[61] The recruiting process led Johnson to contact sources in Austria, England, Germany, Switzerland, the United States, and beyond. He worked closely with the National Refugee Service, but also with other organizations, including the Notgemeinschaft Deutscher Wissenschaftler im Ausland. By January 1939, word of Johnson's plans had reached London. It was there that the chairman of the Notgemeinschaft, Dr. F. Demuth, wrote a letter to Johnson about a young trained agriculturist named Pietrowski.[62] The fate of Pietrowski is unknown, but one can say with certainty that he never set foot on the Van Eeden settlement. In another letter—this one to Johnson's friend Grenville Clark—Johnson confided that he wanted to "get two or three good Spanish agricultural families out of that miserable concentration camp in Spain. The Spaniards from Granada, particularly, are the best gardeners in Western Europe and I want our community to make some wine, at least enough for them to refresh me when I visit them."[63] Unfortunately, Johnson was unable to settle any Spaniards on his farm and thus had to drink store-bought wine.

By the fall of 1939, Johnson had found enough potential settlers. Once initial housing and drainage problems were resolved, the Alvin Corporation settled four families at Van Eeden, giving each a cottage and a ten-acre plot, as outlined in the original plan. The following spring, four more families moved to Van Eden.[64] Each of the eight families was to farm its own plot individually, but Johnson knew that farming could be a discouraging task. Because he had recruited families with mostly urban backgrounds (although a few had some farm experience),[65] he hired a farm manager to supervise the settlers and give them advice when needed. In addition, Johnson relied on soil experts from the Agricultural Experiment Station in New Jersey. The first year of production at Van Eeden failed to yield the level of prosperity that was hoped for. Johnson still considered it a success, however, as 50 percent of the families were already more than half self-sufficient, and morale seemed to be high.[66] Thus the first year report proudly states: "The most concrete evidence of the morale of the settlement consists in the fact that [of] these eight families who have been with us for a year or more, not one wishes to leave us."[67] The settlement was en route to success.

Though not part of Johnson's original vision, the settlers came from diverse backgrounds. The original eight families were Jewish (or had been declared as such by the Nuremberg Laws) and came from Nazi Germany: the Heimanns, Flatows, Loebs, Wolfs, Ladenburgs, Lewins, Willmans, and Collinses. Max Wolf was the only one who had a thoroughly rural background. The others came from academia or had professional careers ranging from accounting to architecture. Van Eeden was a mélange of social classes, generations, and ideologies.

Despite the mediocre start, Alvin Johnson was not expecting Van Eeden to fail. But the settlers ignored major problems from the start. In Johnson's opinion, Van Eeden, with only eight families, was still too small. He believed that at least twenty-five were needed for it to succeed.[68] Some families—such as that of Arthur Flatow, who had been a successful architect in Berlin—were used to a more luxurious lifestyle than what was available at Van Eeden. The farmer who cherished the land and did not care about financial ups and downs remained merely a figment of Johnson's imagined utopia. The main language on the settlement was German, and many families, to Johnson's dismay, did not bother to learn much English. The first and second farm managers—Mr. Mims, a native Wilmingtonian, and A. J. Bruman of the National Refugee Organization—seemed to have largely failed at bringing about speedy prosperity and harmony. In a letter to Leonard Heimann, one of the settlers, Johnson wrote: "It has been a principle of Mr. Bruman to discuss matters as little as possible."[69] The third manager, H. M. Pinckney, was more successful than the first two, but by that point the various problems were too deeply rooted to be fixed.

The years 1941 and 1942 marked a turning point at Van Eeden. Nazi policy in Europe had shifted from forced emigration, plundering, and acts of violence to systematic mass murder, making it impossible for Johnson to recruit settlers from occupied Europe. At Van Eeden, multiple families found the hardships of the small farmer unbearable. Leonard Heimann contracted malaria, so the mosquitos in the southern summer gave him enough reason to leave Van Eeden in 1941. The Flatows left in

14. Life in the Eeden colony: Walter and Fred Loeb coming home from school. "Returning home from the school bus line." In the Manfred and Ann Loeb Collection #P0029, North Carolina Collection Photographic Archives, the Wilson Library, University of North Carolina at Chapel Hill.

1942, hoping to find a better life in a big city than the one they had been leading, just barely getting by, in rural North Carolina. And neither the Lewins nor the Collinses nor the Ladenburgs stayed at Van Eeden longer than two years. Johnson was able to recruit a few more families, but by and large his settlement had failed.

Van Eeden was not without some success stories, however, as the case of the young Austrian couple Felix and Paula Willman illustrates. Before Felix's imprisonment at Dachau and Buchenwald, the couple had lived in a beautiful city apartment in Vienna.[70] Felix was a well-to-do accountant, and Paula was a teacher. After Felix was released from Buchenwald, he and Paula fled to the United States. Once they reached American shores, Johnson tried to dissuade them from moving to the settlement. As Johnson told it, he "urged that in their evening promenades around the Ring in Vienna, they had had no occasion to learn the difference between

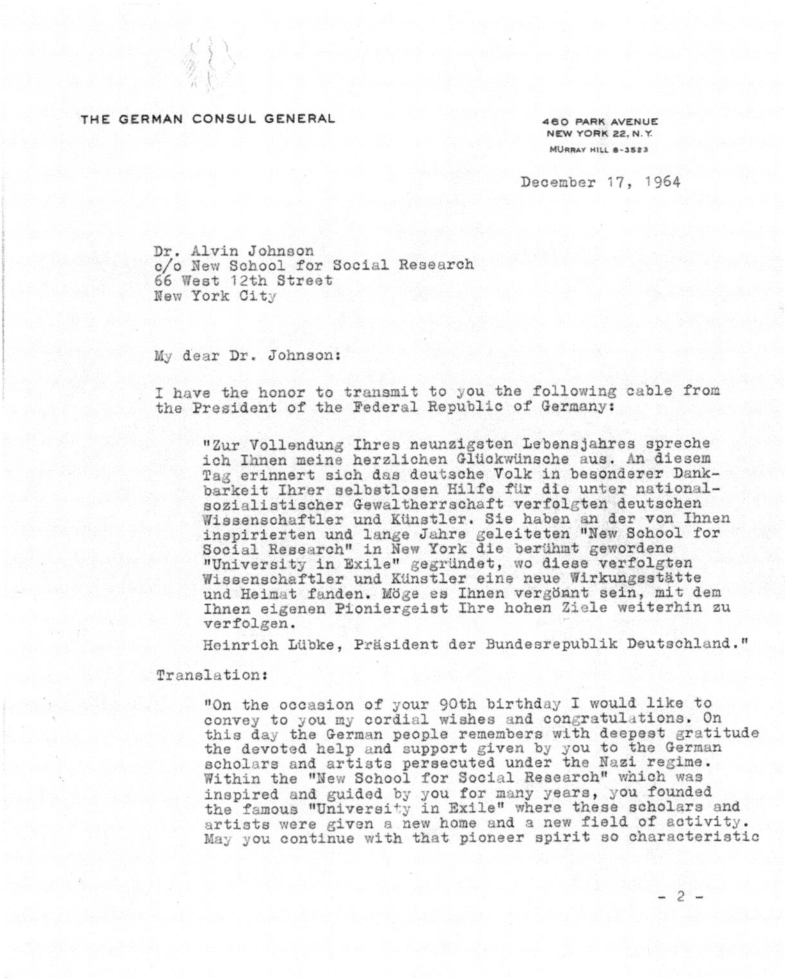
THE GERMAN CONSUL GENERAL

460 PARK AVENUE
NEW YORK 22, N.Y.
MURRAY HILL 8-3523

December 17, 1964

Dr. Alvin Johnson
c/o New School for Social Research
66 West 12th Street
New York City

My dear Dr. Johnson:

I have the honor to transmit to you the following cable from the President of the Federal Republic of Germany:

"Zur Vollendung Ihres neunzigsten Lebensjahres spreche ich Ihnen meine herzlichen Glückwünsche aus. An diesem Tag erinnert sich das deutsche Volk in besonderer Dankbarkeit Ihrer selbstlosen Hilfe für die unter nationalsozialistischer Gewaltherrschaft verfolgten deutschen Wissenschaftler und Künstler. Sie haben an der von Ihnen inspirierten und lange Jahre geleiteten "New School for Social Research" in New York die berühmt gewordene "University in Exile" gegründet, wo diese verfolgten Wissenschaftler und Künstler eine neue Wirkungsstätte und Heimat fanden. Möge es Ihnen vergönnt sein, mit dem Ihnen eigenen Pioniergeist Ihre hohen Ziele weiterhin zu verfolgen.

Heinrich Lübke, Präsident der Bundesrepublik Deutschland."

Translation:

"On the occasion of your 90th birthday I would like to convey to you my cordial wishes and congratulations. On this day the German people remembers with deepest gratitude the devoted help and support given by you to the German scholars and artists persecuted under the Nazi regime. Within the "New School for Social Research" which was inspired and guided by you for many years, you founded the famous "University in Exile" where these scholars and artists were given a new home and a new field of activity. May you continue with that pioneer spirit so characteristic

- 2 -

15a and 15b. A 1964 letter from the German consul general in New York to Alvin Johnson. The West German president congratulated Johnson on his ninetieth birthday and wrote: "On this day the German people remembers with deepest gratitude the devoted help and support given by you to the German scholars and artists persecuted under the Nazi regime." University of Nebraska–Lincoln, University Archives, Alvin Johnson Collection 150813-00013 / 150803-00014.

for you to strive for those high aims you have always lived for.

Heinrich Lübke, President of the Federal Republic of Germany."

Allow me to extend to you on my own behalf the most heartfelt congratulations and warmest wishes for your health and well-being.

Very sincerely yours,

Klaus Curtius

(Klaus Curtius)

a vegetable plant and a weed."[71] To Johnson's great disbelief, the Willmans went to Van Eeden anyway. Despite some early problems with the weeds around their house, the Willmans were among the best settlers. Of Felix, Johnson wrote: "Mr. Willman, who had never grown even a radish before he came to Van Eeden, was offered two managerial jobs at large dairy farms."[72] Felix turned down both offers. The pair stayed at Van Eeden until 1944, when they moved to New York. Johnson continued to guide them, however, getting Felix a job at the New School and Paula enrolled as a student.[73]

The Van Eeden settlement never was able to provide a home for over a hundred families, as Johnson had originally intended. Over time, more and more families continued to leave Van Eden, and in 1948 the Alvin Corporation decided to sell the land to James Wilkins, who continued to farm the land with his son.[74] Johnson had tried his best to help the refugees. He was fully committed to the project and visited the farm every month. Johnson even took personal responsibility for the failure: "If I could have lived in the community," he wrote, "I think it would have succeeded."[75] Despite the unfulfilled expectations, Johnson and the Alvin Corporation did employ some fifty people on the farm. Regardless of the outcome, Van Eeden must be seen as the product of Johnson's relentless efforts to make a difference at a time when many decided to simply stand by.

In 2018 the Jewish American Society for Historic Preservation to the State of North Carolina decided to erect a state highway historical marker recognizing the community established at Van Eeden and Johnson's contribution. The marker reads "Van Eeden: Jewish refugees from Nazi Germany lived, 1939–46, at agricultural colony founded in 1909 and revived by Alvin Johnson."[76]

A Biography to Be Written

Johnson died in 1971 in Upper Nyack, New York. In 2012, he was inducted into the Nebraska Hall of Fame. Although still widely unknown among his fellow Nebraskans, a committed elite in his home state still remember him today. His relative obscurity is surprising, given that the connection between the New School and

Nebraska has persevered. In 2000, the former governor and U.S. senator from Nebraska Bob Kerrey became president of the New School and therefore one of Johnson's successors.

As the Nebraska Hall of Fame Commission noted, Johnson "gained national and international recognition as an economist, educator, humanitarian, social activist, writer and editor."[77] Moreover, Johnson helped to save numerous Central European scholars—many of whom were Jewish or had Jewish ancestors—from Nazi persecution. In addition to his academic writing, Johnson helped to author the nation's first nondiscrimination legislation and wrote two novels, three collections of short stories, and an autobiography. He received honorary doctorates from the New School for Social Research, the University of Nebraska, Brandeis University, Hebrew Union College, Yeshiva University, and the universities of Algiers, Brussels, and Heidelberg.

Johnson is best remembered all over the world as the father of the New School. Much less is known about his other activities, and to this day no biography about him exists. The authors of this paper are in the process of filling in this gap. Archival sources relating to Johnson are scattered all over the United States, with an important collection at Yale University. Unfortunately it seems that most of the New School's own records on Johnson have not survived. According to Krohn, "In investigating the University in Exile at the New School . . . the researcher finds that most of the documents bearing on its history have been lost over the years."[78] In 1991—encouraged by John Braeman, a history professor at the University of Nebraska–Lincoln—Johnson's surviving children donated his personal papers to the university's special collections archive. Despite Johnson's high-profile career and his heroic efforts to aid refugees fleeing from Nazi persecution, his documents have yet to be thoroughly analyzed. Until they are, many aspects of Johnson's personal and academic life will remain elusive.

Questions for Further Discussion

- In 1918 Alvin Johnson argued for a reasonable peace with defeated Germany. World leaders back then would have been wise to listen to Johnson since the Treaty of Versailles had direct repercussions that contributed to World War II. How did each of the following treaty terms contribute to resentful attitudes by Germany toward the Allies: War guilt, Reparations, Territorial losses, Military restrictions?

- Johnson was a private citizen and not a powerful politician. And still, he was able to help people to escape Nazi Germany and to come to the United States. This was anything but easy, given that many Americans did not want refugees to come. What did Johnson do to make this happen and therefore save lives?
- Johnson wanted to create a great farming community to make the newcomers happy. But what were some of the problems he and the citizens of Eeden faced?
- In 2012 Johnson was inducted into the Nebraska Hall of Fame in the State Capitol. Why was Johnson not celebrated as a hero in his home state earlier?
- Johnson's biography is gripping because of the eventful times in which he lived, and also because his identity was complex and multifaceted in ways that flout common expectations or stereotypes. If you want to learn more about concept of identity, and how each of us is made up of many attributes, look at the following websites: www.facinghistory.org, www.pbs.org, www.tolerance.org.

Notes

Gerald Steinacher would like to thank Dr. Jean Cahan, director of the Harris Center for Judaic Studies at the University of Nebraska–Lincoln, for spurring his research interest in Alvin Johnson. Special thanks also go to Tracy Brown and Liz Feldstern for her feedback and final edits of this paper. An earlier version of this chapter was published in *Reassessing History from Two Continents: Festschrift Günter Bischof*, ed. Martin Eichtinger, Stefan Karner, Mark Kramer, and Peter Ruggenthaler (Innsbruck: Innsbruck University Press, 2013), 49–68, and is reprinted here with permission.

1. Peter M. Rutkoff and William B. Scott, *New School: A History of the New School for Social Research* (New York: Free Press, 1986), 32.

2. Alvin Johnson, *Pioneer's Progress: An Autobiography by Alvin Johnson*, with a foreword by Max Lerner (Lincoln: University of Nebraska Press, 1960), 11. The first edition was published in 1952 by Viking Press in New York.

3. Lewis A. Coser, *Refugee Scholars in America: Their Impact and Their Experiences* (New Haven CT: Yale University Press, 1984), 102.

4. "Er verkörpert in jugendlicher Geisteskraft und streitbarer Würde ein Stück typisch amerikanischer Kultur. In seinem ereignisreichen Leben hat er immer auf Seiten der Schwachen gestanden, hat sich für Minderheiten mit Mehrheiten herumgeschlagen, im Namen der Unterdrückten und Verfolgten aufbegehrt." Monika Plessner, "Die Deutsche 'University in Exile' in New York und ihr amerikanischer Gründer" [The German "University in Exile" in New York and its American founder], in *Frankfurter Hefte* 19 (1964): 181–86, 181. All translations are the authors'.

5. Benita Luckmann, "Eine deutsche Universität im Exil. Die 'Graduate Faculty' der 'New School for Social Research'" [A German university in exile: The "Graduate Faculty" of the "New School for Social Research"], in *Soziologie in Deutschland und Österreich 1918–1945*, ed. M. Rainer Lepsius, *Kölner Zeitschrift für Soziologie und Sozialpsychologie*, Sonderheft 23 (Opladen: Westdeutscher Verlag, 1981), 427–41, 427.

6. Max Lerner, foreword to Alvin Johnson, *Pioneer's Progress: An Autobiography* (Lincoln: University of Nebraska Press, 1960), v.

7. Rutkoff and Scott, *New School*, 32.

8. Lerner, foreword to Johnson, *Pioneer's Progress*, xii.

9. *Frederick C. Luebke, Immigrants and Politics: The Germans of Nebraska, 1880–1900* (Lincoln: University of Nebraska Press, 1969).

10. Johnson, *Pioneer's Progress*, 35.

11. "Für eine bessere Welt zu kämpfen, die sich jetzt und hier verwirklichen muss, war der starke Antrieb seines Lebens"; Plessner, "Die Deutsche 'University in Exile,'" 181.

12. "Erziehung der Erzogenen." Plessner, "Die Deutsche 'University in Exile,'" 182.

13. Claus-Dieter Krohn, *Intellectuals in Exile: Refugee Scholars and the New School for Social Research*, trans. Rita and Robert Kimber (Amherst: University of Massachusetts Press, 1993), 61.

14. Alvin Johnson, "In Defence of the Professor Who Publishes," *Midwest Quarterly* 2, no. 4 (July 1915): 343–56, 347.

15. Rutkoff and Scott, *New School*, 31.

16. Rutkoff and Scott, *New School*, 35.

17. Quoted in Luckmann, "Eine deutsche Universität im Exil," 428.

18. Krohn, *Intellectuals in Exile*, 59.

19. Luckmann, "Eine deutsche Universität im Exil,'" 435.

20. Rutkoff and Scott, *New School*, 85.

21. Krohn, *Intellectuals in Exile*, 63.

22. Johnson, *Pioneer's Progress*, 338.

23. Krohn, *Intellectuals in Exile*, 22.

24. Krohn, *Intellectuals in Exile*, 23.

25. Luckmann, "Eine deutsche Universität im Exil,'" 429. Although La Guardia's father was an Italian Catholic and his mother was Jewish and from Trieste (which was, back then, part of the Austro-Hungarian Empire), the future mayor became a member of the Episcopalian Church.

26. Coser, *Refugee Scholars in America*, 104.

27. Krohn, *Intellectuals in Exile*, 59.

28. Plessner, "Die Deutsche 'University in Exile,'" 185.

29. Coser, *Refugee Scholars in America*, 106.

30. Krohn, *Intellectuals in Exile*, 75.

31. Krohn, *Intellectuals in Exile*, 45.

32. "Es war doch ein kleines Stückchen Deutschland in New York." Quoted in Luckmann, "Eine deutsche Universität im Exil,'" 429.

33. Coser, *Refugee Scholars in America*, 106–7.

34. Krohn, *Intellectuals in Exile*, 179. Wirth researched the adaption of Jewish immigrants into urban life in the United States and was very active with the American Jewish Committee and the American Council on Race Relations.

35. Coser, *Refugee Scholars in America*, 104.

36. Coser, *Refugee Scholars in America*, 102ff.

37. Krohn, *Intellectuals in Exile*, 5.

38. Krohn, *Intellectuals in Exile*, 5.

39. See Arthur J. Vidich, foreword to Claus-Dieter Krohn, *Intellectuals in Exile: Refugee Scholars and the New School for Social Research*, trans. Rita and Robert Kimber (Amherst: University of Massachusetts Press, 1993), xii.

40. Krohn, *Intellectuals in Exile*, 161.

41. Coser, *Refugee Scholars in America*, 105.

42. Coser, *Refugee Scholars in America*, 105.

43. Coser, *Refugee Scholars in America*, 106.

44. Coser, *Refugee Scholars in America*, 109.

45. Rutkoff and Scott, *New School*, xi.

46. Johnson, *Pioneer's Progress*, 357.

47. Johnson, *Pioneer's Progress*, 357.

48. Johnson, *Pioneer's Progress*, 364.

49. Letter from Alvin Johnson to Bernard M. Baruch, March 15, 1939, University of Nebraska Archive and Special Collections, the Alvin Johnson Collection (hereafter referred to as AJC), RG 15/8/13, box 15, folder 1.

50. Susan Taylor Block, *Van Eeden* (Wilmington DE: Lower Cape Fear Historical Society, 1995), 6.

51. Block, *Van Eeden*, 7.

52. Johnson, *Pioneer's Progress*, 364.

53. Johnson, *Pioneer's Progress*, 364.

54. Johnson, *Pioneer's Progress*, 365.

55. Report of the President of the Alvin Corporation on the Van Eden Settlement, Watha, North Carolina, February 1941, box 18, folder 5, AJC.

56. Letter from Alvin Johnson to Bernays Heller, March 1, 1939, box 15, folder 1, AJC.

57. Letter from the Hugh MacRae & Co to the Alvin Corporation, August 3, 1939, box 15, folder 1, AJC.

58. Report of the President of the Alvin Corporation.

59. Johnson, *Pioneer's Progress*, 365.

60. Letter from Alvin Johnson to Ernst Elias, January 17, 1940, box 17, folder 2, AJC.

61. Letter from Alvin Johnson to Grenville Clark, June 30, 1939, box 15, folder 1, AJC.

62. Letter from Dr. F. Demuth to Alvin Johnson, January 28, 1939, box 15, folder 1, AJC.

63. Letter from Alvin Johnson to Grenville Clark, June 30, 1939, box 15, folder 1, AJC.

64. Report of the President of the Alvin Corporation.

65. Johnson, *Pioneer's Progress*, 365.

66. Report of the President of the Alvin Corporation.

67. Report of the President of the Alvin Corporation.

68. Report of the President of the Alvin Corporation.

69. Letter from Alvin Johnson to Leonard Heimann, May 29, 1940, box 16, folder 5, AJC.

70. Block, *Van Eeden*, 25.

71. Johnson *Pioneer's Progress*, 365.

72. Letter from Johnson to Dr. Jacob Billikopf, March 23, 1943, box 15, folder 7, AJC.

73. Block, *Van Eeden*, 27.

74. Block, *Van Eeden*, 70.

75. Johnson, *Pioneer's Progress*, 365.

76. This chapter was part of the materials submitted for the approval process to the historical marker advisory committee. For the marker, see http://www.ncmarkers.com/Markers.aspx?MarkerId=D-117. The authors are thankful to Mike Taylor, director of the Pender County Public Libraries in Burgaw, North Carolina, for the information about the marker.

77. "Nebraska Hall of Fame Commission selects Dr. Alvin Johnson as new inductee at 11–15–12 meeting at Nebraska State Capitol," copy of the text in possession of the authors.

78. Krohn, *Intellectuals in Exile*, 7.

Part 2

Teaching about Rescue

7

From Saints to Sinners

Teaching about the Motivations of Rescuers of Jews through Documentary and Feature Films

LAWRENCE BARON

Middle- and high-school teachers face a dilemma in how they should deal with the subject of gentile rescuers of Jews during their units on the Holocaust. The amount of class time allotted to the Holocaust within their courses is usually limited. Since protecting Jews from arrest and deportation by the Germans and their collaborators constituted the exception to the rule of indifference or passivity toward their plight, an emphasis on the inspiring stories of "Righteous Gentiles" distorts their impact on mitigating the numbers of Jews who were incarcerated or murdered in Hitler's attempt to exterminate them. After all, only 5 to 10 percent of the Jews who survived in Germany, its occupied territories, and collaborationist states during World War II received active assistance from gentiles and non-Jewish organizations.[1] As Alvin Rosenfeld observes, "The question that arises with respect to the 'rescuers,' therefore, is not one of their inclusion or exclusion from narrative accounts of the Nazi era but chiefly one of proportion: how central or peripheral are these 'moral heroes' of the Holocaust to the larger history of the Holocaust?"[2]

Within the time constraints imposed on their Holocaust unit, teachers must determine what they intend to convey and cover in the portion devoted to rescuers. Do they merely want students to know that a minority of gentile individuals and groups hid Jews, protested their persecution and deportation, shepherded them to neutral or Allied countries, or supplied them with counterfeit papers that enabled them to pass as Christians? Any introduction of famous rescuers like André Trocmé, Irena Sendler, Oscar Schindler, or Raoul Wallenberg minimally should contextualize their actions historically and chronicle what they did to save Jews.

Screening brief clips from documentaries or feature films about rescuers makes their stories more vivid to students and stimulates further discussion about the risks they ran and what they accomplished. This abbreviated approach to teaching about rescuers implicitly assumes that rescuers responded spontaneously to a dire situation for a variety of unrelated reasons. Indeed, it corroborates one school of interpretation about the rescuers as exemplary but random figures without much in common. Mordecai Paldiel, the former director of Yad Vashem's Department of the Righteous Among the Nations, contends, "Most of the non-Jews who helped Jews during the Holocaust were suddenly drawn into helping without previously having done much that in scope, risk, or sheer magnanimity remotely resembled what they were doing now."[3]

Another perspective on rescuers categorizes them into distinctive groups with shared formative experiences regarding their attitudes towards Jews, empathic sensitivity to the suffering of others, institutional affiliations which could mobilize and support them, personality traits, prior records of altruistic behavior and political activism, or values that predisposed them to shield Jews from harm. This analysis of rescuers views their conduct during World War II as a product of deeply engrained beliefs, habits, or sensibilities that enabled them to become guardians of Jews despite the mortal danger it entailed. Here full disclosure requires me to admit that I served as the historian for the first multinational psychosocial interview study of rescuers, Sam and Pearl Oliner's *The Altruistic Personality*. Subjecting the extensive data they collected about the rescuers to rigorous qualitative and quantitative analysis, the Oliners concluded: "Their involvements with Jews grew out of the ways in which they ordinarily related to other people—their characteristic ways of feeling; their perceptions of who should be obeyed; the rules and examples of conduct they learned from parents, friends, and religious and political associates; and their routine ways of deciding what was wrong and right."[4]

In this chapter I draw on the findings of the Oliners and other scholars like Eva Fogelman, Kristin Renwick Monroe, and Nechama Tec.[5] I recommend clips to show in class or films to be watched at home that illustrate the recurring patterns in the lives of rescuers that inclined them to save rather than abandon Jews.[6] Three caveats should be stressed to students when they learn about rescuers. First, the imminent threats of betrayal, arrest, execution, and collective punishment of family members and associates implicated in their rescue operations deterred many people with similar backgrounds and convictions from acting on their sympathies for the Jewish victims of Nazi oppression. Intervening on behalf of a vilified minority for an indeterminate period with no guarantee Germany and its allies would lose the war was a daunting prospect. Second, as Freud once remarked, human behavior is overdetermined. The rescuers cannot simply be reduced to types who fit into a single category. There is much overlap between the personal, political, or religious forces that impelled them to side with a minority slated for state-sanctioned discrimination and liquidation. Third, rescuers tend to be modest when describing what they did because they felt it was a natural expression of their selves and principles. Conversely, documentaries and feature films often lionize their deeds, making them seem so heroic that it is difficult for audiences to imagine emulating them.

Attachment Rescuers

Although morality is conventionally conceptualized as based on ideological, philosophical, or religious ideals, rescuer studies reveal that in these cases it was also derived from emotional empathy with the suffering of strangers or sympathy for Jews rescuers already knew as colleagues, customers, employers, employees, friends, lovers, neighbors, professionals, relatives, or spouses. Empathy has multiple sources. It can arise from an innate disposition, be inculcated by modeling the consistent caring exhibited by parents and other central figures in one's life, or reflect experiences of having been a recipient of compassion or a victim of exclusion, hardship, and injustice. Positive previous relationships with Jews endowed rescuers with a sense of obligation to assist them. Whether an acute sensitivity to the pain of others or personal ties to specific Jews motivated rescuers to help, their willingness to aid Jews showed that they tacitly recognized the common humanity they and Jews shared, discrediting the virulent racist and religious stereotypes of Jews that the Third Reich and its minions disseminated in Europe during World War II. Approximately 37 percent of the rescuers in the Oliners' interview sample fell into this category.[7]

Miep Gies exemplifies these "attachment rescuers," as the Oliners call them.[8] Her motivations for hiding Anne Frank's family and four of their friends in the attic of the building where Otto Frank's pectin and spice companies were headquartered and supplying them with food and other necessities for over two years initially stemmed from her affection and loyalty toward the Franks. Anne's popular diary and the movies it has inspired present Gies as a benevolent and brave woman without accounting for what motivated her. In her autobiography, the YouTube video of her lecture on the occasion of receiving the Raoul Wallenberg medal in 1994, and the short documentary *Remembering Anne Frank*, she attributes her readiness to join her husband, Henk, and three other of Otto Frank's employees in concealing his family and their friends in the "Secret Annex" and sustaining them through the duration of the war to three causes: 1) her experiences as a starving child with a lung disease who was brought from Austria after World War I to the Netherlands to reside with a foster family who nursed her back to health; 2) her "social-minded" Dutch foster parents who taught her to succor people who were hungry, poor, or persecuted; 3) the bonds of friendship she forged with Otto Frank and his family, particularly Anne. When asked by Otto to participate in his plan, she immediately accepted because "it went without saying" that was this is what she should and would do.[9]

The Attic: The Hiding of Anne Frank, a television movie adapted from Gies's autobiography, will probably hold the attention of students better than her spoken and written recollections.[10] While it portrays primarily the vicissitudes of caring for the occupants of the hideaway and keeping its existence secret, the early scenes of the film disclose some of Gies's motivations. Her invitation to a dinner with the Franks' circle of close friends, her congenial encounters with Anne, and the Franks' attendance at her wedding to Henk depict a warmer relationship with her boss and his family than is usual for an employee. That Otto singled out Gies as the first person he confided in about his scheme to go underground illustrates how much he trusted her. The film does not broach the topic of why she initially came to the Netherlands, but it makes clear that she appreciated her adopted homeland and despised the policies of Nazi Germany, even though her Austrian origins classified her as a German citizen after Hitler's annexation of Austria. Patriotic resistance to what she perceived as the injustice perpetrated against the Jews reinforced her private reasons for helping the Franks. Once the Franks and their friends moved into the attic, Gies's connections to the Dutch underground through her husband were essential in obtaining the extra rations of food required to feed them without arousing the suspicions of the Germans or their Dutch accomplices.

Irene Gut Opdyke was another rescuer who ascribed her hiding of Jews to empathy and friendship.[11] Opdyke was born and raised in Poland, and the outbreak of the war separated her from her parents. While a student nurse, she enlisted to attend to wounded Polish soldiers on the Ukrainian border, where she was raped and left for dead by Soviet soldiers. A Russian doctor acted as both her healer and a maternal figure, restoring her faith in humanity. A German-Russian population exchange allowed her to return to Poland. There she was conscripted to serve meals to German officers and secretaries at a munitions factory and witnessed the relentless onslaught against the Jews in a nearby ghetto. Assigned to supervise Jews who laundered the uniforms of the Germans, she became their friend and smuggled extra food to them. A Gestapo major attracted by both her good looks and fluency in German asked her to be his maid. After he told her the neighboring ghetto in Tarnopol would soon be liquidated, she invited twelve Jewish friends from the laundry to hide in the basement of his villa. One day she forgot to lock the door to the kitchen, where the Jews would congregate when the major was not there. Returning unexpectedly, he stumbled upon them, but decided not to turn them over to the Gestapo if Opdyke agreed to become his mistress.

Though Opdyke prayed to God for guidance, her testimony indicates that she created a haven for her twelve wards out of an emotional kinship with them. As she succinctly but eloquently put it, "We became good friends. I didn't have a family. They were persecuted. It was a human bond. That's how I felt. I did not think of them as different because they were Jews. To me, we were all in trouble, and we had a common enemy."[12] She recalls justifying her actions to the major in similar terms: "I know only one thing. They're my friends. I had to do it. I did not have a home to take them to, I don't have a family. Forgive me, but I would do it again. Nobody has a right to kill and murder because of religion or race."[13] When queried about how she mustered the moral fortitude to offer sanctuary to her friends, she replied, "Courage is a whisper from above. If you think only with your head and not your heart, the head will tell you that it's dangerous and don't do this. So you have to involve the heart."[14]

Oskar Schindler belongs to this cohort of rescuers too. The books and documentaries about him and Spielberg's *Schindler's List* depict him as an unscrupulous rogue who eventually realized that he could spare his Jewish laborers from their precarious existence in the Kraków ghetto and Płaszów concentration camp by transforming his factory into a safe haven for them and transferring them to a new enterprise in Moravia to preempt their deportation to death camps in 1944.[15] Depictions of his moral metamorphosis usually render him an enigmatic figure whose amoral hedonism and opportunism made him an unlikely candidate to endanger himself and squander his wartime profits to insure the survival of his Jewish laborers. The contrast between his personal shortcomings and altruistic behavior during the war intrigued audiences and readers. If someone with Schindler's character flaws could oppose the evil inherent in the Nazi campaign to eradicate the Jews, then other ordinary Germans had no credible excuse for failing to do anything to stop the relocation, torment, or slaying of their Jewish neighbors.[16]

Schindler evolved during the course of the war as he became more appreciative of his Jewish business advisors and fonder of his other Jewish employees, which, in turn, spurred him to assume greater responsibility for their well-being and that of their co-workers. Mietek Pemper, one of his Jewish confidants, opines that Schindler's moral maturation was a consequence of his personal ties to the Jews he saved: "I am quite sure that at first, we were only a source of cheap labor for him. But over the course of the war years, we became human beings he cared for and worried about."[17] In a television documentary about Schindler's life, historian Michael Berenbaum similarly remarks, "He saved them not because he was at the beginning kindhearted, good, moral, noble, and alike, but because on a very deep level he developed a human attachment to these people."[18] Schindler believed his concern for his workers originated in his amicable childhood relationships with Jews.[19]

Psychotherapist Luitgard Wundheiler considers Schindler's ethical evolution an incremental process in which he developed from "an impulsive and sometimes opportunistic helper to a compassionate, more thoughtful helper, and finally to a principled altruist, and from a man whose concern was limited to people he knew personally to someone whose concern included many human beings he did not know at all."[20] These transitions were precipitated by his increasing awareness of the catastrophe befalling the Jews and his broadening perception of the parameters of his moral responsibility, from initially alleviating the threat posed to those closest to him to a more extensive duty to do the same for any Jews whom he could possibly save. Wundheiler posits that his extrapolation from rescuing specific Jews to protecting strangers emerged as Schindler, respectively, internalized and validated the benevolent reputation his Jewish employees bestowed on him as their savior, prompting him to regard any Jews as his extended family meriting his paternalistic protection.[21]

Spielberg's motion picture is an accessible and riveting audiovisual resource. To be sure, it is too disturbingly graphic for younger students and too long to be shown in its entirety in the classroom. Moreover, its reenactment of the Schindler saga suffers from the narrative liberties filmmakers take to heighten the drama and suspense of their creations. For example, Itzhak Stern, played by Ben Kingsley, constitutes a composite character—who parenthetically did not compile the eponymous list—representing several of the Jews Schindler relied upon to finance and manage his business and trade on the black market to obtain the luxury items he plied

16. Oskar Schindler in Paris in 1949. United States Holocaust Memorial Museum, courtesy of Herbert Steinhouse.

high-ranking officers and the commandant of the Płaszów camp with to retain his Wehrmacht contracts and custody over his workers.[22] The powerful scene when Schindler surveys the liquidation of the Kraków ghetto with his mistress from hilltop and glimpses a girl in a red coat meandering through the macabre chaos of the SS looting Jewish apartments and rounding up Jews and shooting them never happened. The girl was not purely a figment of Spielberg's or novelist Thomas Keneally's imaginations. She had existed and either died during the liquidation of ghetto A in 1942 or in an extermination camp. If the former is the case, her cadaver probably was among corpses the Germans exhumed and burnt when they closed Płaszów. Her connection to Schindler was that he had been deeply upset by the massacre of Jewish youngsters housed in the ghetto's "children's home." For Spielberg and Keneally, Schindler witnessing the annihilation of the ghetto and honing in on the girl marked the turning point when he decided to fully dedicate himself to the survival of his Jewish workers. Therefore, the girl personifies the defenseless and innocence of the victims.[23] The scene should elicit a lively student discussion.

Other telling scenes from *Schindler's List* attest to Schindler's growing affection and sympathy for the Jews under his tutelage, but the one I'd recommend showing to students is when a young woman seeks his assistance in getting her parents transferred from Płaszów to his factory. He scoffs at her request and protests to Stern that he does not want either the Jews or the Germans to consider his factory a haven. He excuses Commandant Goeth's brutality by alleging that it is a part of his duties and a byproduct of the war. Under different conditions, Schindler argues, Goeth would be just "a wonderful crook, a man who loves good food, good wine, the ladies, and making money." Of course, this description concisely characterizes Schindler's proclivities, confirming the behavioral and visual parallels between the two men drawn previously in the film. Stern reacts by recounting the summary executions of twenty-five Jews by Goeth as a reprisal for the escape of one prisoner. A moment later Schindler hands Stern a scrap of paper with the names of the woman's parents, whose reassignment to the factory ensues. Schindler's trust in Stern's judgment prods him to strive to deserve the benign reputation his Jewish employees have conferred upon him.

Nevertheless, Spielberg's recurring images of the atrocities perpetrated in the Holocaust contrast Schindler's deeds as a conspicuous exception to the responses of the German army and SS members and officers who commit or condone them. Many Holocaust scholars have decried *Schindler's List* for highlighting the achievements of a "good" German instead of the suffering of the Jews.[24] The movie, however, follows the escalating measures that culminated in the barbaric elimination of the Jews, commencing with their registration, the expropriation of their property, their enslavement as forced laborers, ghettoization, and relentless abuse and privation, and ending in their individual or collective executions or selections for transport to Auschwitz. The corpses of the bodies set ablaze in Kraków represent the massive fatalities Jews incurred there. After a contingent of women from Oskar's factory receive showers instead of being gassed at Auschwitz, the camera pans on the Jews lined up to enter the gas chambers and the smoke rising from the crematoria chimneys. The snow swirling around them visually reminds viewers of the ashes descending from the pyre in Kraków.

In case the staggering death toll of the Holocaust has not permeated the consciousness of the audience, the final scenes of the movie drive home the point. Schindler's Jews and their descendants number more than six thousand, but only four thousand Jews still lived in Poland when the film premiered in 1993. The film is dedicated to the six million Jews who perished. The last two scenes occur in cemeteries. One is a procession of the actors and the survivors they played to Schindler's grave in Jerusalem. Then the credits roll over an image of the street in Płaszów that was paved over with tombstones from the Jewish cemetery in Kraków.

Normative Rescuers

Many rescuers acted in accordance with the humanitarian, political, or religious values espoused by groups with which they were affiliated as part of networks they had belonged to before the war or joined during it to resist the barbarism meted out toward the Jews by Germany and its allies. Their enlistment in collective rescue networks did not preclude that some of the Jews they helped were prior acquaintances, colleagues, or friends, but operating within an organized framework increased the likelihood that they would assist Jewish strangers too. The Oliners chart the chain of events and reasoning that typically elicited the participation of such people in aiding Jews to evade capture and deportation: "The social group, rather than the victim him- or herself, motivates the behavior. The actor perceives the social group as imposing norms for behavior, and, for these rescuers, inaction was considered a violation of the group's code of proper conduct."[25] The Oliners classified 52 percent of the rescuers they interviewed as normative rescuers.[26]

Working through a network magnified the numbers of Jews who could be aided and mitigated the practical burdens and risks associated with hiding them. The group could counterfeit identity papers to permit Jews to pose as gentiles and procure supplemental ration coupons to feed Jews who were in hiding. It could screen confederates from within its ranks for trustworthiness, surveil the local police and Gestapo for tips about impending raids, and relocate Jews to safe houses where they stayed temporarily until the raids were over. If Jews were smuggled to neutral countries, the network could bribe border guards, map secure routes, and recruit *passeurs* to accompany them. The telling word in all the advantages collective action afforded is "could." The arrest of a single member who succumbed to intimidation or torture and revealed the identities of his or her comrades could lead to their arrest, the dismantling of the underground organization, and the apprehension of the Jews under its protection.[27]

The most effective rescue movement during the war occurred when Danish citizens foiled the German plan to round up the Jews residing in their country and mobilized a flotilla of private boats to ferry the vast majority of them to nearby neutral Sweden in October of 1943. A myriad of historical factors contributed to the success of this operation. Denmark had surrendered without much military resistance after Germany invaded it in 1940 and supplied Germany with dairy, meat, and railway access to Norway. The Danish government agreed to suppress the Communist Party and signed the Anti-Comintern Pact against the Soviet Union in 1941. In return for this cooperation by fellow Aryans, Germany neither stationed a large contingent of troops in Denmark nor outlawed parliamentary elections and the Danish monarchy. Cognizant of the lack of government or popular support for enacting legislation against the Jews, German occupation officials decided not the press the issue as long as Denmark remained compliant with other German policies. The situation altered by 1943 in the wake of German defeats at Stalingrad and El-Alamein. To compensate for its losses, Germany tightened its control and economic exploitation of countries it occupied. This provoked a wave of sabotage and strikes in Denmark. The Danish government resigned rather than yield to German demands to quash the resistance, and Germany imposed martial law on the country at the end of August of 1943.

SS Plenipotentiary Werner Best saw this as an opportune moment to rid Denmark of its Jews in one surprise sweep. After confiscating the membership records of the Jewish community, which contained the addresses and names of its members, he devised a plan to raid their homes on Rosh Hashanah. He confided his intentions to his close friend Georg Duckwitz, a German naval attaché in Copenhagen. Dispatched to Denmark in 1939, Duckwitz enjoyed good relations with both gentile and Jewish Danes and leaked Best's secret to a prominent Danish Social Democrat and the Swedish government. The former warned Jewish leaders, who alerted their coreligionists. A grassroots movement grew quickly to hide Jews in Danish churches, homes, and institutions; commandeer vehicles to transport them to the coast; and hire fishermen to shuttle them across the Oresund Sound to Sweden, which had announced in a radio broadcast that it was willing to provide asylum to the refugees. The Germans captured only 468 of 7,800 Jews, 112 remained in hiding in Denmark, and the rest found sanctuary in Sweden.[28]

The documentary *The Danish Solution* and videotaped lecture by Knud Dyby, both of which are available online, provide historical context on the propitious conditions that facilitated the rescue of the Danish Jews and feature eyewitness accounts about the logistical and motivational dynamics of it.[29] From clips, readings, and their teacher's commentary, students should be able to ascertain the conditions that were instrumental to the success of this rescuer operation. Denmark experienced a relatively lenient military occupation, retained much sovereignty until August of 1943, possessed a well-integrated Jewish population, perceived Best's onslaught against the Jews as an integral part of Germany's occupation (since the former occurred within a month of the dissolution of the Danish government), and neighbored near a neutral country open to accepting Jewish refugees. What can be gleaned from the interviewees in *The Danish Solution* and Dyby's reminiscences is that the rescue effort snowballed rapidly because so many Danish gentiles personally knew Jews they could warn and mobilized for a spectrum of reasons that dynamically reinforced one another, like compassion, democratic convictions, patriotism, professional credos, or religious tolerance.

The rescue of the Danish Jews has inspired several feature films.[30] I recommend the Walt Disney production *Miracle at Midnight* for use in middle-school classes, since it is aimed at preteen audiences and can be streamed from the Internet.[31] It is also a useful source because its plotline parallels that of Lois Lowry's *Number the Stars*, which many middle-school students may already have read and that is short enough to be assigned or recommended if they have not.[32] As is true with juvenile movies and books, some of the protagonists are youngsters, heightening the probability that their target audiences will identify with them.

The film opens with a map of Denmark with swastikas inscribed within its borders to indicate the country is occupied by German troops. Brother and sister Hendrik and Else Koster pass beneath a Nazi banner on the way to school, and a German guard stops Hendrik to search his backpack for contraband literature and weapons. Although the security check turns up nothing, Hendrik does belong to a student underground movement and participates that evening in a shootout with the Germans in the course of which one of his fellow resisters is wounded. The injured boy is surreptitiously brought to the hospital, where the doctor who treats him happens to be Hendrik's father. Dr. Koster does not report the shooting and conceals the identity of his new patient. The Best-Duckwitz conversation occurs, conveying the impression that Best's strategy will succeed because he commands the overwhelming manpower to execute it and has the element of surprise in its favor. This enhances dramatic tension, but as already indicated, he lacked full cooperation from the German army and navy.

Following the seizure of the Jewish community records, the Jewish friends of Dr. Koster worry what this portends. The Duckwitz disclosure emboldens the chief rabbi to implore his congregants to abandon their homes on Rosh Hashanah and seek shelter with gentiles they trust until preparations for them to be convoyed to Sweden are completed. The crisis of conscience among Danes is personified in a discussion between Dr. Koster and his wife over whether they should hide their Jewish neighbors. Mrs. Koster fears doing so will endanger her family, but her husband replies, "How do we live with ourselves if we don't? And what is the message we would give our children?" Mrs. Koster relents after discovering the body of her tailor hanging in his shop. His despair over the rumors of the impending raid by the Germans drove him to commit suicide. Dr. Koster utilizes the hospital as an interim shelter for the Jews before they are loaded onto ambulances to be carried to the embarkation point for the journey to Sweden. Mrs. Koster escorts her daughter to the same destination. When she realizes they are being followed, she separates from Else to serve as a decoy for the Germans to apprehend. Meanwhile, Hendrik engages in an armed confrontation with the Germans, adding action to the film, but misleading viewers into thinking that the rescue operation entailed more violence than it actually did. In the end, all but Mrs. Koster manage to reach Sweden.

The following snippets of dialogue reflect the motivations frequently articulated for saving the Jews of Denmark. When asked why he leaked Best's plan and persuaded Sweden to offer asylum to the Jews, Duckwitz answers, "It's easy to persecute the nameless and the faceless, but these people were not faceless to me. A man must live with himself. If he can do something to ease the terrible ache in this world, he must." In a concluding voiceover narration, Dr. Koster declares, "In every language and religion, to be humane is to love your neighbor. People have said, 'You Danes showed enormous courage in that time,' but I felt we only did what was normal." While these quotations may seem platitudinous, they bear a remarkable similarity to Dyby's explanation for why he arranged for Jews to hide in hospitals, captained his own boat to take them to Sweden, and recruited other fishermen to do the same: "To us it was all about fellow human beings in need. These poor people needed to leave and that was the important thing to us. We didn't consider the consequences until later. We just did it."[33]

A portion of normative rescuers were devout Christians who became involved in helping Jews for religious reasons. Some had been approached by their clergy or members of their churches to shield Jews from Hitler's wrath. Others felt a biblical kinship with Jews as the Chosen People and Christ's brethren. Still others deemed Jews innocent victims in dire danger deserving of Christian caritas. In many European countries political parties were based on religious affiliation, thereby making the protection of Jews there a fusion of civic and religious responsibilities. Religious rescuers may have extended aid to Jews originally as an individual act of conscience, but this usually led to involvement in rescue networks that were coordinated by their churches or sectarian relief organizations.[34]

Corrie ten Boom and her family helped hundreds of Jews, Dutch resistance members, and German army deserters during the German occupation of the Netherlands. She is often omitted from the pantheon of rescuers studied by Holocaust scholars because she became a renowned evangelist who believed Jews would recognize Christ as their messiah sometime in the future. She, however, merits inclusion in this section on normative rescuers because her book *The Hiding Place* continues to be a perennial bestseller.[35] It and the eponymous film adaptation of it by Billy Graham's ministry are perhaps the most assigned Holocaust texts in evangelical Christian schools and by evangelical Christian homeschoolers.[36] Teachers in these settings tend to pay less attention to the Holocaust per se and more to the travails of the ten Boom sisters in Ravensbrück and their prediction that the Holocaust was a prelude to the persecution of Christians. Imprisonment and the death of her sister in the German women's camp strengthened ten Boom's consoling faith in Jesus, prompting her, after the war, to forgive the Nazi who had tormented her and her sister there, and propelling her into a lifelong career as an impassioned evangelist.[37]

The film and ten Boom's online interviews amply testify to the Christian tenets underlying her actions and those of her immediate family during the war.[38] Her father, Casper, presided over a Torah and Talmud study group with his Jewish customers and friends, trying to convince them that the New Testament fulfilled the covenant of the Old. Corrie's brother Willem headed the Dutch Reformed Church's Mission to the Jews and erected a nursing home for elderly Jews that became a way station for German Jewish refugees in the Netherlands during the 1930s and a covert agency for hiding Jews during the German occupation. Aware of the ten Booms' reverence for Jews as the descendants of the Patriarchs and Jesus, Jews gravitated to their clock shop seeking temporary quarters and underground connections for finding permanent shelters. The ten Booms allied themselves with the Dutch resistance through Willem to attain the names and addresses of Dutch citizens who might welcome Jews into their homes, furnish food ration coupons, and procure the services of a carpenter who constructed a false wall to create a concealed room where the Jews residing with the ten Booms could retreat if Dutch police or the Gestapo raided their house. They are credited with directly saving eighty Jews.

The ten Booms detested Nazism because its ideology and policies contravened Christian morality and theology. Sometimes their entreaties on behalf of Jews were rejected by pastors or fellow congregants who warned them against disobeying state law and about the harsh punishment they would face if caught. The ten Booms consistently retorted that they were beholden to a higher divine law and the command to love their neighbor. As strict Calvinists they believed that they were predestined to take the Jews under their wings as a test of their faith and rectitude. Given the traditional Christian dogma that Jews collectively bore the stigma for killing Christ, it would have been just as plausible for the ten Booms to perceive Jewish adversity as a preordained punishment. After being betrayed and interned, they regarded their captivity as an opportunity to preach the Gospel inside the concentration camps and transcend their suffering by not succumbing to bitterness and despair.

The ten Booms adhered to an orthodox strain of Dutch Calvinism that retained an acute sense of Christianity's spiritual and genealogical kinship with Judaism and the Jews. Though Calvin believed that the Jews must seek redemption in Jesus Christ, he also taught that God's election "remains with the Jewish people even as the Gentiles are adopted into the covenant."[39] Under the German occupation, the most fundamentalist Calvinist denominations, which constituted only 8 percent of the Dutch population, accounted for 25 percent of the rescues of Jews hidden in the Netherlands.[40] These offshoots of the Dutch Reformed Church seceded from it in the nineteenth century to protest its modernization of liturgy and theology and formed their own political parties as well. Although Corrie and her family belonged to the evangelical wing of the mainstream Dutch Reformed Church, their interpretation of Scripture, particularly of how Jews and Judaism should be treated and viewed, more closely resembled that of the schismatic Reformed churches.

There is a long legacy of Christian anti-Judaism, discrimination against Jews, and stereotypes fostered by the polemics and charge of deicide leveled against the Jews and the Pharisees, Sadducees, and Temple priests in the New Testament and by Christian theologians during the Roman Empire. These subsequently informed church and state policies and popular attitudes toward the Jews until the eighteenth century, when anticlericalism, democratization, secularization, and toleration challenged them, and countries subsequently conferred citizenship upon Jews. In the wake of the Holocaust, various Christian denominations revised or repudiated the theological doctrines and scriptural passages that had been invoked to justify Christian complicity in or indifference toward Hitler's attempt to annihilate European Jewry. Both Christian and Jewish Holocaust scholars have advocated these reforms. Yet the fact that conservative Christian rescuers like Corrie ten Boom drew on a philosemitic tradition inherent in the Gospels and the Christian practice of caritas has tended to be overlooked. Remembering Corrie ten Boom and other gentiles like her reminds us of David Gushee's advice in his study of religiously motivated Christian rescuers: "Given the desperate importance of neighbor-love in a world full of suffering and needy neighbors, all paths that *genuinely lead Christians in love's direction* should be accorded legitimacy and warmly welcomed."[41]

Autonomous Rescuers

The rarest type of rescuer identified by the Oliners, only 11 percent in their interview pool, acted on "autonomous principles rooted in justice and caring."[42] They exhibited a high degree of moral independence in arriving at their decisions to help Jews. To fail to undertake steps to save Jewish lives would have contradicted their deep personal commitments to human equality and justice. To be sure, autonomous rescuers often were in the position to aid Jewish friends, empathize with the plight of Jewish strangers, and work with or even lead rescue networks. Nevertheless, emotional impulses and the efficacy of joining collective endeavors were not the primary reasons they intervened on behalf of Jews. The baselessness of Nazi antisemitism and the savagery of its translation into genocidal policies compelled them to preserve Jewish lives. These rescuers had cultivated virtuous consciences and strong loci of control. In Kristen Renwick Monroe's judgment, they acted to maintain their own "need for self-esteem and cognitive consistency, in order to provide moral salience to the perceived needs of another."[43]

One of the few autonomous rescuers I had the privilege to interview during my collaboration with the Oliners was Marion Pritchard (née van Binsbergen). Although a feature film chronicling her life has not been produced, interviews with Pritchard as well as her Wallenberg Award lecture are available to stream online. She also appears in the documentary *The Courage to Care*.[44] There are published transcripts of her interviews and analyses of her motivations.[45] Listening to and watching her tell her story with a calm detachment that masks her firm moral resolve is bound to affect students profoundly.

Pritchard was enrolled in the school of social work at the University of Amsterdam when Germany occupied the Netherlands in 1940. Outraged by the firing of a Jewish professor in her program in 1941, she joined an underground student group that transcribed BBC broadcasts and clandestinely disseminated printed copies. The Germans imprisoned her for seven months for this activity. In the summer of 1942, she rode her bicycle past a Jewish orphanage where the Gestapo was conducting a raid. When some children refused to climb into the back of an awaiting truck, the Germans grabbed their limbs and heaved them into it. At that moment Pritchard decided she must shield other Jews from the same fate and formed a rescue ring with ten of her friends, two of whom were Jewish.

Most of Pritchard's activities entailed procuring clothing, food ration cards, hiding places, and medical care for Jewish "submarines," the epithet bestowed on those who evaded arrest and deportation by going into hiding, and moving them to temporary safe houses when there were credible tips about imminent German roundups. She also supplied counterfeit identity papers to Jewish infants and adults whose appearance enabled them to pass as Aryans and served as a courier between the resistance and the fugitives they placed in Dutch homes.

When Pritchard could not locate a hiding place for a Jewish man and his three children, she approached an elderly friend of her parents about letting the four stay in a vacation cottage outside of Amsterdam. She moved into the home to care for the Jewish family and constructed a hideout under the floorboards. Her wards repeatedly practiced escaping into the cubbyhole as quickly as possible in case the Germans unexpectedly searched the house. Shortly after one such raid, a Dutch collaborator returned, assuming that the fugitives would believe the danger was over and come out of wherever they were hiding. To avert their arrest, Pritchard grabbed a pistol and killed him. She contacted a local baker and persuaded him to remove the body in his delivery truck and bring it to an anti-Nazi undertaker, who buried it in a coffin along with another corpse. Marion regretted killing him, but felt she had no alternative. She continued to hide the father and his children and assist Jewish "submarines" for the duration of the war.

Although Pritchard modestly focused in her interview on one particular family that she harbored, I learned in the course of the interview of others—Jews and gentiles—who had managed to survive using false papers or in hiding due to her efforts. When I tracked some of them down and spoke to them, I realized how many more people owed their lives to her. Pritchard subsequently estimated that the total may have been as high as 150.

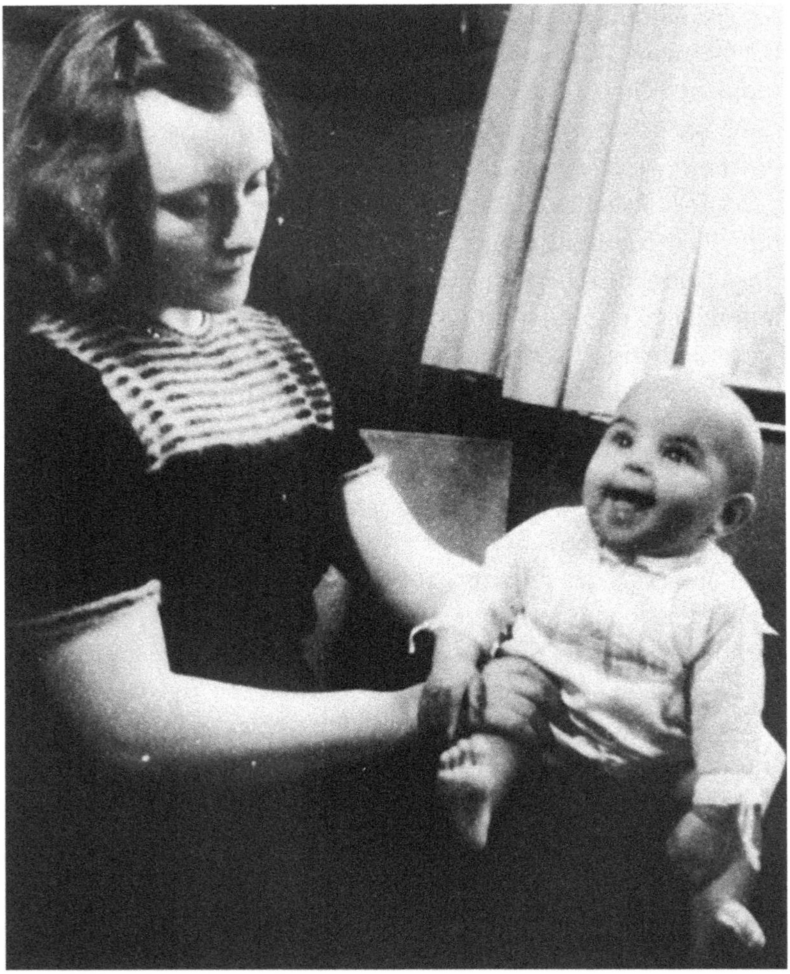

17. Marion Pritchard, who rescued Jewish children during the Nazi occupation of the Netherlands, ca. 1944, in Amsterdam (?). She died in 2016. United States Holocaust Memorial Museum, courtesy of Marion Pritchard.

As Pritchard responded to a litany of questions I posed about her childhood, she attributed her acute sense of responsibility for the innocent victims of Nazi injustice to the way her parents raised her and embodied the values they inculcated in her. Her British mother insisted that she attend an Anglican church and sent her daughter to a boarding school in England during her high school years. This multicultural experience militated against ethnocentrism. As a girl she had taken ballet lessons and asked her parents why her fellow students had mocked an instructor who was a homosexual. Her parents, whose attitudes were remarkably progressive for that era, discussed homosexuality with her and warned her against stereotyping people on the basis of their gender orientation. Her father was a liberal Dutch judge who hated the Nazis and the antisemitic policies they imposed on the Netherlands. He was indignant when Jewish judges were dismissed from their positions by the Germans.

Reflecting on the formative influences on her life that inclined her to work for the resistance and help Jews, Pritchard opined:

> I believe that courage, integrity, and a capacity for love are neither virtues, nor moral categories, but a consequence of a benign fate, in my own case, parents who listened to me, let me talk, and encouraged in every way the development of my own authentic self. It may be redundant to add that they never used corporal punishment in any form. Being brought up in the Anglican Church was a positive experience for me and imbued me early on with a strong conviction that we are our brothers' keepers. When you truly believe that, you have to behave that way in order to be able to live with yourself.[46]

Before most Americans had heard of Oskar Schindler, Raoul Wallenberg was the best-known Righteous gentile. In 1957 Philip Friedman dubbed Wallenberg "the hero of Budapest" for pulling Jews off deportation trains, furnishing them with bogus Swedish protective papers, and finding housing for youngsters in children's centers run by the International Red Cross and for adults in safe houses rented by Sweden and other neutral countries. According to Friedman, 660 Jews worked for Wallenberg; 8,000 Jewish children found refuge in the centers; 10,000 Jews received Swedish protective passports, and 15,000 Jewish adults lived in the 32 buildings.[47] Ten years later Wallenberg loomed large in Arthur Morse's book *While Six Million Died* as a belated exception to the rule of American apathy toward the wartime plight of European Jewry. Wallenberg's mission constituted the most successful rescue operation sponsored by the War Refugee Board that President Roosevelt created in 1944 to help those displaced and persecuted by the Third Reich and the war in Europe.[48] Wallenberg's fame reached its apex in the 1980s as a joint consequence of the growing consciousness of the Holocaust in the United States and of Cold War tensions with the Soviet Union. Such tensions were exacerbated by revelations that the Soviet Union had arrested Wallenberg in 1945 and imprisoned him for the rest of his life.[49] In 1983 he was granted honorary American citizenship. The documentary *Raoul Wallenberg: Buried Alive* provides a fascinating portrait of Wallenberg, his wartime exploits, and postwar incarceration.[50]

The television miniseries *Wallenberg: A Hero's Story* broadcast in 1984 portrayed Wallenberg as a courageous hero battling the twin foes of Nazism and Communism.[51] It highlighted Wallenberg's disdain for Hitler and his eagerness to accept the American mission to protect the Jews of Hungary. Bright lighting, the casting of the dashing actor Richard Chamberlain as Wallenberg, melodramatic background music, and upwardly tilting camera angles enhance his bravery and stature as he defiantly prevents the Germans from rounding up and deporting Jews whom he claims have Swedish ancestry or relatives. The NBC trailer for the film glorifies Wallenberg for leaving "his world of wealth for a mission no one else would dare to accomplish, a mission to stop the Nazis and the crime of the century."[52] The viewers' guide to the docudrama similarly lauded him for volunteering to "go to the storm center of war-torn Europe on a dangerous and purely humanitarian mission to rescue Hungary's besieged Jews." The film gingerly broaches the issue of the late and limited help accorded to European Jews by the United States while castigating the Soviet Union for arresting and imprisoning Wallenberg.[53]

The movie understandably devotes most of the story to Wallenberg's rescue of Jews in Budapest, but it drops a number of clues about what kind of person he was and the concerns that motivated him. The initial glimpse of him occurs when he berates a German businessman during a celebration of Walpurgisnacht in Sweden at the end of April of 1944 and parodies Adolf Hitler. Wallenberg accuses the Nazis of burning and gassing Jews, and expresses dismay that his wealthy banking family looks askance so long as it can profit from commerce with Germany. He emerges as a rebel who bucked his family's wishes that he work for one of its enterprises or pursue a prestigious career in government. Instead, he attended the University of Michigan and earned his degree in architecture. His mother recalls that he always had an adventurous streak and mentions that he had worked for a bank in Haifa in the mid-1930s, obliquely hinting at his encounters with German Jewish refugees immigrating there. His uncle criticizes him for being an idealist "in search of perfect justice." Wallenberg partnered with a Hungarian Jew to run a food import company and visited Hungary as his proxy several times during the war. Bored with his mundane career when Europe was "in the middle of a nightmare," he leaps at the offer from the War Refugee Board and the Swedish government to galvanize a rescue operation in Hungary via his position as the undersecretary of the Swedish legation. Upon hearing he has accepted this risky mission, his mother wonders why, and Wallenberg simply replies, "I would explode if I missed this opportunity." With some background readings, students should be able to tease out the motivations and traits to which the miniseries alludes.[54]

Conclusion

Holocaust rescuers illustrate that there were viable nonviolent alternatives to countenancing the Holocaust. Teachers must embed these rescuers' notable achievements within the less gratifying realities of the "Final Solution," which only a minority of Jews survived and only a minority of gentiles opposed. If time permits, students should delve more deeply into the patterns of motivations and traits among distinctive categories of rescue. Films put a human face on the few who withstood the temptation to play it safe by standing idly by while Jews were persecuted and butchered. Movies, whether they are dramatizations or documentaries, tend to fashion their protagonists to conform to genre expectations. Wallenberg becomes a Rambo of rescue, Schindler a scoundrel with a golden heart. More sophisticated analysis of their motivations belies their representation as stock characters. Using outside reading assignments and classroom discussions can enable students to discern the ordinary qualities like empathy for the pain of others, coordinated political or religious activism against blatant travesties of ethics and justice, loyalty toward associates and friends, or upholding core values that pushed the individuals portrayed on the screen to help Jews against the Germans and their allies. Perhaps these lessons will inspire students to cultivate these virtues to prepare themselves for the extraordinary moral challenges they may face during their lives.[55]

Questions for Further Discussion

- In this chapter, we are presented with two schools of thought regarding what made rescuers do what they did. The first posits that non-Jews helped Jews in an almost "random" way, with nothing in their background predisposing them to do so. In this understanding, there is no way to "predict" who might become a rescuer. The second school of thought identifies specific social and psychological factors that made particular individuals more likely to attempt rescue efforts. Which viewpoint is more compelling to you? If the first is true, how can a society strive to cultivate rescuers? If the second is true, how can a society strive to cultivate rescuers?
- Thinking about rescuers discussed in this chapter (Miep Gies, Irene Gut Opdyke, Oscar Schindler), do you see any differences between the terms "help" and "rescue"? How, if at all, are these terms different? Were the risks of trying to help someone the same as the risks of trying to rescue someone? Would you characterize as heroes both the individuals who helped Jews and the individuals who rescued Jews? Why/why not?
- How are group rescue efforts different from individual efforts? Are the motivations different? The risks?
- Think about the various, organized social and religious groups in your community or that you might be a part of. Have these groups taken a stand on any difficult issues or worked to help individuals in need?

- How are "autonomous rescuers" different from "attachment rescuers" and "normative rescuers"? Think of rescuers you have studied. What category would best describe them? Can rescuers in all three categories be considered altruistic? Should those in each category be considered heroes?

Notes

1. Peter Hayes, Introduction to Chapter 8, "Rescuing Jews—Means and Obstacles," in *How Was It Possible? A Holocaust Reader*, ed. Peter Hayes (Lincoln: University of Nebraska Press, 2015), 645.

2. Alvin H. Rosenfeld, *The End of the Holocaust* (Bloomington: University of Indiana Press, 2011), 81.

3. Mordecai Paldiel, *The Path of the Righteous: Gentile Rescuers of Jews during the Holocaust* (Hoboken NJ: KTAV), 8.

4. Samuel P. Oliner and Pearl M. Oliner, *The Altruistic Personality: Rescuers of Jews in Nazi Europe* (New York: Free Press, 1988), 260.

5. Eva Fogelman, *Conscience and Courage: Rescuers of Jews during the Holocaust* (New York: Anchor Books, 1994); Kristen Renwick Monroe, *The Heart of Altruism: Perceptions of a Common Humanity* (Princeton NJ: Princeton University Press, 1996), 91–120; Kristen Renwick Monroe, *The Hand of Compassion: Portraits of Moral Choice during the Holocaust* (Princeton NJ: Prince University Press, 2004); Nechama Tec, *When Light Pierced the Darkness: Christian Rescue of Jews in Nazi-Occupied Poland* (New York: Oxford University Press, 1986).

6. For an overview of how and which films teachers should consider for use in their courses, see Lawrence Baron, "Incorporating Film into a Study of the Holocaust," in *Essentials of Holocaust Education: Fundamental Issues and Approaches* (New York: Routledge, 2016), 169–88. For helpful essays on how to use films as a teaching tool in general, see Alan S. Marcus, *Celluloid Blackboard: Teaching History with Film*, ed. Alan B. Marcus (Charlotte NC: Information Age Publishing, 2007).

7. Oliner and Oliner, *The Altruistic Personality*, 221.

8. Oliner and Oliner, *The Altruistic Personality*, 171–86.

9. Miep Gies and Alison Leslie Gold, *Anne Frank Remembered: The Story of the Woman Who Helped to Hide the Frank Family* (New York: Simon & Schuster 13–98; Miep Gies, "1994 Wallenberg Lecture," Wallenberg Endowment Committee and Rackham School of Graduate Studies, University of Michigan, accessed July 30, 2017, https://www.youtube.com/watch?v=7exvJQWHueg; *Anne Frank Remembered*, directed by Jon Blair (Netherlands, UK, and United States: Anne Frank House, BBC, Disney Channel, and Jon Blair Film Company, 1995); *Dear Kitty: Remembering Anne Frank*, directed by Wouter van der Sluis (Netherlands, 1998), accessed July 30, 2017, https://www.youtube.com/watch?v=kci_AXVxVY0.

10. *The Attic: The Hiding of Anne Frank*, directed by John Erman (UK and United States: Yorkshire Television and Telecom Entertainment, 1988).

11. Irene Gut Opdyke and Jennifer Armstrong, *In My Hands: Memories of a Holocaust Rescuer* (New York: Alfred A. Knopf, 1999); Monroe, *The Hand of Compassion*, 139–63; Carol Rittner and Sondra Myers, *The Courage to Care: Rescuers of Jews during the Holocaust* (New York: New York University Press, 1986), 44–51; *The Courage to Care*, directed by Robert Gardner (United States: United Way Production, 1986); "A Whisper from Above," ABC *Primetime Live* (United States: American Broadcasting Corporation, n.d.), accessed August 1, 2017, https://www.youtube.com/watch?v=jn2g6cNcbPo; Irene Gut Opdyke, "Talk," Institute for Holocaust and Genocide Studies of Indiana Purdue University-Fort Wayne, n.d., accessed August 1, 2017, https://www.youtube.com/watch?v=r6VcKx5z-2o.

12. Rittner and Myers, *The Courage to Care*, 47.

13. Rittner and Myers, *The Courage to Care*, 49.

14. "A Whisper from Above."

15. David Crowe, *Oskar Schindler: The Untold Account of His Life, Wartime Activities, and the True Story Behind the List* (Cambridge MA: Westview Press, 2004); Thomas Keneally, *Schindler's List* (New York: Simon & Schuster, 1982); Mietek Pemper and Victoria Hertling, *The Road to Rescue: The Untold Story of Schindler's List*, trans. David Dollenmayer (New York: Other Press, 2011); *Oskar Schindler: The Documentary*, directed by Jon Blair (UK: Thames Television, 1982); *Oskar Schindler: The Man behind the List*, directed by Martin Kent (United States: Actuality Productions, 1998), accessed August 5, 2017, https://www.youtube.com/watch?v=pDumJVv6GP8&list=PL63008A1D7D4BDC18; *Schindler's List*, directed by Steven Spielberg (United States: Amblin Entertainment and Universal Studios, 1993).

16. Peter Krämer, "The Good German? Oskar Schindler and the Movies, 1951–1993," in *Hollywood's Chosen People: The Jewish Experience in American Cinema*, ed. Daniel Bernardi, Murray Pomerance, and Hava Tirosh-Samuelson (Detroit MI: Wayne State University Press, 2013), 125–40.

17. Pemper and Hertling, *The Road to Rescue*, 126.

18. Michael Berenbaum, quoted in *Oskar Schindler: The Man behind the List*.

19. Crowe, *Oskar Schindler*, 206.

20. Luitgard N. Wundheiler, "Oskar Schindler's Moral Development during the Holocaust," *Humboldt Journal of Social Relations* 13, nos. 1 and 2 (1986): 342.

21. Wundheiler, "Oskar Schindler's Moral Development," 351–55.

22. Crowe, *Oskar Schindler*, 99–105.

23. Crowe, *Oskar Schindler*, 192–208.

24. This is the consensus of a majority of the essays on the film featured in Yosefa Loshitzky, ed., *Spielberg's Holocaust: Critical Perspectives on* Schindler's List (Bloomington: Indiana University Press, 1997).

25. Oliner and Oliner, *The Altruistic Personality*, 199.

26. Oliner and Oliner, *The Altruistic Personality*, 221.

27. Fogelman, *Conscience and Courage*, 203–20. Fogelman calls these people "network rescuers."

28. *Rescue of the Danish Jews: Moral Courage under Stress* (New York: New York University, 1988); Herbert Pundik, *In Denmark It Could Not Happen: The Flight*

of the Jews to Sweden (Jerusalem: Gefen, 1998); Emmy Werner, *A Conspiracy of Decency: The Rescue of Danish Jews during World War II* (Boulder CO: Westview Press, 2002); Leni Yahil, *The Rescue of Danish Jewry* (Philadelphia: Jewish Publication Society, 1969).

29. *The Danish Solution*, directed by Karen Cantor and Camilla Kjaerilff (United States: Singing Wolf Documentaries, 2003), accessed August 10, 2017, https://www.youtube.com/watch?v=rTpqI2kkU5g; Knut Dyby, "Rescue and Resistance in Denmark during the German Occupation. '40–45," Holocaust Memorial Committee of Oregon State University, April 15, 1996, accessed August 10, 2017, https://www.youtube.com/watch?v=pDumJVv6GP8&list=PL63008A1D7D4BDC18.

30. *Across the Waters*, directed by Nicolo Donato (Denmark: SF Studios, 2016); *A Day in October*, directed by Kenneth Madsen (Denmark: Kenmad, Panorama Film International, and Det Danske Film Institut, 1991); *The Only Way*, directed by Bent Christensen (Denmark and United States: Hemisphere Pictures and Laterna Film, 1970).

31. *Miracle at Midnight*, directed by Ken Cameron (United States: Davis Entertainment, Disney Education Productions, and Walt Disney Television, 1998), accessed August 12, 2017, https://www.youtube.com/watch?v=4O5DI4z7BDU.

32. Lois Lowry, *Number the Stars* (Boston: Houghton-Mifflin, 1989). For the similarities between the novel and the film, see Lawrence Baron, *Projecting the Holocaust: The Changing Focus of Contemporary Holocaust Cinema* (Lanham MD: Rowman & Littlefield, 2005), 191–95.

33. Dyby, "Rescue and Resistance"; Martha Loeffler, *Boats in the Night: Knud Dyby's Involvement in the Rescue of the Danish Jews and the Danish Resistance* (Blair NE: Lur Publications, 1999); Monroe, *The Hand of Compassion*, 165–85.

34. David P. Gushee, *The Righteous Gentiles of the Holocaust: A Christian Interpretation* (Minneapolis MN: Fortress Press, 1994); Pearl M. Oliner, *Saving the Forsaken: Religious Culture and the Rescue of Jews in Nazi Europe* (New Haven CT: Yale University Press, 2004).

35. Corrie ten Boom, Elizabeth Sherrill, and John Sherill, *The Hiding Place* (Old Tappan NJ: Fleming H. Revell, 1971); Lawrence Baron, "Supersessionism without Contempt: The Holocaust Evangelism of Corrie ten Boom," in *Christian Responses to the Holocaust: Moral and Ethical Issues* (Syracuse NY: Syracuse University Press, 2003), 119–31.

36. *The Hiding Place*, directed by James F. Collier (United States: Worldwide Pictures, 1975), accessed August 15, 2017, https://www.youtube.com/watch?v=XX0GwjXExFE. The sequel, *Return to the Hiding Place*, directed by Peter C. Spencer and Josiah Spencer, focuses on the role of the ten Booms in helping the Dutch resistance.

37. Simone Schweber and Rebekah Irvin, "'Especially Special': Learning about Jews in a Fundamentalist Christian School," *Teachers College Record* 105, no. 9 (2003): 1693–1719.

38. Corrie ten Boom, interview by Kathryn Kuhlman, n.d., accessed August 17, 2017, https://www.youtube.com/watch?v=1OaP_aSjyC0.

39. Gushee, *The Righteous Gentiles*, 122–25.

40. Bob Moore, *Victims and Survivors: The Nazi Persecution of Jews in the Netherlands 1940–1945* (London: Arnold, 1997), 162–67.

41. Gushee, *The Righteous Gentiles*, 172.

42. Oliner and Oliner, *The Altruistic Personality*, 221, 249.

43. Monroe, *The Hand of Compassion*, 240.

44. Marion Pritchard, USC Shoah Foundation, May 14, 1998, accessed August 20, 2017, https://www.youtube.com/watch?v=PB6S4f_QRVI, ; Marion Pritchard, "1996 Wallenberg Lecture, Wallenberg Endowment Committee and Rackham School of Graduate Studies, University of Michigan, October 16, 1996, accessed August 22, 2017, https://www.youtube.com/watch?v=CHzCMno5fC0; *The Courage to Care*, directed by Gardner.

45. Rittner and Myers, *The Courage to Care*, 28–33.

46. Rittner and Myers, *The Courage to Care*, 33.

47. Philip Friedman, *Their Brothers' Keepers* (New York: Crown Publishers, 1957), 159–67.

48. Arthur Morse, *While Six Million Died: A Chronicle of American Apathy* (New York: Hart, 1967), 350–74.

49. Per Anger, *With Raoul Wallenberg in Budapest* (New York: Holocaust Library, 1981); John Bierman, *Righteous Gentile: The Story of Raoul Wallenberg, Missing Hero of the Holocaust* (New York: Viking, 1981); Elenore Lester, *Wallenberg: The Man in the Iron Web* (Englewood Cliffs NJ: Prentice Hall, 1982); Kati Marton, *Wallenberg: Missing Hero* (New York: Random House, 1982); Harvey Rosenfeld, *Raoul Wallenberg: Angel of Rescue* (Buffalo NY: Prometheus Books, 1982); Frederick E. Werbell and Thurston Clarke, *Lost Hero: The Mystery of Raoul Wallenberg* (New York: McGraw-Hill, 1982). For more recent books on Wallenberg, see Alex Kershaw, *The Envoy: The Epic Rescue of the Last Jews of Europe in the Desperate Closing Months of World War II* (Cambridge MA: De Capo Press, 2011); Bengt Jangfeldt, *The Hero of Budapest: The Triumph and Tragedy of Raoul Wallenberg*, trans. Harry Watson (London: I. B. Tauris, 2014); Ingrid Carlberg, *Raoul Wallenberg: The Heroic Life and Mysterious Disappearance of the Man Who Saved Thousands of Hungarian Jews from the Holocaust*, trans. Ebba Segerberg (London: MacLehose Press, 2016).

50. *Raoul Wallenberg: Buried Alive*, directed by David Harel (Canada: Wayne Aaron Films, 1983).

51. *Wallenberg: A Hero's Story*, directed by Lamont Johnson (United States: Dick Berg-Stonehenge Productions and Paramount Television, 1985). For a less uplifting depiction of Wallenberg that documents the defeats as well as victories he experienced in his battle to save Jews, see *Good Evening, Mr. Wallenberg*, directed by Kjell Grete (Hungary, Norway, and Sweden: FilmTeknik, Filmhuset, Hungarian Filmproduction, Hunnia Filmstúdió, Invik & Co., Sandrews, Svenska Filminstitutet (SFI), and TV3 Sverige, 1990).

52. "NBC *Wallenberg: A Hero's Story* 1985 TV Promo," accessed August 25, 2017, https://www.youtube.com/watch?v=KeGczrRl9Nc.

53. "Poster and Guide for Viewers," *Wallenberg: A Hero's Story*, April 8–9, 1985; Elie Wiesel, "*Wallenberg: A Hero's Story*, The Brave Christians Who Saved Jews from the Nazis," *TV Guide*, April 6–12, 1985, 2–3.

54. Bierman, *Righteous Gentile*, 18–37; Kershaw, *The Envoy*, 51–56; Marton, *Missing Hero*, 9–41.

55. Samuel P. Oliner and Pearl M. Oliner, *Toward a Caring Society: Ideas into Action* (Westport CT: Praeger, 1995); Kristen Renwick Monroe, *Ethics in an Age of Terror and Genocide: Identity and Moral Choice* (Princeton NJ: Princeton University Press, 2011).

8

Complicating the Narrative

Oskar Schindler, *Schindler's List*, and the Classroom

MARK GUDGEL

"Nobody uses *Schindler's List* anymore," my colleague stated casually from across the table, as together with a team of seven other teachers we sat discussing lessons we were going to share at the upcoming sessions of the Arthur and Rochelle Belfer Conference on Holocaust Education at the United States Holocaust Memorial Museum (USHMM).

"Actually," I responded, eager to chime in, if somewhat hesitant to call attention to the error, "on a national scale, that film is used two-to-one more than any other for teaching about the Holocaust." My colleague wasn't unfamiliar with what I was researching, nor did she question my results. But knowing what was actually being used, rather than making even seemingly logical assumptions, helped guide our thinking in a meaningful way as we continued preparations for our work that summer.

My colleague's assumption was understandable, and had I not just finished surveying 420 teachers across the United States about precisely this very subject, that is, how they use film to teach about the Holocaust, I almost certainly wouldn't have second-guessed her on the matter. I had been surprised myself, a month before, to discover through my research that the now twenty-plus-year-old black-and-white film was in fact the most widely utilized film by quite a wide margin. In fact, I had learned that more than 25 percent of American teachers who teach about the Holocaust used *Schindler's List* in their classes. I felt confident then, as I do now, that these data can help to improve the ways in which we teach, and teach teachers, about the Holocaust.

What happens when the lights go down, when the projector warms up, and the opening credits begin to roll in an American secondary classroom is a strikingly underinvestigated phenomenon. What my 2015 study showed for certain was, first, that many of the academic and educational communities' respective assumptions about what is used were not entirely accurate, and, second, that more than two decades after the release of the film, *Schindler's List* enjoys widespread popularity in the classroom like no other.

But why *Schindler's List*? Why Schindler at all? What are the difficulties with using this film? How can it be used effectively? Can it? And, perhaps the most urgent question, is this the best way to teach young people about the Holocaust? Once I learned about the popularity of the film, I wanted to know more about how it was being used, and if it was being used effectively. The second phase of my study involved interviewing teachers, many of whom used *Schindler's List* to teach about the Holocaust, and many of whom did not. A discussion of their interviews, as well as the survey that preceded them, coupled in places with my own personal experiences as an educator, make up the bulk of this chapter.

How *Schindler's List* Is Used by Classroom Teachers

In order to address such questions as the ones posed above, it is important first to have an understanding of what is already taking place. How teachers utilize the film matters when considering if it works or not. As previously stated, more than 25 percent of teachers surveyed across the United States reported using *Schindler's List* in whole or in part. Contrasted against the next-most-popular feature film, Roman Polanski's *The Pianist*, at just less than 11 percent, or the most popular documentary films—the award-winning *One Survivor Remembers* at nearly 17 percent and *I'm Still Here* at just more than 11 percent—one gets an idea of just how significant the greater-than-one-in-four figure actually is.

Just as, if not more, significant than how many teachers say they use the film is the question of how they are using it. Just less than 58 percent of those surveyed reported using the three-hour-and-fifteen-minute film from start to finish, while the remaining slightly more than 42 percent of those who use it indicated that they in some way cut or abbreviated the film.

The fact that most teachers who use the film use it from start to finish is especially startling when juxtaposed next to the amount of class time in total these same teachers have allotted to teach about the Holocaust. Table 1 shows a breakdown of the amount of time survey respondents said they had to teach about the Holocaust.

Table 1. Amount of time teachers report having to devote to the Holocaust, by percentage

Amount of class time devoted to the Holocaust	% of teachers
1 week or less	25.8
2–3 weeks	20.0
4–5 weeks	13.3
6–8 weeks	16.1
9 weeks/One term	13.1
One semester	8.9
Full year	1.7

With such limited time at their disposal, it may be difficult to imagine why so many teachers would still opt for using such a lengthy film, especially in its entirety. The next section deals with potential answers to that question.

Why Schindler?

The shortest answer to the question "Why Schindler?" is as concise as the query itself: Spielberg. Though Thomas Keneally's 1982 novel, originally titled *Schindler's Ark*, enjoyed some popularity,[1] it was Steven Spielberg who directed the movie that made "Schindler" into a household name. The movie, released in 1993, grossed an estimated $96,067,179 worldwide.[2] It is not unreasonable to suggest that had Spielberg selected as his subject the story of Chiune Sugihara, Irene Gut Opdyke, or even Raoul Wallenberg, rather than Oskar Schindler, then perhaps one of those would be the name synonymous with "hero" that is so frequently used in American classrooms.

Of course, while Spielberg deservingly receives much credit for the success of the movie, the work of actors like Liam Neeson, who played Oskar Schindler, as well as Ralph Fiennes (Amon

Goeth), not to mention arguably less substantial roles played by Ben Kingsley (Itzhak Stern) and Embeth Davidtz (Helen Hirsch), undeniably contributes to the quality and eventual success of the movie by making the story both believable and riveting. Between the actors and actresses, the director, and the production crew, the film won seven Oscar awards, three Golden Globes, six BAFTA awards, and seemingly countless others.[3] Considering the accolades for the cast and crew, there is little question that the movie accomplished what it set out to do, which is what all Hollywood movies are meant to do, namely be popular and make money. But while this may explain why students often enjoy it over, say, some documentary films, student enjoyment is not necessarily correlated to the choices of teachers. Why teachers choose to use the film may be another matter entirely.

The second phase of the research study I conducted in 2015 involved interviewing teachers who had taken my survey. After surveying 420 American teachers, I then interviewed 44 of them, a little more than 10 percent. When conducting these interviews, I had already of course seen the results of the survey, and had taken note of the surprising popularity of *Schindler's List*. This fact worked its way into my line of questioning, and whenever I contacted a teacher who was among the 25+ percent who show the film, I made it a point to ask them about it.

Teachers primarily cited three distinct things they liked about the movie. The first commonly reported point of appreciation was that the film covers a lot of ground. "Great story, great message," said one teacher from Kentucky. "It covers so many aspects of the Shoah." Said another, a history teacher from Ohio, "You can see ghettos, camps, resistance—a whole Holocaust narrative." Teachers reportedly appreciated that many of the individual aspects of the Holocaust that they tried to include in their units were portrayed in some way in the film.

The second aspect of the film that teachers expressed appreciation for was that Schindler's transformation was a message that they wanted to share with young people. An English teacher in Nebraska, a colleague of mine, expressed great enthusiasm for Spielberg's storyline and the transformation that Oskar Schin-

18. Oskar Schindler (*seated*) with Leopold Pfefferberg, who was saved by Schindler, November 1964. United States Holocaust Memorial Museum, courtesy of Leopold Page Photographic Collection.

dler goes through. Of her students, she told me "They see his change, and they can see themselves changing their attitudes towards others if they get to know them. . . . They want to talk." When asked about issues of historical inaccuracy, her answer indicated that she had already given this matter much thought: "Those are teachable moments . . . those are concerns we can discuss to make the lesson even more complex." Other interviewees expressed similar sentiments about Schindler's transformation and the message they hoped their students would take from viewing it on the screen.

The line "they want to talk" encompasses the final, oft-repeated aspect of *Schindler's List* that teachers reported enjoying about the film. Teachers reported that the movie inspired their students to want to speak about the Holocaust. A history teacher in Colorado expressed appreciation for the discussions that were born of the film in his classroom. "I like the moral ambiguity," he told me. "It creates dialogue. And if people are going to become less ignorant, then that dialogue is necessary."

The notion that the film inspired dialogue in a unique way was reiterated again and again. Clearly, and understandably, teachers enjoy that Spielberg's version of events made young people want to discuss the Holocaust. And yet, in spite of the enthusiasm that so many teachers profess for *Schindler's List*, these same teachers were often the ones to point out problems with the film. The next part of this chapter addresses some of those issues.

Problems with the Film

There are multiple issues that did not prevent *Schindler's List* from being powerful from an entertainment standpoint, which as previously observed was the primary purpose for which it was created, yet seem to get in the way of the film being used efficaciously in the classroom. These issues can be broken down into three major categories, including pedagogical problems, historical inaccuracies, and philosophical objections. Being aware of the issues that fall within each of these categories gives teachers the best chance to address them with students when using the film, or perhaps compelling cause to reconsider doing so at all.

Pedagogical Problems

THE LENGTH OF THE FILM

My 2015 study revealed many of the obstacles that teachers face in teaching about the Holocaust. More than 25 percent of teachers—almost exactly the same number of teachers who use *Schindler's List*, reported having less than one week to teach about the Holocaust, while more than 45 percent had less than three weeks. Those of us, such as myself, who have been fortunate enough to teach whole classes on the topic, are in a stark minority; less than 2 percent of teachers reported having a full year to teach about the Holocaust.

This factor doesn't jive perfectly with the fact that, in the same study, more than 50 percent of teachers reported that the length of a film influenced their decision about whether to show it or not. This notion was further fleshed out during the interview stage of the mixed-methods study. Said one California teacher when asked why he opted not to screen *Schindler's List*, "Showing that movie would take 4.5 percent of a 180-day year." Numerous teachers made similar remarks, until the formidable length of the film was a response I came to expect to hear about from teachers who told me they didn't use it in class.

While undeniably engaging, *Schindler's List* is notoriously long by almost any standard. At three hours and fifteen minutes in length, it could take as many as five class periods to show from beginning to end, depending on the structure and duration of the classes, without any consideration for pre-teaching, which is an important part of showing any film, especially one with so much graphic content as this one.

GRAPHIC CONTENT

Another concern, and perhaps an obvious one, expressed by teachers is the graphic nature of the movie. The film is rated "R" for violence, sexuality, and strong language. The movie contains bloody scenes of executions and wanton killing, necropornographic images of the mass incineration of the dead, scenes depicting nudity and sexual acts, and other visuals that young people—as well as their parents and other school stakeholders—may find disturbing or deem inappropriate.

Many of my colleagues have suggested that they would not show the movie, simply because of the school environment in which they teach. This is especially true among those in Jewish, Catholic, and other religious institutions.

Similarly, while I stated above that many teachers interviewed in my study expressed enthusiasm for the film, it is important to note that some did not. A teacher based in Indiana, when asked if she taught the film, replied that she once had, but not anymore, due to "nudity, the gas chamber scene, the beatings, execution of the architect, corpses, shootings, and other scenes of gratuitous violence." It seems that, over time, specific scenes had weighed heavily on the teacher, and she had witnessed them having an adverse affect on many of her students. Concluded the veteran educator: "Testimony of real people, survivors, is far more powerful."

Another social studies teacher in California spoke at length about their decision not to use the film in class:

> I ask myself, what is my objective in the use of any particular film; what will the students know after they watch the film that they did not know before they watched the film? It seems to me that students come to *Schindler's List* knowing that the Holocaust was terrible and that it is this prior knowledge which is reinforced by watching the film. Other than additionally learning something about Schindler and his story, they learn very little else. At the end of the film they have not increased their knowledge of the historical, political or social factors which led to the Holocaust.

After this, the discussion continued. The length of the film was brought up as another difficulty in using it. Then the teacher concluded with a very personal and thought-provoking response:

> A friend of mine, a rabbi who was born in Bergen-Belsen shortly after the war, has argued that many of the victims of the Holocaust were highly observant Jews for whom modesty was a profound value. They would never have allowed themselves to be seen in the nude. My friend argues that we should respect their wishes, in death as in life. Thus, I have removed all photographs of disrobed victims from my teaching of this topic, whether in primary source photographs or cinema.

This response stood out to me then, as it still does today. I have pondered it at length since that time, so very simple yet undeniable. It has altered my approach to teaching about the Holocaust.

In the public school where I teach, a Sensitive Materials Form must be sent home to screen any film with content of the nature described above. Just as important as parent permission, however, is teacher rationale. Parents may very well grant me permission to show such a film to their children, but they do so because they trust me to have thought it through. They trust my judgment that this film is important to help their students understand what I am trying to teach them. They trust me to help contextualize the material for their son or daughter, and for all of their classmates as well. Any time a teacher shows a film to students, it is important that they consider their rationale for selecting that film, and for teaching about the Holocaust in general. Teachers are strongly urged to think hard about what it is they hope their students will take away from lessons on the Holocaust, and equally hard about whether or not *Schindler's List* is the only, or best, means of getting them there.

DO NOT ROMANTICIZE HISTORY AND OTHER GUIDELINES

The final pedagogical concern with *Schindler's List* might best be termed "romanticizing history." It is difficult when watching the film not to be entranced by the debonair Schindler, brilliantly portrayed by Liam Neeson, as he manipulates his way to the top in a very American-style narrative of making something out of nothing. The very nature of a Hollywood film coupled with this particular storyline makes for viewing that is engaging, yes, but also potentially problematic.

The United States Holocaust Memorial Museum's (USHMM) guidelines for teaching about the Holocaust have long served teachers by giving them a framework for evaluating and thinking through their classroom practices and lessons.[4] Intended not as a set of rules, but to help talented teachers give deeper thought to what they're doing in an attempt to foster more efficacious teaching about the Holocaust, several of the guidelines come immediately to mind when considering *Schindler's List*. "Do not romanticize history" and "Contextualize the history" are difficult to reconcile to the use of Spielberg's film. Another, "Strive for balance in establishing whose perspective informs your study of the Holocaust," seems also to suggest that content from *Schindler's List* in some ways goes against the guidelines offered by the museum, as the perspective offered by the film all but neglects that of the Jews in favor of other characters.

However, other guidelines from the USHMM appear perhaps to support the use of the film. "Translate statistics into people" is something the film inherently seems to accomplish, both in the characters of Schindler and Stern as well as, and perhaps most notably, in the little girl with the bright red jacket. Furthermore, the film seems to "Avoid simple answers to complex questions," masterfully, and even raises a few complex questions of its own. In the end, the final USHMM guideline, "Make responsible methodological choices," is left largely in the hands of teachers, who must determine their own rationale for teaching about the Holocaust and then ask themselves whether Oskar Schindler helps them to meet it.

Whether a close examination of these or other pedagogical guidelines would land one in the "for" or "against" camp is largely a matter of opinion. The case can certainly be made both ways. What is difficult to ignore, however, going back to the romanticizing of history, is the fact that, at base, Spielberg's is a film about a Nazi, in which Jews are largely tertiary characters who help to advance the plot and add depth to the character of Schindler, often without doing the same for themselves. This is problematic for several reasons, but most of all because, even if you regard him solely as a hero, the Holocaust is not a story about heroes, and using *Schindler's List* perhaps puts disproportionate emphasis on those who engaged in acts of rescue. The horrible reality is that for every act of heroism during the era of the Holocaust, there were multiple, perhaps even countless acts of collaboration, perpetration, or simple cowardice. And while Schindler's story touches on certain aspects of that reality, to make the story of Oskar Schindler the story of the Holocaust is certainly to romanticize history.

Historical Inaccuracies

In addition to pedagogical problems, there are some noteworthy historical inaccuracies in the film, ranging from the seemingly superfluous to those that would almost certainly confuse the understanding of viewers who did not know better. Web pages are full of dramaturgical analyses and criticisms of the film, pointing out everything from the existence of a 1950s Mercedes, a Billy Holiday song from the 1950s, and a bottle of Hennessy (cognac) from the 1990s (the film is set prior to and in 1945). These things, though interesting perhaps, do not confuse the meaning of the film (though they are apparently quite distracting to some people). What does confuse meaning, however, are implausible, impossible, and untrue events that take place without context or explanation.

With few exceptions, classroom teachers were not unaware of this difficulty with the film. Again, many, when interviewed, including those who show the film as well as those who don't, spoke to the problems of a Hollywood version of the Holocaust being their students' introduction to the subject. "Cinematically it's a well-made movie," explained a teacher from Pennsylvania. She then added, "Historically, it's a train-wreck." Others, like the English teacher from Nebraska cited earlier, suggested that the inaccuracies of the film became teachable moments, and something that inspired discussion.

However, it is important to recall that every teacher interviewed came to me from a bank of contacts compiled by USHMM at their numerous trainings for educators. This certainly suggests that those surveyed and later interviewed have a solid background in Holocaust education, perhaps substantially more so than the average classroom teacher, who, for inexperience, lack of training, or other reasons, may not have spent time in professional development related to how best to teach about the Shoah. For those teachers, spotting the significant and potentially dangerous historical inaccuracies may not be so easy. The following is a brief analysis of some of the most egregious historical mistakes made in the film.

EVENTS FROM THE FILM

There are numerous, seemingly small events and details from the film that are undeniably inaccurate from an historical standpoint. To say that these details, for example, featuring a vehicle that was produced at least half a decade after the conclusion of World War II, are "small" is not to diminish the significance of good dramaturgical work, but to contextualize the significance of events that do not impact the storyline against events that do. Among those that do, the one that stands out the most is that of the scene in which Schindler arrives in Auschwitz, demanding that the women and children who were transported there be released and sent to his new camp at Bruennlitz. He meets with, and bribes, the camp commandant, and has them released in what is compelling and powerful cinema in which he even bodily pulls children away from SS guards.

However, according to Oskar's wife, Emilie, Oskar never went to Auschwitz. Rather, he beseeched an old friend, a woman by the name of Hilde, to use her apparent influence to have the transport redirected to Bruennlitz.[5] Further, the person who attempted to bribe the SS with a bag of diamonds (unsuccessfully) was a man named Schoeneborn, an employee of the factory.[6] Finally, the transport of workers that arrived at Auschwitz was there for a substantial amount of time, days if not weeks, and contained women but no children as portrayed in the movie. In her memoir, Emilie Schindler describes the women arriving at Bruennlitz as being in "disastrous condition—fragile, emaciated, weak," suggesting that their time in Auschwitz was not brief. Children who arrived at Auschwitz-Birkenau, like those depicted in the movie being saved by Schindler's heroics, were almost without exception murdered upon arrival.[7] To portray them as prisoners of Auschwitz, as Spielberg does, calls into question the horrific reality that awaited children, as well as pregnant women, the mothers of infants, the elderly, and the disabled, at the Nazi's most notorious killing center.

It is this part of the film that is perhaps most confusing to student viewers, students no doubt aware of Auschwitz on some level but who are unlikely to understand the historical realities of the camp well enough to pick up on details such as this one. This is similar to one of the arguments often made against using *The Boy in the Striped Pajamas*, namely, that the very suggestion that Shmuel (a young Jewish boy) is a child-prisoner of Auschwitz is destructive to students' understandings of Auschwitz. Any teacher using *Schindler's List* in the classroom must make a point of correcting Spielberg on this point, or risk convoluting their pupils' understanding of history.

EXCLUDING EMILIE SCHINDLER

A second troubling historical inaccuracy is the nearly complete omission of Emilie Schindler from the storyline as anything more than a witness. In Spielberg's version of events, Emilie is but a reserved and troubled girl whose dashing husband is having an affair. While the real Oskar Schindler was indeed often having an affair of one kind or another, in Emilie's version of events, published in *Where Light and Shadow Meet* in 1996, she was nevertheless pres-

19. Oskar Schindler plants a tree on the Avenue of the Righteous Among the Nations at Yad Vashem, 1962. United States Holocaust Memorial Museum, courtesy of Leopold Page Photographic Collection.

ent in Kraków a great deal of the time, assisting her husband and interacting with "his" Jews as much or more than he was.

It is unfortunate that Emilie Schindler and her brave acts seem to have been unnecessarily excluded from her husband's story. There is little debate that Emilie, in reality, played a substantially larger role in assisting those who would become known as "Schindler Jews" than the film gives her credit for. Perhaps that is why they have never (to my knowledge) been referred to as "Oskar Schindler Jews." In 1993, Yad Vashem bestowed the title of Righteous Among the Nations on Oskar *and* Emilie Schindler for their successful efforts to save Jews during the era of the Holocaust.[8]

THE LIST ITSELF

The biggest issue with the movie, however, is that it has a fundamentally flawed premise. David Crowe, the preeminent Schindler historian of our day, pens a damning line in his 2004 biography of Schindler: "In reality, Oskar Schindler had absolutely nothing to do with the creation of his famous transport list."[9] In the movie, Schindler dictates by name the list of more than one thousand people whom he ultimately helped to rescue. In real life, he could never have done this.

Emilie Schindler confirms Crowe's assertion in her memoir. Therein, she quotes her former husband as stating during their dinner discussion about the making of such a list: "Another problem that worries me is the list of people we are to submit to him [Camp Commandant Amon Goeth]. I don't really know the men, their families; I barely know the names of the few who come to our office when something is needed."[10]

It is not that there never was a list. In fact, there were nine of them. But Oskar Schindler did not—could not—write them. Instead, Marcel Goldberg, a corrupt member of the security police, and a Jew himself, probably put most of them together. Goldberg is accused of favoritism and even accepting bribes as he did so, and it quickly becomes evident why his was not a story destined for the big screen. And yet, in many ways that's the story Spielberg attempted to tell with Schindler, a story of an arguably "bad" man doing an inarguably good thing, or as Itzhak Stern refers to it in the movie, an "absolute good."[11]

Further, it may not be fair to take all the credit away from Schindler, or better, the Schindlers, when it comes to the salvation of the Jews of their factory. Thomas Keneally, the author of *Schindler's Ark*, the book on which the film is based, is quoted in response to Crowe as saying that Schindler was "personally responsible for the fact there was a list."[12]

In the end, we know that the story portrayed on film is not the story as it truly unfolded, in this and other ways. The very name of the movie appears to be flawed, the result of a novel, and a legend, and not the reality that took place during that horrible time. Still, it would surely be unfair to take all credit away from Oskar for his role in saving "his" Jews at that time. To my knowledge, no one has convincingly argued that Schindler did not undergo a seeming moral transformation, nor have they suggested that without Schindler, any of the Jews on the nine lists would have been better off.

Philosophical Objections

Finally, there are philosophical objections to the film, objections that include the "sexualization of female suffering" and the demeaning and problematic portrayal of Jews going "like sheep to the slaughter," an oft-referenced phrase that is considered by most to be objectionable, if not downright offensive.[13] The Jews of the movie are indeed tertiary characters, as pointed out before, while Neeson and Fiennes, Schindler and Goeth, respectively, share or dominate the screen much of the time. The portrayal of Jews in *Schindler's List* thus deserves a closer look.

Many have argued that the Jews in *Schindler's List* wind up as "extras in their own tragedy."[14] Their often two-dimensional nature and brief screen time renders them simplistic, while the screenplay and directing render them "extras." Haim Bresheeth, writing in Yosefa Loshitzky's *Spielberg's Holocaust*, argues that "By concentrating on the good Nazi, it became impossible to give center stage to any of the Jews featured in the story."[15]

Writing in the *Jewish Chronicle*, Nathan Abrams framed the argument like this:

> Some feel the film, which won a best picture Oscar, serves to embed a narrative of Jewish weakness and passivity, in which Jews were nearly always portrayed as undeserving victims. . . . Spielberg marginalizes the Jews to supporting roles (with the exception of Schindler's accountant Itzhak Stern). Spielberg portrayed them as cardboard cut-outs, a monolithic mass of feebleness, lacking in psychological depth, to be saved or murdered at the whim of the non-Jews. From this point of view, then, *Schindler's List* is not about the Holocaust or the Jews at all, but a biopic of Schindler and his conversion from ambivalent antihero to righteous gentile.[16]

While other films do perhaps an even worse job of portraying Jews as two-dimensional props who exist only to further a separate narrative during the era of the Holocaust (think *The Boy in the Striped Pajamas*), Abrams's critique resonates when one thinks back over Spielberg's film, struggling to find examples to contradict his argument. We know that Jews were not only the primary victims of the Nazi extermination machine but were also often weakened by their circumstances and up against unthinkable odds. In fairness to Spielberg, an act of spiritual resistance is indeed portrayed in the concentration camp wedding that takes place in *Schindler's List*, yet this isolated instance arguably doesn't go far enough to enable viewers—especially students—to see the victims of the Holocaust as the same sort of deep, complex, *human* characters that Schindler and Goeth are portrayed to be.

Schindler's List is a film that presents many problems for teachers who choose to use it in their classrooms, and yet, if you ask teachers, they'll tell you that this is true of almost every film. An entire canon of literature exists around *The Boy in the Striped Pajamas*, and almost all of it is criticism (perhaps rightfully so). Unbiased, historically unflawed resources are few and far between, if in fact they exist at all, and they are rarely if ever favorites among young people. In the end, the difficulties examined above related to *Schindler's List* are not a warning against using the film as much as they are a reminder of the tremendous importance of thinking through the materials we select, and giving careful consideration to how best to use them to meet our objectives.

Suggestions for Using *Schindler's List*

If you are among the 25 percent of teachers who already use *Schindler's List*, or else you plan to be among them soon, then you are in good company. Some of the best teachers I know, and some of the most experienced that I interviewed, have an affinity for this movie as a teaching tool that borders on zealotry, and they use it in their classes to great effect. Though I have pointed out a number of difficulties with the film, I would not suggest that any teacher not use this film simply because of those difficulties. As stated above, all films have flaws, and many films have more than *Schindler's List*. That said, if you are using the film, be it for the first or fiftieth time, doing so reflectively is, of course, always the right approach.

Rescue and resistance are parts of the Holocaust narrative that students often insist upon. They captivate their attention and fit nicely with the unfortunate, two-dimensional white knight narrative of World War II that so often appears in American history books. They fit equally well with a distinctly American worldview: the vague notions that good always triumphs over evil, that David is *destined* to slay Goliath, and that when things get too bad,

God will intervene. These ideas are deeply imbedded in American culture and perhaps serve to enhance the intrigue of a movie like Spielberg's for students and teachers alike.

If you ask a young person what they know about Rwanda, you will most likely discover quickly that the very name of the country has for far too many people become synonymous with genocide, and that their knowledge is based largely, perhaps entirely, on one account. The reason that students, and in many instances teachers as well, have such limited knowledge of Rwanda is in part because of the great influence of Hollywood. *Hotel Rwanda* is one of the best-produced, best-acted, most engaging, and most easily accessible films that have been made about the 1994 genocide against the Tutsi in Rwanda. It is also considered a work of fiction, and an egregious and offensive misconstruing of events, by many, if not most, in Rwanda today.[17] The problem with narrative films is that the story they present can become the entire story for students, and even when the story they present is accurate, it is always incomplete.

Here, it falls once again upon the teacher to help fill in the endless blanks, to take what can be learned from a film and help transform it into a broader, more accurate, and more complete historical narrative. This is difficult work, and yet not to do so would be to allow *Schindler's List* to stand alone as *the* story of the Holocaust, with marginalized and weak Jewish victims, a litany of various historical inaccuracies, and everything else examined above.

There are many activities and supplemental materials that exist to help teachers add to their Holocaust lessons. The difficulty expressed before about limited time in which to teach the subject being further complicated by a lengthy film hasn't gone away, but every teacher has a different environment, different school, different district, different mandates, different interests, and all of this leads to differing amounts of time to spend teaching about the Holocaust. Assuming a teacher has chosen to use a three-hour-plus film, we can hope that they have significantly more than three hours to teach about the Holocaust.

Below are some activities that are easily available to teachers and may help to add complexity and depth to a Holocaust unit that relies heavily on *Schindler's List.*

One Survivor Remembers: A film made available by Teaching Tolerance that portrays in her own words the life of Holocaust survivor Gerda Weissmann Klein. The kit, which is free to teachers, includes the video; her memoir, *All But My Life* (1996); and other teaching tools. It is available at tolerance.org.[18]

Salvaged Pages/I'm Still Here: Alex Zapruder's *Salvaged Pages* (2002) is a collection of diary entries from young people who wrote during the Holocaust, while *I'm Still Here* is an MTV documentary based on some of those accounts. The book and the film are well done, revealing tremendous depth and humanity in the victims of the Holocaust, specifically young victims with whom students can often closely relate.[19]

USHMM Timeline Activity: The United States Holocaust Memorial Museum has long been a leader in Holocaust education. The Timeline Activity, developed by USHMM staff, adds layers of depth and complexity to the history of the Holocaust through historical events, the stories of individuals, and more. Downloadable lessons and materials are available for free at ushmm.org.

Where Light and Shadow Meet: Emilie Schindler's (1996) memoir is a brief and fascinating companion to the film. Utilized frequently in this essay, in many places it affirms the known story, while in others it complicates or even contradicts it. As a primary source read alongside the film it can complicate the narrative for students, and lead to deeper thinking.[20]

Oskar Schindler: David Crowe's (2004) historical account of Schindler is nearly eight hundred pages long, and leaves no stone unturned. Appropriate for higher-level classes, it excerpts well, and again serves to complicate the story, challenging prior assumptions and assertions made by the film.[21]

USC Shoah Foundation Visual History Archive: Founded by Steven Spielberg in 1994 (shortly after the release of *Schindler's List*), this amazing resource contains some fifty-five thousand survivor testimonies from sixty-two countries in forty-one languages. In addition, the USC Shoah Foundation offers a host of resources and programs for educators and students alike. If *Schindler's List* is in any way a sin, the Visual History Archive more than atones for it. Testimony from those saved by Schindler is available and, in the broader picture, access to so many different testimonies is an invaluable way to help students connect to the Holocaust, whether paired with the movie or not. Visit sfi.usc.edu/vha for information and access.

Of course, there are so many other things that a creative and dedicated teacher can do with *Schindler's List*. One teacher I interviewed said that he used the film to pose moral dilemmas for his students. There are seemingly limitless questions of this nature raised by Spielberg's movie, but most interesting to me was this one: "If the Nazis had won the war, would Oskar Schindler have attempted to save anyone at all?" I have asked classes similar questions in the past about the professed regret of Hitler's minister of armaments, Albert Speer, for his role in Nazi Germany, but, in all honesty, this teacher's question about Oskar Schindler seems the stronger one to me. These sorts of creative approaches to teaching place movies in their proper places as supplements to lessons, rather than making them lessons unto themselves. For teachers to develop their own lessons around the materials they use is still, in this author's opinion, the best means of ensuring that those individual educators' objectives can be met by their students.

Several years ago, I had the opportunity to work as a Fulbright Scholar at what was then the University of London's, today the University College of London's, Institute of Education, studying the use of the words that are often used to teach about the Holocaust. To make a long story short, what I found was that, while terms like "resister" and "bystander" and "collaborator" were important for teaching people who were unfamiliar with the subject, as soon as students begin to understand the Holocaust, they repeatedly reject the use of such simplistic terms in favor of more thoughtful—and accurate—descriptions. From this conclusion I developed a brief activity to help illustrate the point. It can be seen below.

Beyond Labels

Name:________________Class:____________Date:____________

Directions: Each of the statements below is true of probably many people who lived during the era of the Holocaust. Using the word bank below, write the term that you think is being described underneath the description.

WORD BANK:

Collaborator	Rescuer	Bystander
Perpetrator	Victim	Resister

A person who, at great personal risk, rescued the lives of more than a thousand people who otherwise would have been victimized by the Nazi regime.

A person who collaborated with SS and other Nazi entities, following the German invasion into Poland, and making deals to further their own career and ambitions.

A person who, as a member of the Nazi Party, perpetrated crimes against others by utilizing Jewish slave labor in a factory, stolen from its previous (Jewish) owners, and that manufactured goods for the Nazis.

A person who stood up against the Nazi regime and resisted their authority by saving Jews and also sabotaging German supply lines.

A person who had countless opportunities, even prior to the start of the war, to assist people in need, yet chose to stand by and watch the crimes being perpetrated against the Jews.

A person who, along with others, gathering what few belongings they could, fled to Buenos Aires, Argentina, to avoid persecution.

Of course, as they are written here, the answers are obvious even to those who have no experience with the Holocaust. I have multiple versions of this activity, each with varying degrees of complexity and nuance depending on for whom I am teaching this lesson. The big reveal at the end is that each of these statements was written about one person: Oskar Schindler. Of course, I am quick to point out that I would never define Schindler as a victim of the Holocaust, but the fact that he was, at one point or another, a rescuer, a resister, a bystander, a perpetrator, and a collaborator, is a fascinating realization, and serves to remind students just how complex their fellow human beings, and they themselves, truly are.

And that, to me, is the most substantial value that lies in Spielberg's film about Oskar Schindler. It is not the transformation from sinner to saint, but the potential to dig deeper, to see a man conflicted, complicated, in some ways ugly, and in others perhaps divine. I rarely teach about the Holocaust using *Schindler's List*, but when I have, I have supplemented it with numerous primary sources, testimonies, academic articles, and more intended to help students, as Elie Wiesel once put it to me, "think higher, feel deeper." Those who knew Oskar Schindler do not often describe him as "good" nearly so much as they express gratitude for what he did, and the message that we do not have to live the lives of saints to do the right thing when the opportunity presents itself is one that both my students and I alike deeply appreciate.

Conclusion

It was near the end of the writing process for my dissertation when my wife, Sonja, and I sat down to watch *Schindler's List* together. Sonja was a film studies major in college, and I, of course, had just completed a raft of research about Schindler. Both of us had seen the film previously, though for both of us, it had been quite a long time ago. It dawned on me as we watched the movie that I had been so caught up in academic conversations about it back when I first saw it that I had forgotten its sheer and unmistakable power. I had forgotten how emotionally moving the film is, and how it had, at a time when I knew very little, inspired me to learn more. Undeniably, it is powerful and inspired cinema.

I have taught many students about the Holocaust by using *Schindler's List*. I have taught many more about it using other, or no, films. In the end, I remain torn between the seemingly countless difficulties with Spielberg's masterpiece and the undeniable power of it. I think of those moments when students have professed to realizing that although they had made poor choices, they realized they could also still make good ones, and it makes me long to show the film to everyone I meet. Then I think about the time that I got so caught up in the film that I forgot to watch the clock, and the bell rang on a Friday afternoon during the middle of the scene depicting the violent and bloody ghetto raid. My students left the room with horrifying images still playing in their heads and no time to decompress and process them as a group. At the end of the term, many of them rightfully chastised me for this in their end-of-class reviews. When I remember this event, I think there must be a better, *safer*, more effective way to teach about the Holocaust.

To this day, I teach about the Holocaust, and to this day, I remain on the fence about showing this film. Sometimes I do it. Sometimes I do not. I can rationalize both decisions convincingly for parents, principals, and anyone else who cares to inquire, yet in the end it's the man in the mirror whose opinion I've come to dread the most. Am I doing this most important subject the justice it deserves? Am I teaching my students in the best way I am able? Would my friends who survived the Holocaust appreciate what I am doing? Will my students be changed for the better by my efforts? Such questions keep me up at night.

Our students are being brought up in a world that is significantly more removed by time from the era of the Holocaust than it was when those who teach them were learning for themselves. Black-and-white images of events that happened long ago in faraway lands to people they have never met do not naturally resonate with an increasingly tech-savvy and unfocused generation, and yet the lessons of the Holocaust have never been more apt. The lessons of the 1938 Évian Conference, at which thirty-two countries, with the lone exception of the Dominican Republic, decided not to admit additional Jewish refugees fleeing Europe, have clearly been lost to a world in which xenophobia drives public policy, and the alt-right and neo-Nazis have been emboldened in ways we never could have imagined but a few short years ago. With that in mind, perhaps our children are in need of heroes, imperfect yet effective heroes with whom they can relate.

Questions for Further Discussion

- Should educators use film in the classroom and how should they make decisions about which film/s to use? How might films impact the classroom experience of learning about the Holocaust?
- If the majority of a student's classroom experience of learning about the Holocaust is from watching *Schindler's List*, what aspects of the Holocaust might they be missing? Chimamanda Ngozi Adichie's TED Talk on "The Danger of a Single Story" provides an interesting and related perspective.
- The three main reasons that teachers choose *Schindler's List*, discussed in this chapter, would serve as a good "test" for other films and materials that one might want to bring into the classroom: 1) Does this resource demonstrate multiple Holocaust narratives? 2) Does this resource allow students to make a connection to their own lives/experiences? 3) Does this resource engage students in dialogue and to ask further questions?

Notes

1. Thomas Keneally, *Schindler's Ark* (London: Hodder & Stoughton, 1982).

2. Internet Movie Database, *Schindler's List*, accessed February 2, 2018, http://www.imdb.com/title/tt0108052/.

3. Internet Movie Database, *Schindler's List*.

4. "Guidelines for Teaching about the Holocaust," United States Holocaust Memorial Museum, accessed August 2, 2017, https://www.ushmm.org/educators/teaching-about-the-holocaust/general-teaching-guidelines.

5. Emilie Schindler, *Where Light and Shadow Meet* (New York: Norton, 1996), 68–69.

6. Schindler, *Where Light and Shadow Meet*, 66.

7. Schindler, *Where Light and Shadow Meet*, 69.

8. United States Holocaust Memorial Museum, "Oskar Schindler," https://www.ushmm.org/wlc/en/article.php?ModuleId=10005787, accessed February 2, 2018.

9. David M. Crowe, *Oskar Schindler: The Untold Account of His Life, Wartime Activities, and the True Story behind the List* (New York: Basic, 2004), 361.

10. Schindler, *Where Light and Shadow Meet*, 63.

11. *Schindler's List*, directed by Steven Spielberg (United States: Amblin Entertainment and Universal Studios, 1993).

12. O. Burkeman and B. Aris, "Biographer Takes Shine off Spielberg's Schindler," *Guardian*, November 25, 2004, https://www.theguardian.com/world/2004/nov/25/germany.film.

13. Nathan Abrams, "Is *Schindler's List* Fatally Flawed?," *Jewish Chronicle*, March 27, 2013, https://www.thejc.com/culture/features/is-schindler-s-list-fatally-flawed-1.43304.

14. Haim Bresheeth, "The Great Taboo Broken: Reflections on the Israeli Reception of Schindler's List," in *Spielberg's Holocaust: Critical Perspectives on* Schindler's List, ed. Yosefa Loshitzky (Bloomington: University of Indiana Press, 1997), 202.

15. Bresheeth, "The Great Taboo Broken," 202–3.

16. Abrams, "Is *Schindler's List* Fatally Flawed?"

17. Alfred Ndahiro and Privat Rutazibwa, *Hotel Rwanda: Or the Tutsi Genocide as Seen by Hollywood* (Paris: L'Harmattan, 2008); Edouard Kayihura, *Inside the Hotel Rwanda: The Surprising True Story . . . and Why It Matters Today* (Dallas TX: Benbella, 2014). For more resources on teaching about the genocide against the Tutsi in Rwanda, see https://sfi.usc.edu/blog/lesly-culp/resources-teaching-about-genocide-against-tutsi-rwanda.

18. Gerda Weissmann Klein, *All but My Life* (New York: Hill & Wang, 1996).

19. Alexandra Zapruder, *Salvaged Pages* (New Haven CT: Yale University Press, 2002).

20. Schindler, *Where Light and Shadow Meet.*

21. Crowe, *Oskar Schindler.*

9

Teaching the Lesson of Moral Courage through Writing

LIZ FELDSTERN AND AMANDA RYAN

To those of us involved in Holocaust studies and Holocaust education, the inspirational story of the Danish people's collective effort to rescue their Jewish neighbors during the Nazi occupation is well known. The Danish example is unique in many ways and has been well researched and rightfully commended as the exception to the rule. In Denmark, friends, neighbors, and often strangers took great risks to hide and then evacuate their Jewish countrymen. Though under military occupation and taking actions punishable by death, the Danes defied the Nazi orders to arrest and deport Jews and instead arranged and largely financed escape routes across a narrow waterway—a trip of less than one hour—to Sweden.

The heroic effort made by the Danes is a story familiar to many, if not all, in the field of Holocaust education. However familiar the story is, it makes it no less remarkable and valuable in the retelling. The Danes' spontaneous, decentralized rescue effort was everything we like to think that civil unrest can achieve—working-class fishermen lent their boats to the cause, underground newspapers encouraged the populace to stand in solidarity with their Jewish countrymen, religious and political leaders publicly denounced the Nazis, those with means financed the hiding and evacuation—and more than seven thousand lives were saved.[1] After the war, Danes who had been targeted for persecution by the Nazis returned to Denmark and received a warm welcome. Unlike other Nazi-occupied countries, Denmark had cared for their neighbors' homes and belongings and kept their jobs waiting for them. For many returning Danes, this welcome reestablished their dignity as human beings and provided them the strength to rebuild their lives.

Years later, these events inspired the creation of the Tribute to the Danes and Other Rescuers Organization in 1966. That organization subsequently merged with the national Anti-Defamation League (ADL) in 1999. In 2003 the ADL's Omaha office; the Institute for Holocaust Education (IHE); Dana College in Blair, Nebraska; and the Danish Immigrant Museum in Elk Horn, Iowa, organized a collaborative effort to use the story of the Danes as a teaching tool for regional high school students. Together, these organizations launched the Tribute to the Rescuers High School Essay Contest. Since the inception of the contest, the museum was renamed the Museum of Danish America, and Dana College unfortunately closed its doors. However, the essay contest has continued, due to the valuable experience it grants youth in exploring complicated concepts of moral courage and personal action. In 2017 we marked the fifteenth anniversary of the annual contest, which is now run by the IHE.

The Tribute to the Rescuers High School Essay Contest is open to all ninth-through-twelfth-grade students in Nebraska and western Iowa. It asks young people to analyze the concept of moral courage, the idea of risking one's personal safety or well-being for the benefit of others. Over the contest's fifteen years of history, we have received nearly 8,000 essays, with an average of 350 to 500 essays per year in more recent years. The essays are judged in a three-round process that involves forty plus volunteer judges from many different backgrounds and sectors of the Omaha community. These include educators of all levels, lawyers, bankers, retirees, nonprofit professionals, Jews, and non-Jews. Some judges are well versed in Holocaust history, and some learn quite a bit from reading the essays. The students whose essays are judged to be the first, second, third place, and honorable mention winners receive cash prizes. To date, the IHE has distributed more than $50,000 in prizes.

It must be noted that because the essay contest is named for the Danish rescuers, and because the prompt for the contest is to choose an example of someone who demonstrated moral courage, the Holocaust history and stories that students uncover are about people who stood up for good in the face of evil. An issue we face with this is that these stories were, in fact, a very rare type of interaction in the grand scheme of the Holocaust, and students should know that. The IHE philosophy is that while we must be careful not to overemphasize the "feel good" stories of Holocaust rescuers, at the same time we must continue to teach and explore these accounts in the hope that they hold clues as to how moral courage and humanity in the face of inhumanity can be encouraged. In short, we want these stories to inspire others. The Tribute to the Rescuers Essay Contest can be one part of a course of Holocaust studies, but it is not intended to stand on its own as a way to provide Holocaust education.

To be eligible to win, students must follow instructions detailing the criteria for a successful essay. Essayists must select one person or group whom they believe demonstrates moral courage. The subject of the essay can be from the Holocaust era, or students may select other individuals tackling issues of social justice and human rights. Students write about their chosen example, their example's connection to the Holocaust, and how they personally connect or feel inspired by the illustration. These essays require a high level of critical analysis, and students must thoroughly display their understanding of moral courage and adequately articulate how their historical example exemplifies this quality. Further, if the student chooses a subject that is not from the Holocaust era, they must also adequately relate it to the Danes' outstanding example. In concluding the essay, each student must take an introspective view of his or her own life and how he or she can best display moral courage. This can be a difficult task for students to tackle in only 750 to 1,000 words. However, the participants in the essay contest have a chance to be moved by a history they might not have had time to learn in their everyday classes.

Now that the contest has celebrated its fifteen-year anniversary, it seems a fitting time to look back and see what has been learned along the way about how students view moral courage, to which examples of moral courage they are drawn, and how they feel this attribute might be relevant in their own lives. The IHE spent time looking over the broad range of the more than eight thousand essays that have been submitted through the years. While it would be beyond the time constraints of this project to read or catalog all of the essays, a sampling were reviewed with an eye to answering a few key questions. Namely, which morally courageous people or general categories of people do students choose to write about? What do these choices reveal? How do students feel about participating in the essay contest? How are they impacted or changed by their participation? What (if any) larger lessons remain with the students after the contest is completed? We sought to collect this information through three different channels: A review of the winning essays from the past ten years, discussions with staff members and essay contest judges who have been involved for multiple years, and online surveys of previous essay contest winners and teachers who have participated in the essay contest. Regarding the online surveys (one version for students and one for teachers, each comprising four questions), it should be noted that the ability to collect data in this method is limited. In many cases, the contact information on file for essay contest participants is no longer current. If the student used a school-provided email address when they originally participated in the contest, upon graduation the email address would no longer be reachable. Similarly, if an educator has transferred to a different school (or retired) since their participation, the email address on record may no longer be current. While the surveys were short and did not require a significant time commitment to complete, we also did not offer an incentive. As such, the pool of respondents was relatively small. Of the student surveys sent, nine students completed the survey. The educator survey had a total of ten respondents. While the limited size means that the survey results are not conclusive and cannot be fully extrapolated to the overall participants of the essay contest, the results (coupled with the general review of past essays and anecdotal information from staff and essay contest judges) provide a window of insight to the significance and impact of the essay contest.

As a start to our reflections on the essay contest, who are these morally courageous people that students write about? Some of the topics that students choose every year are connected to the American civil rights movement. Dr. Martin Luther King Jr., Rosa Parks, and Harriet Tubman are always well represented. It is likely that students choose these examples because they are familiar with them from their school studies, and so they come immediately to mind as examples of individuals of moral courage. Students must conduct research to flesh out their essays, but the underlying examples in these cases were already known to them. In recent years, we have had other examples of subjects that likely came to students' minds because they were widely covered in mainstream media. These include Paul Rusesabagina of Rwanda, Malala Yousafzai of Pakistan, and American World War II POW Roddie Edmonds, who was recognized by Yad Vashem as Righteous Among the Nations in 2015. Another category of examples of moral courage that students choose (presumably) before doing any research is family members. Students have written about grandparents who were Holocaust survivors or U.S. military liberators. They have also written about struggling single parents and special-needs siblings.

Over the years, we have seen a trend in the subjects students choose based on the extent to which they have conducted research. Unsurprisingly, if students have heard of any Holocaust-era rescuer, it is probably Oskar Schindler, and we receive essays about Schindler every year. From those who do a minimal amount of research, we often receive essays about Irena Sendler, Jan Karski, Raoul Wallenberg, the White Rose, and Chiune Sugihara. Some students delve more deeply into research before choosing a subject, and we have had students write about LGBTQ activists in Uganda, freedom fighters in the Dominican Republic, and little-known heroes of the Holocaust.

Looking specifically at essays related to the Holocaust, it is clear that students are fascinated by individuals who were not Jewish, who were not particularly persecuted because of any other aspect of their identities, and yet deliberately took actions that put their lives in danger. While that is the very definition of moral courage, in the oft-chosen examples students are confronted with the consequences of that risk: when Irena Sendler's legs are broken, when the members of the White Rose—just a few years older than our essayists—are sentenced to death, and so on. The drama of these examples—consuls hurriedly penning life-saving visas and thrusting them into desperate hands just before the train pulls out of the station, Jewish babies hidden in packages and suitcases to smuggle them out of the ghetto—this drama captures the students' interest and imagination. They are in awe of the people who did these things, and their admiration for these real-life heroes is evident in their essays.

As you might imagine, the writing skills of high school students have a broad range. Some are more adept than others, but overwhelmingly the essays demonstrate that the students have made great efforts to do their subject justice. The language has a tendency to be flowery—peppered with stunning hyperbole and SAT-prep-induced adjectives. We regularly run across sentences such as:

> My moral courage is but a small seed compared to Janusz Korczak's lush garden.
>
> Bystanders need to leave the safe confinement of their shadows and embrace the light that moral courage exudes.
>
> No bully will ever again penetrate the wall of my identity, built with bricks made of moral courage.

But the IHE truly believes that students are moved to use such colorful language both by their desire to impress the judges and because of the enormity of the subject matter.

In addition to describing someone who exemplified moral courage and connecting that example to the Holocaust, the final component of the essay requirements is that the writer makes a personal connection to the idea of moral courage. The IHE provides a standard definition for moral courage: "The ability to take a strong stance on a specific issue and to defend it based on one's personal beliefs or convictions regardless of danger or threats to personal safety—physical, emotional or otherwise."[2] Some students interpret this to mean that they should share an example of when they themselves displayed moral courage. Fortunately, most of the students in Nebraska and western Iowa have had no such opportunity and probably never will. We hope they will not be called upon to risk their lives in service of others. But some try to elevate the time they "sat next to the unpopular kid at lunch" or "volunteered at the soup kitchen" to the level of moral courage. These students are doing something decent and important, even though it cannot rightfully be called moral courage. But there are students, perhaps those with a level of maturity beyond their young years, or those whom life has genuinely challenged to a greater degree—who manage to reflect on the idea of moral courage in a way that is both profound and genuine. These students restore our faith in the next generation. They write gems like:

> Anyone anywhere can make a difference as long as they believe in what they are doing and care enough to see it through to the end.
>
> We cannot always stop injustice entirely, but we have a duty to try.
>
> The Partisans taught me about the impact that we can have when we follow our morals and beliefs. Although I may never experience a tragedy like what they lived through, I will frequently face challenges where my courage to stand up for my beliefs will be tested. My goal in life is to make a difference and to make the world a better place. I am inspired by the courage of the Bielski brothers and hope that one day I too will have the courage to make a difference.
>
> Too often I find myself in a situation where I'm thinking "Why on earth didn't I just do what was right?" To have morals is one thing, to have courage is another. I hope that what I have learned will result in more situations where I make the right choice.
>
> I understand now that what I say does matter, and that it has impact on the lives of others.
>
> While I may not live in a nation fraught with war or oppression, I still have a responsibility to help those in need around me.
>
> Yes, the environment is doomed and the Earth will eventually be absorbed by the Sun, but I can still lead a life full of aspiration and happiness if I devote myself to cultivating the goodness that is left in the world.
>
> Someday I want to be a superhero—not because of any special powers—but because of the sacrifices I am willing to make for what I know is right.[3]

These students are not done thinking about moral courage and what it means to them—as none of us should be—but they have started to examine a concept that lies at the very root of our shared humanity.

In surveying the past winners, the IHE found that most students believe the essay contest helped them to think of ways to be personally responsible for responding to prejudice and discrimination. Seven students responded "Very Much" on this measure and two students answered "Somewhat." No students responded "Not Really" or "Not at All" in regard to the essay contest's impact on their sense of personal responsibility to respond to prejudice and discrimination. For instance, one student wrote, "Something that stuck with me was how standing by is just as bad as contributing to the crime." Another student stated, "You can't always win, but you can always lose well. Mordechai knew he would not survive his resistance efforts but did what he could to fight for what he knew was right."

While these are positive statements and show growth and introspection on their own lives, other students offer frank honesty when faced with thoughts of whether they could act with moral courage. "I realized that as much as I want to believe I would be a hero in an emergency situation, I am not so sure that I would have the courage," stated one student. While a response like this may sound pessimistic, it may also show that the students have been impacted by the stories they learned and better recognize the magnitude of the actions that their subjects completed. Students were asked to what extent the essay contest deepened their understanding of the meaning of moral courage. On this measure as well, the respondents had a clear inclination. Six answered "Very Much" and three answered "Somewhat." None of the responding students described their growth in understanding moral courage as "Not Really" or "Not at All."

Not only does the IHE see the merit in providing an opportunity for students to conduct research, analyze human behavior, and form a connection to personal experiences, but the teachers that participate each year do as well. Some of the educators that participate in the Tribute to the Rescuers Essay Contest do so because they already teach a unit on the Holocaust, and the essay contest serves as a supplemental project for their students. Others participate due to the deep, reflective nature of the essay prompt. From the teacher survey results, 100 percent of educators believe the essay contest helps their students better understand our personal responsibility to show moral courage, while 70 percent (seven out of the ten respondents) believe it allows students to better analyze moral behavior, understand the harm of prejudice and discrimination, and learn Holocaust history. It is notable that the students and teachers have a striking similarity in their responses. The teachers' version, however, had an additional question about whether the essay contest successfully helps students consider *ways* to personally act to prevent the repetition of history. Only four of the teachers felt this goal is met successfully. So there is strong consensus among teachers that while students are internalizing their *responsibility* to show moral courage, there is more to be done in terms of providing real options for *how* they can do so.

Educators do believe the essay contest has a positive impact on their students and the role they play in society. As one educator noted, "I think this contest assignment allows students to consider how they are connected to history, even though they live in modern times. Especially in light of our current world, my students were able to see how damaging the discrimination and hatred toward a single group of people can be. We had several discussions on if the treatment of Syrians, Muslims, and refugees could turn into a genocide—I think my students were shocked to see the connections between modern society and 20th century history." Other educators also noted that the essay contest allows their students to consider the behaviors that made their subjects moral exemplars, which allows them to be reflective of their own behaviors.

Although one essay contest may not be the cure to our societal problems, the Tribute to the Rescuers Essay Contest does serve as a meaningful tool for educators to use. A decade and a half in, the evidence—both anecdotal and from a small-scale survey—seems to indicate that the essay contest does well in achieving its goals for general Holocaust awareness/education, for promoting examples of moral courage, and for starting students on the path to understanding their own moral responsibilities and potential ways to fulfill them. While our outreach is limited to Nebraska and western Iowa, other essay contests may serve a similar purpose in other regions.

To put our essayists in good company, we would like to conclude by pointing out that they are not the only ones prone to flowery language on the topic of moral courage. Robert F. Kennedy once said:

> Each time a man stands up for an ideal, or acts to improve the lot of others, or strikes out against injustice, he sends forth a tiny ripple of hope, and crossing each other from a million different centers of energy and daring those ripples build a current which can sweep down the mightiest walls of oppressions and resistance. . . . Few men are willing to brave the disapproval of their fellows, the censure of their colleagues, the wrath of their society. Moral courage is a rarer commodity than bravery in battle or great intelligence. Yet it is the one essential, vital quality for those who seek to change the world which yields most painfully to change.[4]

The IHE and educators across the state would like to think that our young essayists, inspired by the moral courage of others, really can be the tiny ripples of hope that together form an unstoppable current.

Questions for Further Discussion

- Students can learn about the Danish rescue efforts here: https://www.ushmm.org/outreach/en/article.php?ModuleId=10007740.
- Which examples of Holocaust rescuers do you think would make for a compelling essay about moral courage?
- Which examples come to mind of individuals or groups, not connected to the Holocaust, that demonstrated moral courage?
- Which aspects of your study of the Holocaust most stuck with you as especially compelling or memorable?

- If you are or if you know a student in Nebraska or western Iowa, check out the Tribute to the Rescuers High School Essay Contest and other programs for students, teachers, and the public at www.ihene.org.

Notes

1. See Carol Rittner, Stephen D. Smith, and Irena Steinfeldt, eds., *The Holocaust and the Christian World: Reflections on the Past, Challenges for the Future* (New York: Continuum, 2000), 97–100. For a comparison between Swedish, Danish, and Swiss rescue operations and humanitarian relief, see Gerald Steinacher, *Humanitarians at War: The Red Cross in the Shadow of the Holocaust* (Oxford: Oxford University Press, 2017).

2. Holocaust Education, "Essay Contest Research and Prep," accessed February 4, 2018, http://www.ihene.org/essay-contest-1/.

3. Tragically, the student who wrote this winning essay in 2016 was murdered in 2017. We hope that her message can serve as an inspiration to others.

4. Robert F. Kennedy Day of Affirmation Address, University of Cape Town, Cape Town, South Africa, June 6, 1966, https://www.jfklibrary.org/Research/Research-Aids/Ready-Reference/RFK-Speeches/Day-of-Affirmation-Address-as-delivered.aspx.

Suggested Further Reading and Films

Selected Bibliography

Bystanders and Perpetrators

Barnett, Victoria. *Bystanders: Conscience and Complicity in the Holocaust*

Baum, Steven. *The Psychology of Genocide: Perpetrators, Bystanders, and Rescuers*

Blumenthal, David. *The Banality of Good and Evil*

Browning, Christopher. *Ordinary Men: Reserve Police Battalion 101 and the Final Solution in Poland*

Cesarani, David, and Paul Levine. *Bystanders to the Holocaust: A Reevaluation*

Gross, Jan Tomasz. *Neighbors: The Destruction of the Jewish Community in Jedwabne*

Hilberg, Raul. *Perpetrators, Victims, Bystanders*

von Kellenbach, Katharina. *The Mark of Cain*

Kelman, Herbert, and V. Hamilton. *Crimes of Obedience*

Klee, Ernst, et al., eds. *The Good Old Days: The Holocaust as Seen by Its Perpetrators and Bystanders*

Pollack, Martin. *The Dead Man in the Bunker*

Posner, Gerald L. *Hitler's Children: Sons and Daughters of Leaders of the Third Reich Talk about Their Fathers and Themselves*

Roseman, Mark. *The Villa, the Lake, the Meeting: Wannsee and the Final Solution*

Schrafstetter, Susanna, and Alan E. Steinweis, eds. *The Germans and the Holocaust*

Stangneth, Bettina. *Eichmann before Jerusalem: The Unexamined Life of a Mass Murderer*

Staub, Erwin. *The Roots of Evil*

Steinacher, Gerald. *Nazis on the Run: How Hitler's Henchmen Fled Justice*

Waller, James. *Becoming Evil: How Ordinary People Commit Genocide and Mass Killing*

Wiesenthal, Simon. *The Sunflower: On the Possibilities and Limits of Forgiveness*

National Rescue Operations

Bartoszewski, Wadyslaw. *The Blood Shed Unites Us* (Poland)

Bar-Zohar, Michael. *Beyond Hitler's Grasp: The Heroic Rescue of Bulgaria's Jews* (Bulgaria)

Bauer, Yehuda. *American Jewry and the Holocaust* (USA and the Holocaust)

Brachfeld, Sylvia. *A Gift of Life* (Belgium)

Breitman, Richard, and Allan J. Lichtman. *FDR and the Jews* (USA and the Holocaust)

Caracciolo, Nicola, ed. *Uncertain Refuge: Italy and the Jews during the Holocaust* (Italy)

Celinscak, Mark. *Distance from the Belsen Heap: Allied Forces and the Liberation of a Nazi Concentration Camp* (Germany)

Chary, Frederick. *The Bulgarian Jews and the Final Solution, 1940–1944* (Bulgaria, Balkans)

Erbelding, Rebecca. *Rescue Board: The Untold Story of America's Efforts to Save the Jews of Europe* (USA and the Holocaust)

Fenyvesi, Charles. *When Angels Fooled the World: Rescuers of Jews in Wartime Hungary* (Hungary, Romania)

Flender, Harold. *Rescue in Denmark* (Denmark)

Gitman, Esther. *When Courage Prevailed: The Rescue and Survival of Jews in Croatia* (Croatia, Yugoslavia)

Goldberger, Leo, ed. *The Rescue of Danish Jewry: Moral Courage under Stress* (Denmark, Sweden)

Gross, Leonard. *The Last Jews in Berlin* (Germany)

Herzer, Ivo, ed. *The Italian Refuge: Rescue of Jews during the Holocaust* (Italy)

Iranek-Osmecki, Kazimierz. *He Who Saves One Life* (Poland)

Lazan, Marion Blumenthal. *Four Perfect Pebbles* (The Netherlands)

Lazare, Lucien. *Rescue as Resistance* (French Jewish rescue networks)

Leuner, H. D. *When Compassion Was a Crime: Germany's Silent Heroes* (German righteous)

Levine, Paul A. *From Indifference to Activism: Swedish Diplomacy and the Holocaust: 1938–1944* (Sweden, neutral nations)

Loeffler, Martha. *Boats in the Night* (Denmark)

Mieszkowska, Anna. *Irene Sendler: Mother of the Children of the Holocaust* (Poland)

Moore, Bob. *Victims and Survivors* (the Netherlands)

Moore, Bob, and Johannes Houwink ten Cate, eds. *The Secret Diary of Arnold Douwes* (the Netherlands)

Paldiel, Mordecai. *German Rescuers of Jews* (Germany)

Paulson, Gunnar. *Secret City: The Hidden Jews of Warsaw* (Poland)

Pundik, Herbert. *In Denmark It Could Not Happen* (Denmark)

Schreiber, Marion. *The 20th Train* (Belgium)

Stein, Andre. *Quiet Heroes: Rescue of the Jews by Christians in Nazi-Occupied Holland* (the Netherlands, Righteous)

Stille, Alexander. *Benevolence and Betrayal: Five Italian Jewish Families under Fascism* (Italy, Fascism)

Tammeus, Bill, et al. *They Were Just People: Stories of Rescue in Poland* (Poland)

Toldorov, Tzvetan. *Fragility of Goodness: Why Bulgaria's Jews Survived the Holocaust* (Bulgaria)

Tomasewski, Irene. *Zegota: The Rescue of Jews in Wartime Poland (Codename Zegota)* (Poland)

Vromen, Suzanne. *Hidden Children of the Holocaust: Belgian Nuns and Their Daring Rescue of Young Jews from the Nazis* (Belgium)

Werner, Emily. *Conspiracy of Decency: The Rescue of the Danish Jews during World War II* (Denmark, Sweden)

Wyman, David S. *The Abandonment of the Jews: America and the Holocaust 1941–1945* (USA, Holocaust)

Yahil, Leni. *The Rescue of Danish Jewry: Test of a Democracy* (Denmark)

Zuccotti, Susan. *The Holocaust, the French, and the Jews* (France, Vichy)

Zuccotti, Susan. *The Italians and the Holocaust* (Italy, fascism)

Zuccotti, Susan. *Under His Very Windows: The Vatican and the Holocaust in Italy* (Italy, Catholic Church)

Psychosocial Studies

Baron, Lawrence, et al. *Embracing the Other*

Blum, Lawrence. *Moral Perception and Particularity*

Fogelman, Eva. *Conscience and Courage*

Monroe, Kristen. *The Heart of Altruism*

Oliner, Samuel, and Pearl Oliner. *The Altruistic Personality*

Tec, Nechama. *When Light Pierced the Darkness*

Rescuer Narratives (c = written for children, adolescents)

Axelrod, Toby. *Rescuers Defying the Nazis* (c)

Block, Gay and Malka Drucker. *Rescuers: Portraits of Moral Courage in the Holocaust*

Friedman, Philip. *Their Brother's Keeper*

Geier, Arnold. *Heroes of the Holocaust* (c)

Gilbert, Martin. *The Righteous: Unsung Heroes of the Holocaust*

Grunwald-Spier, Agnes. *The Other Schindlers*

Gutman, Israel, et al. *The Encyclopedia of the Righteous Among the Nations*

Johnson, Alvin. *Pioneer's Progress: An Autobiography*

Halter, Marek. *Stories of Deliverance*

Hellman, Peter. *When Courage was Stronger than Fear* (Original: *Avenue of the Righteous*)

Klempner, Mark. *The Heart Has Its Reasons*

Marshall, Robert. *In the Sewers of Lvov*

Meltzer, Milton. *Rescue* (c)

Monroe, Kristen. *The Hand of Compassion*

Morgenstern, Naomi. *The Daughter We Had Always Wanted—The Story of Marta* (c)

Paldiel, Mordecai. *The Path of the Righteous*

Paldiel, Mordecai. *Sheltering the Jews* (c)

Rittner, Carol, and Sondra Myers. *The Courage to Care*

Silver, Eric. *The Book of the Just*

Werber, Jack. *Saving Children: Diary of a Buchenwald Survivor and Rescuer*

ATTACHMENT RESCUERS

Crowe, David. *Oskar Schindler: The Untold Story of His Life*

Gies, Miep. *Anne Frank Remembered*

Huneke, Douglas. *The Moses of Rovno: Fritz Graebe*

Keneally, Thomas. *Schindler's List/Schindler's Ark*

Meyers, Odette. *Doors to Madame Marie*

Opdyke, Irene Gut. *In My Hands*

Stolzfus, Nathan. *Resistance of the Heart*

DIPLOMATS WHO RESCUED JEWS

Berman, John. *Righteous Gentile: The Story of Raoul Wallenberg*

Borden, Louise. *His Name Was Raoul Wallenberg* (c)

Deaglio, Enrico. *The Banality of Goodness: The Story of Giorgio Perlasca*

Fralon, Jose Alain. *A Good Man in Evil Times: The Story of Aristide De Sousa Mendes*

Gold, Alison Leslie. *A Special Fate: Chiune Sugihara: Hero of the Holocaust*

Handler, Andrew. *A Man for All Connections*

Isenberg, Sheila. *A Hero of Our Own: The Story of Varian Fry*

Kershaw, Alex. *The Envoy*

Kranzler, David. *The Man Who Stopped the Trains*

Levine, Hillel. *In Search of Sugihara*

Levine, Paul. *Raoul Wallenberg in Budapest: Myth, History and Holocaust*

Marton, Kati. *A Death in Jerusalem*

Rosenfeld, Harvey. *Raoul Wallenberg*

Skogland, Elizabeth. *A Quiet Courage: Per Anger*

Smith, Danny. *Lost Hero*

Smith, Michael. *Foley: The Spy Who Saved 10,000 Jews*

Strauss-Rosenat, Eleanor. *Do Right and Fear No One: The Paul Grüninger Story* (c)

Tschuy, Theo. *Dangerous Diplomacy: The Story of Carl Lutz*

Wasserstein, Bernard. *The Ambiguity of Virtue: Gertrude van Tijn and the Dutch Jews*

RELIGIOUSLY MOTIVATED RESCUERS

Eman, Diet. *Things We Couldn't Say*

Gushee, David. *The Righteous Gentiles of the Holocaust: A Christian Interpretation*

Fleischner, Eva, and Michael Phayer et al. *Cries in the Night*

Ford, Herbert. *Flee the Captor*

Grose, Peter. *A Good Place to Hide*

Hallie, Philip. *Lest Innocent Blood Be Shed*

Henry, Patrick. *We Only Know Men*

Joffroy, Pierre. *A Spy for God*

Kurek, Ewa. *Your Life Is Worth Mine*

Leboucher, Fernand. *Incredible Mission*

Lubac, Henri. *Christian Resistance to Anti-Semitism*

Moorehead, Caroline. *Village of Secrets*

Phayer, Michael. *The Catholic Church and the Holocaust, 1930–1965*

Oliner, Pearl. *Saving the Forsaken*

Ramati, Alexander. *The Assissi Underground*

Riebling, Mark. *The Church of Spies: The Pope's Secret War Against Hitler*

Satloff, Robert. *Among the Righteous*

Ten Boom, Corrie. *The Hiding Place*

Unsworth, Richard. *A Portrait of Pacifists*

Zasloff, Tela. *A Rescuer's Story: Pastor Pierre-Charles Toureille in Vichy France*

Walker, Stephen. *Hide and Seek: The Irish Priest in the Vatican Who Defied the Nazi Command*

Selected Filmography

Documentaries

As If It Were Yesterday. Directed by Myriam Abromowicz and Esther Hoffenberg (1980)

Assignment Rescue. Directed by Richard Kaplan (1997)

Avenue of the Just. Directed by Samuel Elfert (1978)

The Children of Chabannes. Directed by Lisa Gossels, Dean Wetherell (1999)

The Courage to Care. Directed by Robert Gardner (1985)

The Danish Solution. Directed by Karen Cantor (2005)

Defying the Nazis: The Sharps' War. Directed by Ken Burns, Artemis Joukowsky (2016)

Diamonds in the Snow. Directed by Mira Reym Binford (1994)

Diplomats for the Damned. History Channel (2001)

Fifty Children: The Rescue Mission of Mr. and Mrs. Kraus. Directed by Steven Pressman (2013)

Hiding and Seeking. Directed by Oren Rudavsky and Menachem Daum (2004)

Hitler's Children. Directed by Chanoch Ze'evi (2011)

Into the Arms of Strangers. Directed by Jonathan Mark Harris (2000)

Jacoba. Directed by Joram ten Brink (1988)

My Italian Secret: The Forgotten Heroes. Directed by Oren Jacoby (2014)

Nicky's Family. Directed by Matej Minac (2011)

An Open Door: Jewish Rescue in the Philippines. Directed by Noel Izon (2016)

The Optimists. Directed by John Comforty (2000)

The Power of Conscience. Directed by Alexandra Isles (1994)

The Power of Good (Original: *Síla lidskosti: Nicholas Winton*). Directed by Mattej Minac (2002)

Raoul Wallenberg: Between the Lines. Directed by Karin Altmann (1984)

Rescue in the Philippines. Directed by Russell Hodge (2013)

Schindler: The Documentary. Directed by Jon Blair (1982)

Secret Lives: Hidden Children and Their Rescuers. Directed by Aviva Slesin (2002)

So Many Miracles. Directed by Victor Sarin (1987)

They Risked Their Lives. Directed by Gay Block (1991)

Villa Bel Air. Directed by Jorg Bundschuh (1987)

Voices from the Attic. Directed by Axel Engstfeld (1982)

Wallenberg: Buried Alive. Directed by David Harel (1983)

Weapons of the Spirit. Directed by Pierre Sauvage (1987)

Tzedek. Directed by Marek Halter (1994)

Zegota: A Time to Remember. Directed by Sy Rotter (1992)

Feature Films

Across the Water. Directed by Nicolo Donato (2016)

All My Loved Ones. Directed by Matej Minac (1999)

The Assisi Underground. Directed by Alexander Ramati (1985)

The Attic: The Hiding of Anne Frank. Directed by John Erman (1988)

The Blind Love of Otto Weidt. Directed by Kai Christiansen (2014)

Conspiracy of Hearts. Directed by Ralph Thomas (1960)

Defiance. Directed by Edward Zwick (2008)

The Consul of Bordeaux. Directed by Francisco Manso Joao Correa (2011)

The Courageous Heart of Irene Sendler. Directed by John Kent Harrison (2010)

A Day in October. Directed by Kenneth Madsen (1993)

Disobedience: The Sousa Mendes Story. Directed by Joel Santoni (2008)

The Flat. Directed by Arnon Goldfinger (2011)

Forbidden. Directed by Anthony Page (1984)

Free Men. Directed by Ismäel Ferroukhi (2011)

Good Bye Children. Directed by Louis Malle (1987)

Good Evening, Mr. Wallenberg. Directed by Kjell Grade (1990)

The Grüninger File. Directed by Alain Gsponer (2013)

Hidden Children: The Flight of the Innocent. Directed by Leone Pompucci (2004)

Hidden in Silence. Directed by Richard Colla (1996)

The Hiding Place. Directed by James Collier (1975)

The Hill of a Thousand Children. Directed by Jean-Lous Lorenzi (1996)

In Another Lifetime. Directed by Elisabeth Scharang (2011)

In Darkness. Directed by Agnieszka Holland (2011)

Journey to Jerusalem. Directed by Ivan Nitchev (2003)

Judgment in Nuremberg. Directed by Stanley Kramer (1961)

Just This Forest. Directed by Jan Lomnicki (1990)
Miracle at Midnight. Directed by Ken Cameron (1998)
Miracle at Moreaux. Directed by Paul Shapiro (1986)
Naked among Wolves. Directed by Philipp Kaddelbach (2015)
Not All Were Murderers. Directed by Jo Baier (2006)
The Only Way. Directed by Bent Christensen (1970)
Perlasca: An Italian Hero. Directed by Alberto Negrin (2002)
Persona Non Grata. Directed by Cellin Gluck (2015)
The Quality of Mercy (Original: *Hasenjagd*). Directed by Andreas Gruber (1994)
Rosenstrasse. Directed by Margaretha von Trotta (2003)
Run Boy Run. Directed by Pepe Danquart (2013)
Saviors in the Night. Directed by Ludi Boeken (2009)
The Scarlet and the Black. Directed by Jerry London (1983)
Schindler's List. Directed by Steven Spielberg (1993)
Sophie Scholl: The Final Days. Directed by Marc Rothemund (2005)
13 Minutes (Original: *Elser*). Directed by Oliver Hirschbiegel (2015)
Turkish Passport. Directed by Burak Arliel (2011)
Under the Earth. Directed by Beda Docampo Feijoo (1987)
Varian's War. Directed by Lionel Chetwynd (2001)
The Zookeeper's Wife. Directed by Niko Caro (2017)

Contributors

Brian Barmettler obtained his Matura with concentrations in Latin and history from the Kollegium St. Fidelis in Stans, Switzerland, before moving to the United States to attend the University of Nebraska–Lincoln. He earned a BA in history and political science with a minor in classics in 2016 and then interned on Capitol Hill and worked at a boutique lobbying firm in Washington DC. Barmettler is currently pursuing a JD at the University of Michigan–Ann Arbor.

Lawrence Baron (PhD, University of Wisconsin–Madison) is Professor Emeritus of Modern Jewish History at San Diego State University, where he held the Nasatir Chair from 1998–2012 and served as director of the Lipinsky Institute for Judaic Studies until 2006. He is the author of *Projecting the Holocaust into the Present: The Changing Focus of Contemporary Holocaust Cinema* (Rowman & Littlefield, 2005) and an extensive list of peer-reviewed journal articles. In the fall semester of 2015, he served as the Ida King Distinguished Visiting Professor of Holocaust and Genocide Studies at the Richard Stockton University of New Jersey.

Mark Celinscak (PhD, York University) is the Louis and Frances Blumkin Professor of Holocaust and Genocide Studies in the Department of History and the executive director of the Sam and Frances Fried Holocaust and Genocide Academy at the University of Nebraska–Omaha. His award-winning book, *Distance from the Belsen Heap: Allied Forces and the Liberation of a Nazi Concentration Camp*, was published by the University of Toronto Press in 2015. Celinscak was a Pearl Resnick Postdoctoral Fellow at the United States Holocaust Memorial Museum and a fellow at the Holocaust Educational Foundation of Northwestern University.

Michael Dick is the Frank A. Belousek Doctoral Student in the University of Nebraska–Lincoln's History Department. He has participated in competitive seminars on the Holocaust at both the United States Holocaust Memorial Museum and the Holocaust Research Institute at the University of London. His master's thesis examined the Americanization of the Holocaust, specifically how Raoul Wallenberg's memory has been represented in the United States. In his dissertation he compares postwar Europe and postconquest Native America using the work of American social worker Aleta Brownlee, who directed child welfare operations for the United Nations in Europe and later the Bureau of Indian Affairs in the United States.

Rebecca Erbelding is the author of *Rescue Board: The Untold Story of America's Efforts to Save the Jews of Europe* (Doubleday, 2018), which won the National Jewish Book Award. She is a historian, curator, and archivist at the United States Holocaust Memorial Museum and served as the lead historian on the museum's special exhibition *Americans and the Holocaust*, on display 2018–2021. Her work has previously been featured in the *New York Times*, the *Washington Post*, the *New Yorker*, and on the History Channel and National Geographic.

Liz Feldstern holds a bachelor's degree in Jewish studies from Rutgers University and a master's degree in conflict management from the Hebrew University of Jerusalem. She is a certified mediator and lives in Israel. During studies for both of her university degrees Liz conducted extensive research on the Displaced Persons camps that housed survivors of the Holocaust in the years immediately following World War II. For five years she coordinated Foreign Relations for the Israel Center for Excellence through Education, located in Jerusalem. In this capacity she planned and implemented teacher training and professional development seminars for hundreds of teachers in Israel, the United States, and Singapore. Feldstern directed the Institute for Holocaust Education in Omaha, Nebraska, from 2013 to 2018.

Benjamin Frommer (PhD, Harvard University) is an associate professor of history at Northwestern University and the author of *National Cleansing: Retribution against Nazi Collaborators in*

Postwar Czechoslovakia (New York: Cambridge University Press, 2005), which was also published in Czech translation (Academia: Prague, 2010). His current book project, *The Ghetto without Walls: The Identification, Isolation, and Elimination of Bohemian and Moravian Jewry, 1938–1945*, examines the wartime destruction of one of the world's most integrated and intermarried Jewish communities. At Northwestern Frommer has held the Charles Deering McCormick Professorship of Teaching Excellence (2013–16) and the Wayne V. Jones Research Professorship in History (2010–12).

Mark Gudgel (EdD, Regent University) teaches English, humanities, and world religions at Omaha North High Magnet School, as well as multiple courses in the MEd program at Nebraska Wesleyan University. A Fulbright Scholar and fellow of both the United States Holocaust Memorial Museum and the Imperial War Museum in the area of Holocaust education, Gudgel's dissertation focused on the use of film to teach about the Holocaust in American secondary classrooms. Gudgel is the author of numerous articles and essays, in addition to poetry and other genres of writing. His 2012 TED talk focuses on genocide education and empowering young people to change the world.

Roy G. Koepp (PhD, University of Nebraska–Lincoln) is an assistant professor of Modern European History at Eastern New Mexico University. Koepp's specialties are modern Germany, Nazi Germany/Holocaust, and the World War I–II era. His current research looks at the paramilitary scene in post–World War I Bavaria. He is working on a book manuscript on this topic, and his 2015 article for *The Historian*, "Gustav von Kahr and Emergence of the Radical Right in Bavaria," is a result of that research.

Ari Kohen (PhD, Duke University) is an associate professor of political science and the Schlesinger Professor of Social Justice at the University of Nebraska–Lincoln. His most recent book, *Untangling Heroism: Classical Philosophy and the Concept of the Hero*, was published by Routledge in 2014. His previous book, *In Defense of Human Rights: A Non-Religious Grounding in a Pluralistic World*, also from Routledge, was published in 2007. He is the author of a dozen articles on human rights, genocide, transitional justice, and heroism.

Amanda Ryan holds a bachelor's degree in religious studies from the University of Nebraska at Omaha and is currently completing her master's degree in sociology from UNO. Her current research interests include religion in public life, human rights, and the intersection of race/ethnicity and religion for Jews of color. Before moving to Omaha Amanda became interested in learning about the Holocaust from her high school English teacher in Minden, Nebraska. Through personal narratives about Holocaust survivors and literature she became invested in sharing the lessons of the Holocaust with others. Ryan served as the administrative assistant for the Institute for Holocaust Education from 2016 to 2019.

Gerald J. Steinacher (PhD, University of Innsbruck) is an associate professor of history and the Hymen Rosenberg Professor of Judaic Studies at the University of Nebraska–Lincoln. Prior to his appointment he served as the Joseph A. Schumpeter Research Fellow in the Center for European Studies at Harvard University. He is the author of numerous publications on German and Italian twentieth-century history, most recently *Humanitarians at War: The Red Cross in the Shadow of the Holocaust* (Oxford University Press, 2017). His previous book, *Nazis on the Run: How Hitler's Henchmen Fled Justice* (Oxford University Press, 2011), was awarded the National Jewish Book Award and translated into four languages.

Donna Walter was the education coordinator for the Institute for Holocaust Education from 2012 to 2018. She was an eighth-grade language arts teacher and language arts coordinator at St. Pius X–St. Leo in Omaha, Nebraska, for many years. Walter is the recipient of the 2012 National Catholic Educational Association Distinguished Teacher Award and is an alumna of the Belfer National Conference of the United States Holocaust Memorial Museum and of the Anti-Defamation League "Bearing Witness" and "Bearing Witness—Advanced" programs.

Index

In the Contemporary Holocaust Studies series

Unlikely Heroes: The Place of Holocaust Rescuers in Research and Teaching
Edited by Ari Kohen and Gerald J. Steinacher